THE OFFICIAL HISTORY OF THE
ICC CRICKET
WORLD CUP

BATTING ORDER

THE ICC CRICKET WORLD CUP – THE ORIGINS

The game of cricket was undeniably slow on the uptake when it came to holding a World Cup. Indeed, in the old days the sport seemed to make a virtue of deliberating extensively, even excessively, before accepting anything new. That, combined with how cricket grew – imported to a few far-flung countries which were part of the British empire – meant that a World Cup was not an easy thing to organise.

International cricket was the plaything of England and Australia alone from 1877 until South Africa joined the party in 1889. It was almost 30 years later that West Indies made it four (1928), with New Zealand (1930) and India (1932) being added to the mix in relatively quick succession. Pakistan bumped the numbers up to seven – still hardly enough for a bona fide multi-team tournament – in 1952. And by the time a World Cup was first mooted in the early '70s, South Africa was in sporting isolation, meaning there were just six Test-playing nations.

A tournament of half a dozen sides playing Test matches against each other over a concentrated period of time was, and is, logistically close to impossible. So for a World Cup to come into being, the game would have to change. And until 1971, one-day international cricket did not exist, the first game of this type being played between Australia and England in January of that year more to give the crowd some entertainment after the first three days of the Melbourne Test had been washed out than in any far-sighted strategy to introduce a new format of the game.

In England, one-day cricket had been played domestically since 1963, and the influx of overseas players in 1969 – as well as the introduction of the 40-over league in that year – meant that short-form cricket had been normalised around the world. Eventually, the go-ahead for the first global tournament was given by the ICC in the summer of 1973 and off we went, the competition scheduled for a fortnight in June in England two years later.

Fast forward 44 years and we are on the verge of another English ICC Cricket World Cup. Twenty nations have now taken part in these tournaments, seven have been ever-presents and only five have been crowned winners.

In the chapters that follow, 11 different writers tell the stories of the 11 ICC Cricket World Cups to date.

Matt Thacker, May 2019

1975

THE START OF SOMETHING SPECIAL

BY JON HOTTEN

The weather in Melbourne can be capricious, and on the last day of 1970, it turned. The skies above the MCG opened as the Australian batsmen took the field for the first morning of the third Ashes Test and rained down for the next three days. By the time the front blew through, the match had been abandoned without a ball bowled. A total wash-out of a Test was rare, so rare that it had happened only twice before, in 1890 and 1938, both times at Old Trafford and both times in games between England and Australia.

The Australian Board went into conference with the MCC tour manager David Clark and arrived at a solution. The Melbourne Test was rescheduled to fit between the games at Sydney and Adelaide, and to appease a disappointed Victorian public, the teams agreed to play a limited overs match at the MCG on what would have been the final day of the original game, 5 January 1971.

MCG management told their caterers to prepare for a crowd of 20,000, but when the gates opened that Tuesday morning, 46,006 paying customers walked through them. They watched England bat first and score a tepid 190 from 39.4 of their allotted 40 eight-ball overs. On an outfield that had been submerged for three days, they managed an underwhelming seven boundaries, their total overhauled by Australia with 42 deliveries to spare. After play, an astute Don Bradman told the crowd: "You have seen history made."

It seemed like an ad hoc interlude on a long and at times fractious tour, yet it became ODI No.1, the inaugural match in a sequence that now stretches beyond 4,000 games. Ashley Mallett, Australia's spinner at Melbourne, said: "They called it the first one-day international, which rather surprised me... that game we thought was a bit of a joke."

Climate has shaped cricket, its grounds and its pitches, its methods and its tactics, but rarely as radically as it did that day. Domestic limited overs contests in England and Australia had gained an immediate popularity that was reflected in the roll-up crowd at the MCG. At last, the game was accelerating to meet the needs of the time in which it existed, and the public were ahead of the curve. Over the next four years, the game's administrators crawled towards them, staging another 17 one-day internationals, 14 of them involving England. Then they made a far bolder move.

***

The first intimations of the "Festival of Cricket" that would become the World Cup began with the ICC (then the International Cricket Conference) at their 1972 meeting, made possible when the heads of the India and Pakistan boards began informal discussions on resuming cricket relations that had been suspended in the dispute over Kashmir. Any World Cup could not have happened without them. By 1973 the women's game had struck out ahead, with the financial support of Sir Jack Hayward, and staged their inaugural World Cup that summer in England. The ICC meeting that rubber-stamped the men's tournament came, coincidentally, three days after the women's event had concluded.

The meeting resolved that an "International Tournament" would take place in two years' time and England should host: it was a small country around which travel was relatively easy, the population had diasporas from which support for each of the competing teams could be drawn and, if the weather gods smiled down, had enough midsummer daylight hours to stage 60-over-a-side matches. There was also the undeniable lure of history, with a showpiece final at cricket's most storied ground, Lord's.

The Test and County Cricket Board (TCCB) drove the tournament forwards, using the domestic Gillette Cup as a model for the format and inviting Australia to stay on for an Ashes series at the conclusion of the World Cup, a financial backstop that reduced uncertainty over cost. That fear – always the greatest for any administrator – was alleviated further when a British insurance company called Prudential bought the sponsorship rights for £100,000, a fee that meant that gate receipts and ticket sales could be split as profit between the ICC and the TCCB. It was serendipitous reward for taking a leap into the unknown, and more was to follow.

***

The English summer got its dirty work out of the way early in 1975. On 2 June, a week before the World Cup began, a freak snowstorm swept southwards from the Peak District and blanketed the Midlands. An inch of the white stuff halted play in the County Championship match between Derbyshire and Lancashire at Buxton and a flurry alighted on Birmingham airport. A few flakes fell in the capital, the first time snowfall had been recorded in London in June for two centuries.

It proved an odd and good omen for the two weeks and 15 matches planned for the eight teams that had assembled. There were six Test playing nations in 1975: the hosts England, plus Australia, India, Pakistan, New Zealand and West Indies, who would compete alongside Associates Sri Lanka, invited by ICC, and East Africa, a newly named portmanteau team of club players from Kenya, Tanzania, Uganda and Zambia. The competition was billed as "the Prudential Trophy" rather than the World Cup, although the public were in little doubt what they were watching: knock-out cricket in a form never seen at men's international level.

It looked like any other first-class match. The players wore whites, used the red ball and took breaks for lunch and tea along with the change between innings. There were no fielding restrictions, no 30-yard circles, no boundaries brought in for the safety of the fielders. Cricket grounds did not have floodlights, so there was no day-night play. Deliveries slipping past leg stump were not given as wides. The notions of one-day specialists, or pinch hitters, yorker bowlers and mystery spinners lay in an unmapped future. Instead, here stood pioneers.

It is worth remembering cricket's world order in 1975, when so much was still to happen. West Indies were the slender pre-tournament favourites, granted the honour by virtue of the spectacular vision of cricket they were moving towards under their bespectacled captain Clive Lloyd. Six feet five inches tall and ursine, with sloping shoulders and a gunslinger's moustache, Lloyd showed rather than told his team how he wanted them to play. In his first series as skipper, in the winter just gone, he had taken India for 165 in Bangalore and then scored 242 not out in Mumbai, the latter sealing a series victory by three matches to two. Shorn of the great all-rounder Sobers by injury, Lloyd's squad nonetheless glittered with promise. The batting included the 23-year-old Antiguan Vivian Richards, 24-year-old Bajan Gordon Greenidge, and a wildly talented all-rounder with echoes of Sobers, the 25-year-old Trinidadian Bernard Julien. Andy Roberts, a brooding, lightning-quick bowler from the same island as Richards, was just 24, too. Lloyd's Guyanese countrymen were at the heart of the team's batting, the veteran Rohan Kanhai joined by Alvin Kallicharran, a diminutive powerhouse entering his prime, and the hard-hitting left-handed opener Roy Fredericks. They also had a vintage spinner in the record-breaking Lance Gibbs, Lloyd's cousin.

What was yet to emerge, Roberts aside, was the fast-bowling battery with which Lloyd's teams would come to dominate cricket. Instead, the world's most hostile bowling belonged to Australia, in the form of a terrifying opening pair, the raw slingshot pace of Jeff Thomson and the sublime seam and swing of Dennis Lillee (it would be West Indies' defeat at their hands in the winter of 1975–76 that prompted Lloyd's plan to fight fire with fire). Under the sharp, attacking captaincy of Ian Chappell and his vice captain, brother Greg – a batsman of supreme elegance and class – Australia appeared the other side to watch. To the opening pair of Lillee and

Thomson they'd added, astutely, a left-arm swing bowler who, given the right kind of English day, might wreak some havoc – the hard-living, easy-going, big-hitting Gary "Gus" Gilmour.

England were shorn of their leading batsman Geoffrey Boycott, who had elected to make himself unavailable, but their bowling looked strong. John Snow, now a veteran but still in possession of effortless menace, Chris Old, Geoff Arnold and Peter Lever knew pretty much all there was to know about the seamer's art in England, while Derek Underwood was a freakishly talented bowler of left-arm spin at almost medium pace, who operated in tandem with the game's greatest wicket-keeper, Alan Knott. Tony Greig added some all-round swagger to a batting line-up that had know-how rather than raw power.

New Zealand brought no less than three Hadlee brothers – Barry, Dayle and the 23-year-old tyro Richard, and two Howarths, Geoff and Hedley, plus their supreme opener and captain Glenn Turner and a glorious left-arm pacer whose run-up began somewhere in the middle-distance, Richard Collinge, a man on his way to becoming New Zealand's leading wicket-taker – a record the youngest Hadlee would in turn make his own.

India were a team on the rise, their strength in spin augmented by the emergence of Sunil Gavaskar, a player who would become the first great batting superstar of Indian cricket and establish a lineage that runs through Sachin Tendulkar to Virat Kohli. Gavaskar had been a sensation in his first Test series, making 774 runs in the West Indies as India won for the first time there, and although he had slumped to a degree, he had played in consecutive series wins over England.

India's eternal rivals Pakistan glistened with batting talent too, the magisterial Majid Khan, silky Zaheer Abbas, waspish Asif Iqbal, the Mohammed brothers Mushtaq and Sadiq, and a player already described as "the find of the century", Javed Miandad, who would turn 18 the day after he debuted against West Indies on 11 June. Their other young hope, still a year off graduating from Oxford, was one Imran Khan.

Playing at home didn't offer England the advantage it might have been. In county cricket every side except Yorkshire employed an overseas star or two. Clive Lloyd was a fixture at Lancashire, along with India's suave keeper-batsman Farokh Engineer. Glenn Turner played like a god under the spire of Worcester cathedral. At Hampshire, Gordon Greenidge opened the batting and Andy Roberts the bowling, Viv Richards was flat-sharing with Ian Botham in Taunton, Imran had played at Worcestershire and would move to Sussex, Zaheer Abbas made hundreds for fun at Gloucestershire, ditto Asif Iqbal at Kent. Sarfraz Nawaz and Bishan Bedi were bedrocks of the Northants bowling, and so on. Many would come to regard England as a second home.

This carnival rolled into town for a competition that was tightly structured, scheduled for two weeks and 15 matches. The teams had been divided into groups of four under the caveat that Australia and England and India and Pakistan would be kept apart during the initial phase. Each team would play three matches, with the top two sides in both groups advancing to the semi-finals. The hosts were joined by India, New Zealand and East Africa in Group A, with West Indies, Australia, Pakistan and Sri Lanka duking it out in Group B.

From the moment it began and until its drama-packed conclusion in the midsummer gloaming, the tournament was in possession of that other great indefinable – luck. Both its opening match, between England and India at The Oval, and the final at Lord's were matches so extraordinary that they have entered the folklore of the game.

The players were invited to Buckingham Palace the day before the World Cup opened, where the Queen found an unlikely fan in Jeff Thomson. The scourge of English batsmen pronounced Her Majesty "just great". Suitably and regally endorsed, the competition opened with four matches played simultaneously, every team in action under a golden sun in its blameless sky.

***

Australia and Pakistan began at Headingley, where Asif Iqbal's men were contesting just their fourth ODI, a game that would be settled by Dennis Lillee. Australia batted first and compiled 278 for 7 from their 60 overs, a score that showed some of the uncertainty batsmen had over how to play. Rick McCosker assembled a patient 25 from 76 deliveries, a knock that would not have been out of place in the tense first overs of a Boxing Day Test, the Chappell brothers cruised along with strike rates around 90, and Ross Edwards struck an unbeaten 80 from 94. The sole six of the day was hit by Jeff Thomson, perhaps still high on his brush with royalty.

Pakistan's reply folded under the hostility of Lillee's conclusive spell. There were eight single-digit scores in their 205 all out, Lillee posting figures of 12-2-34-5. Thommo's day hadn't quite stayed on course: he was no-balled repeatedly during his eight overs. Luckily for him, the concept of the free hit lay decades ahead.

The outsiders suffered two harrowing defeats. At Old Trafford, Sri Lanka folded to 86 all out against West Indies, who knocked them off for the loss of Roy Fredericks. Viv Richards, making an ODI debut along with Andy Roberts, didn't get a bat. Glenn Turner did though, tucking into the East Africa attack at Edgbaston to the tune of an unbeaten 171 out of New Zealand's 309 for 5. East Africa deserved credit for surviving their 60 overs, albeit if their total of 128 for 8 failed to set the pulse galloping, Mehmood Quaraishy's 88-ball 16 not out remaining to this day the slowest World Cup innings of more than 75 balls.

That go-slow was understandable, but at Lord's came one of the most mysterious innings ever played as England beat India by 202 runs. The hosts batted first and made what was then an unprecedented total: 334 for 4, quaint now (there were 11 scores higher in the 2015 World Cup) and less than a run a ball, but in 1975 the highest ODI total ever scored. It contained hints of the future too, as England batted around Dennis Amiss's 137 and then launched in the final overs, Chris Old producing a belt-and-braces 51 from 30, including a couple of sixes.

What happened next remains a curio that not even its central character can explain. Sunil Gavaskar felt the second ball of the innings, delivered by John Snow, brush the edge of his bat, a nick so faint that England didn't bother appealing. Years later, he would say: "I asked myself, 'Why the hell did I not walk the second ball?' I was caught behind and would have been out for zero. But nobody appealed. I had flashed outside the off stump... it was just such a faint nick that nobody appealed. The bowler went "Aah" and the keeper, Alan Knott, who was standing some way back, did the same. There was no real appeal, no proper 'How's that?' That little moment of hesitation got me so much flak all these years."

As it was he stayed in, and his lucid nightmare began. At first it seemed that Gavaskar and Solkar were seeing off the new ball. England's bowlers were fresh and buoyed by the record total they were defending, and when Solkar went, caught by Peter Lever from the bowling of Geoff Arnold for eight scraped from 34 deliveries, they had certainly won the early skirmishes. Overs ticked past. Gavaskar tried briefly to lift his torpor, but instead became more entrenched. "In the first few overs [I played] some shots which I'd never want to see again – cross-batted slogs," he said. "I wasn't overjoyed at the prospect of playing non-cricketing shots and I just got into a mental rut after that." Anshuman Gaekwad, best known for the resistance that would bring him Test cricket's then slowest double hundred, was next out with the score on 50, having contributed 22 to a partnership of 29. Gundappa Viswanath made 37 of the next 58 runs, and, as the innings crawled desperately on, reality hit home for the flag-waving Indians in the crowd. Several broke through the cordon of stewards and ran out to the middle to plead with Gavaskar, and the atmosphere soured as fans were left bewildered and ashamed at this apparent surrender. When it was over, Gavaskar had made 36 not out from 174 deliveries (a marginally quicker strike rate than Quraishy's innings but incontrovertibly, and for all time, the slowest World Cup innings of over 100 balls), hit one four and been the architect of overwhelming defeat. India's 132 for 3 had come at 2.2 runs per over. He returned to a silent dressing room.

Outside, bewilderment turned to anger. On the BBC broadcast Ted Dexter said that India should have called Gavaskar off the field. India's team manager GS Ramachand told the *Daily Express*: "It was the most disgraceful and selfish performance I have ever seen... his excuse was, the wicket was too slow to play shots but that was a stupid thing to say after England had scored 334." Speculation over why Gavaskar had batted as he did settled on conscious choice: either a mute protest at the impossibility of the task, a response to the psychic scars of the team being bowled out for 42 the last time they had appeared at Lord's, a protest over team selection, even a pragmatic decision to get some practice in for the games ahead.

As Gavaskar assumed the mantle of greatness across his epic career, the game became one of cricket's great oddities, an out-of-time, I-was-there moment, and yet the mystery at its heart remained. Why had he played that way, how had he become wedged in that mental rut from which he could not escape? He admitted he had thought about simply standing aside and letting the ball hit his stumps, anything to end the agony, but couldn't bring himself to do it. "It is something even now that I really can't explain."

But it was Dennis Lillee's spectacular detonation of the Pakistan middle order that made most of the next day's headlines, as the notion of tournament cricket caught the public imagination. Advance ticket sales for the second round of matches had been sluggish, but the glorious weather and the novelty of watching the world's best players compete in meaningful games concluded in a single day stirred something in the fans, and the tournament gathered a momentum that it would never lose.

There was a slightly lop-sided quality to the groups. On England's side of the draw, the hosts' progress was one of unruffled calm. After the non-event of India's chase at Lord's, they went to Trent Bridge to play New Zealand, where Keith Fletcher provided the hundred for the rest to bat around, and the bowlers, after they had Lever-ed out New Zealand's one real threat in Glenn Turner, again easily defended an above-par score, Tony Greig bagging four wickets as New Zealand fell to 186 all out.
East Africa were brushed aside in England's final game at Edgbaston, where another imposing total of 290 for 5 proved way too much for the minnows, for whom future England all-rounder Derek Pringle's father Don opened the bowling. Once John Snow had sliced the top from the East Africa batting with a four-wicket burst, they fell to 94 all out.

It left New Zealand's encounter with India as the pivotal game for the second semi-final place. They met in Manchester on a day when Glenn Turner would again hold sway. India went in first, their total of 230 all out coalescing around 70 from Abid Ali and a doughty, unexpected 26 from Venkat at No.10, before Turner took hold of the game and the destiny of the group with his second unbeaten hundred in three innings, this time 114.

Group B offered the real fireworks, where West Indies followed up their opening victory over Sri Lanka with a nipper against Pakistan, who showed for the first time in a world tournament, but certainly not the last, their love of a scrap. Robbed of skipper Asif Iqbal through injury and Imran Khan, who had returned to Oxford for his end-of-year exams, Majid stepped up to win the toss and elect to take first dig on an excellent Birmingham pitch. The Pakistan middle order prospered in conditions familiar to its county players, Majid's 60 supported by half centuries from Mushtaq and Wasim Raja and a cameo 24 from Javed. Majid was happy enough with 266 for 7, though wary of West Indies' batting depth.

They were to need all of that depth, and then some. Sarfraz Nawaz, a supremely skilful operator with the new ball and the man generally recognised as the inventor (or at least the discoverer) of reverse swing, opened up the top order, knocking over Roy Fredericks, Gordon Greenidge and Alvin Kallicharran, and by the time Viv Richards was sent back from his first one-day knock for 13, West Indies' hopes seemed to lie with Clive Lloyd. The skipper duly rebuilt with a half-century, only to fall caught behind to Javed's occasional leg spin. It left West Indies at 151 for 7, with more than a hundred still to get and just wicket-keeper Deryck Murray and the tail to get them.

Somehow, Murray dug it out, adding 37 with Vanburn Holder and then a knife-edge last wicket 64 with Andy Roberts. The keeper played out a penultimate over maiden from Pervez Mir, and with his frontline seamers bowled out, Majid gave the final over to Wasim Raja. Roberts, via a combination of leg byes, overthrows and a bunt through midwicket, got West Indies home with two balls to spare. A note of good old English farce capped the excitement: the man of the match award went to Sarfraz after the adjudicator Tom Graveney had to leave early and missed Murray's heroics. The last-wicket partnership of 64 is still, after more than 4,000 matches, the highest 10th-wicket stand in any successful ODI chase.

It was the key result in the group. West Indies reasserted their tag as favourites with a powerful seven-wicket win over Australia at a packed and partisan Oval. The Windies' fans provided an uplifting and cacophonous chorus of beer-can beats that would become famous as the soundtrack to most of their greatest victories in England. Chappell's Australians had already cemented their semi-final place with a 52-run win over Sri Lanka, who nonetheless offered hints of their own history in the making by responding to Australia's 328 with a gutsy 276 for 4, despite two of their batsmen being retired hurt and hospitalised by a rampant Jeff Thomson.

***

So after a triumphant group phase that occupied no more than a week, the semi-finals were set. England would face Australia at Headingley, while New Zealand headed south to meet West Indies at their Oval stronghold. As with the simultaneous group rounds, both games were scheduled for the same day, 18 June, a feast of cricket for a nation that was now caught up in the unfolding narrative of this new-fangled thing.

In the north, all of the pre-match talk was of Lillee and in particular Jeff Thomson, the human threat to life and limb who was fresh in the psyches of the English batsmen he had terrorised in the Ashes series of the previous winter, when he bowled as quickly as any man on earth ever had, and perhaps faster. As so often in cricket, the cards were to fall another way.

Chappell won the toss and, under cloud cover and seeing plenty of grass on the wicket, elected to field. Both Lillee and Thomson wanted to come down the hill from the Kirkstall Lane End, so Chappell held Thommo back and threw the new cherry to left-armer Gary Gilmour for a go from the Football Stand End. It was to prove one of cricket's great hunches. Gilmour may have been from Waratah on the New South Wales coast, but English conditions were to offer the natural environment for his probing swing. Bowling unchanged for his 12 overs, "Gus" reduced England's dreams to rubble. When he was done, the innings stood at 36 for 6, all of the wickets to Gilmour's booming inswing save that of Tony Greig, whom he'd fooled with a ball that slid across the stumps and took the edge. England stumbled blinking from the wreckage, captain Mike Denness with 27 and Geoff Arnold's 18 the only scores exceeding single figures. Needing 94 to reach the inaugural World Cup final, Australia's ambitions teetered on the brink as England's bowlers fought back. Rod Marsh's dismissal left Australia in mirror-image disarray at 39 for 6 in the only ODI ever in which both sides have been six down for less than 40, but when it's your day, it's your day, and Gilmour partnered with Doug Walters to knock off the remaining runs. He hadn't featured in any of the group games – and he was to play only five ODIs in his career – but there would be no leaving Gus out of the big match at Lord's.

There, Australia would once again face West Indies. Lloyd's team moved ominously past New Zealand, taking wickets with dread regularity once they'd overcome Glenn Turner and Geoff Howarth, and then chasing down a way-under-par 158 thanks to another gem from Kallicharran and a meaty half-century from Greenidge. Although they'd been drawn in the same group, the tournament had arrived at a final featuring its two outstanding teams. Lord's would be full for the shoot-out, and what drama they would witness.

***

The great day dawned in sunshine, and once the teams were under way at 11am, they would require all the daylight that remained to settle things. Both had proven one thing about this new format: that it was about attacking cricket. It may seem a statement of the obvious now, some 4,000 games later, but this was a form in embryo with a counter-theory that winning matches was about containing the opposition. That may have fitted with the more conservative nature of England's cricket, but not Ian Chappell's bullish aggression or Clive Lloyd's visions of athletic dominance.

As he had in the semi-final, Chappell won the toss and fielded, keen to deploy his heavy artillery while there was some early juice in the pitch. The first wicket went quickly, a perfect miniature of what both sides were trying to achieve as Roy Fredericks hooked Dennis Lillee into the stands only to tread on his wicket as he did so. Thomson found the edge of Greenidge's bat, Gilmour took the choice scalp of Alvin Kallicharran and the West Indies were rocking at 50 for 3 as their skipper walked out to meet Rohan Kanhai. The innings – and the final itself – turned when Ross Edwards dropped Lloyd at midwicket soon afterwards. "After that," Lloyd said, "everything hit the middle of the bat."

"He battered us from one side of Lord's to the other," Ian Chappell admitted, as the potent Australian attack met an even more powerful opponent. Lloyd wielded his famously heavy bat, bringing it down as straight as the railway sleeper it resembled. He and Kanhai added 149, of which Lloyd made 102 from just 85 deliveries. It was a genuine captain's innings, played from a place of peril in the spirit that he wanted his team to follow. Gilmour's golden arm found him four more wickets, but when the innings was done, West Indies had 291 on the board, riches that a few hours earlier had seemed too much to hope for.

Australia lost McCosker early but at 81 for 1 they were on top. There had been much talk about bowling power, but their innings was about to be derailed in another way that would come to shape the limited-overs game: the brilliance of the fielding. Viv Richards had not yet made his mark as a batsman – his first great year would come in 1976 – but with stunning athleticism and a rocket arm, he ran out first Alan Turner then, catastrophically for Australia, both of the Chappell brothers, two of the three with direct hits. Australia scrabbled to hold on, but when the ninth wicket went down, they were still 58 short with seven overs to come. At the crease were Dennis Lillee and Jeff Thomson, often Australia's match-winners, albeit not with the willow. There was nothing to lose, and they set about the task with a breezy fatalism, edging closer amid ratcheting tension and a dipping sun.

The clock ticked past eight, the runs required came down to 26 with two overs left, the crowds encroaching towards the boundary ropes as they anticipated the decisive moment. Thomson flicked the first ball of Holder's over to long leg and sprinted two, surviving with a dive and a spray of dust, umpire Dickie Bird shaking his head and ordering over-excited spectators back off the pitch. Order restored, Holder ran in again and Thomson hit him straight to the only fielder anywhere near him, Roy Fredericks at extra-cover, who held the catch. Tumult ensued. The crowd thought it was over and ran on but the batsmen, having heard umpire Tom Spencer's call of no-ball, began charging up and down. Fredericks shied at the stumps, missed and saw the ball disappear into the mob. Lillee and Thomson kept running as the crowd tried to pinch the players' sweaters from around Dickie Bird's neck. For a while, chaos reigned. When the spectators were eventually pushed back, Thomson asked Spencer: "How many are you giving us for that?"

"Two," Spencer said.

Lillee told Dickie Bird they'd run "about 17…"

Eventually they settled on four. The drama extended for three more deliveries until Thomson really was run out, the fifth such dismissal of the innings – still the joint ODI record – and West Indies had the first World Cup in their hands.

It was a wonderful ending, entirely unscriptable, and one that still resonates today. It seemed somehow perfect that such a happy, inspired couple of weeks should end in that way, with the best two teams gracing the old ground before a buoyant crowd. One-day cricket had started because the game needed a shot in the arm, and suddenly it had new momentum to carry it forwards. Almost 160,000 fans had come to the 15 matches, and the ICC were quick to schedule the next iteration for four years' time. When the *Wisden Almanack* bestowed its verdict the following April, it summed up perfectly what this "Festival of Cricket" had achieved: "It might not be termed first class, but the game has never provided better entertainment in one day."

1975

RESULTS AND STATISTICS

GROUP A TABLE

		P	W	L	Pts	RR
1	England	3	3	0	12	4.944
2	New Zealand	3	2	1	8	4.071
3	India	3	1	2	4	3.237
4	East Africa	3	0	3	0	2.036

GROUP B TABLE

		P	W	L	Pts	RR
1	West Indies	3	3	0	12	4.346
2	Australia	3	2	1	8	4.595
3	Pakistan	3	1	2	4	4.630
4	Sri Lanka	3	0	3	0	3.390

ENGLAND V AUSTRALIA

PRUDENTIAL WORLD CUP 1975 (SEMI-FINAL)

Venue: Headingley, Leeds
Date: 18th June 1975
Toss: Australia
Result: Australia won by 4 wickets
Umpires: WE Alley, DJ Constant
Man of the Match: GJ Gilmour

ENGLAND		R	b	SOUTH AFRICA		R	b
DL Amiss	lbw b Gilmour	2	7	A Turner	lbw b Arnold	7	20
B Wood	b Gilmour	6	19	RB McCosker	b Old	15	50
KWR Fletcher	lbw b Gilmour	8	45	*IM Chappell	lbw b Snow	2	19
AW Greig	c Marsh b Gilmour	7	25	GS Chappell	lbw b Snow	4	9
FC Hayes	lbw b Gilmour	4	6	KD Walters	not out	20	43
*MH Denness	b Walker	27	60	R Edwards	b Old	0	3
+APE Knott	lbw b Gilmour	0	5	+RW Marsh	b Old	5	8
CM Old	c GS Chappell b Walker	0	3	GJ Gilmour	not out	28	28
JA Snow	c Marsh b Lillee	2	14	MHN Walker	did not bat		
GG Arnold	not out	18	30	DK Lillee	did not bat		
P Lever	lbw b Walker	5	13	JR Thomson	did not bat		
Extras	(5 lb, 2 nb, 7 w)	14		Extras	(1 b, 6 lb, 6 nb)	13	
Total	(all out, 36.2 overs)	93		Total	(6 wickets, 28.4 overs)	94	

Fall of wickets: 1-2 (Amiss), 2-11 (Wood), 3-26 (Greig), 4-33 (Hayes), 5-35 (Fletcher), 6-36 (Knott), 7-37 (Old), 8-52 (Snow), 9-73 (Denness), 10-93 (Lever)

Fall of wickets: 1-17 (Turner), 2-24 (IM Chappell), 3-32 (GS Chappell), 4-32 (McCosker), 5-32 (Edwards), 6-39 (Marsh)

AUSTRALIA	O	M	R	W	Wd	Nb	ENGLAND	O	M	R	W	Wd	Nb
Lillee	9	3	26	1	-	-	Arnold	7.4	2	15	1	-	-
Gilmour	12	6	14	6	-	-	Snow	12	0	30	2	-	-
Walker	9.2	3	22	3	-	-	Old	7	2	29	3	-	-
Thomson	6	0	17	0	-	-	Lever	2	0	7	0	-	-

NEW ZEALAND V WEST INDIES

PRUDENTIAL WORLD CUP 1975 (SEMI-FINAL)

Venue: Kennington Oval, Kennington
Date: 18th June 1975
Toss: West Indies
Result: West Indies won by 5 wickets
Umpires: WL Budd, AE Fagg
Man of the Match: AI Kallicharran

NEW ZEALAND		R	b	WEST INDIES		R	b
*GM Turner	c Kanhai b Roberts	36	74	RC Fredericks	c Hastings b Hadlee	6	14
JFM Morrison	lbw b Julien	5	26	CG Greenidge	lbw b Collinge	55	95
GP Howarth	c Murray b Roberts	51	93	AI Kallicharran	c and b Collinge	72	92
JM Parker	b Lloyd	3	12	IVA Richards	lbw b Collinge	5	10
BF Hastings	not out	24	57	RB Kanhai	not out	12	18
+KJ Wadsworth	c Lloyd b Julien	11	21	*CH Lloyd	c Hastings b McKechnie	3	8
BJ McKechnie	lbw b Julien	1	9	BD Julien	not out	4	5
DR Hadlee	c Holder b Julien	0	10	+DL Murray	did not bat		
BL Cairns	b Holder	10	14	KD Boyce	did not bat		
HJ Howarth	b Holder	0	1	VA Holder	did not bat		
RO Collinge	b Holder	2	4	AME Roberts	did not bat		
Extras	(1 b, 5 lb, 7 nb, 2 w)	15		Extras	(1 lb, 1 nb)	2	
Total	(all out, 52.2 overs)	158		Total	(5 wickets, 40.1 overs)	159	

Fall of wickets: 1-8 (Morrison), 2-98 (Turner), 3-105 (GP Howarth), 4-106 (Parker), 5-125 (Wadsworth), 6-133 (McKechnie), 7-139 (Hadlee), 8-155 (Cairns), 9-155 (HJ Howarth), 10-158 (Collinge)

Fall of wickets: 1-8 (Fredericks), 2-133 (Kallicharran), 3-139 (Richards), 4-142 (Greenidge), 5-151 (Lloyd)

WEST INDIES	O	M	R	W	Wd	Nb	NEW ZEALAND	O	M	R	W	Wd	Nb
Julien	12	5	27	4	-	-	Collinge	12	4	28	3	-	-
Roberts	11	3	18	2	-	-	Hadlee	10	0	54	1	-	-
Holder	8.2	0	30	3	-	-	Cairns	6.1	2	23	0	-	-
Boyce	9	0	31	0	-	-	McKechnie	8	0	37	1	-	-
Lloyd	12	1	37	1	-	-	HJ Howarth	4	0	15	0	-	-

AUSTRALIA V WEST INDIES

PRUDENTIAL WORLD CUP 1975 (FINAL)

Venue: Lord's Cricket Ground, St John's Wood
Date: 21st June 1975
Toss: Australia
Result: West Indies won by 17 runs
Umpires: HD Bird, TW Spencer
Man of the Match: CH Lloyd

WEST INDIES		R	b	AUSTRALIA		R	b
RC Fredericks	hit wkt b Lillee	7	13	A Turner	run out (Richards)	40	54
CG Greenidge	c Marsh b Thomson	13	61	RB McCosker	c Kallicharran b Boyce	7	24
AI Kallicharran	c Marsh b Gilmour	12	18	*IM Chappell	run out (Richards->Lloyd)	62	93
RB Kanhai	b Gilmour	55	105	GS Chappell	run out (Richards)	15	23
*CH Lloyd	c Marsh b Gilmour	102	85	KD Walters	b Lloyd	35	51
IVA Richards	b Gilmour	5	11	+RW Marsh	b Boyce	11	24
KD Boyce	c GS Chappell b Thomson	34	37	R Edwards	c Fredericks b Boyce	28	37
BD Julien	not out	26	37	GJ Gilmour	c Kanhai b Boyce	14	11
+DL Murray	c and b Gilmour	14	10	MHN Walker	run out (Holder)	7	9
VA Holder	not out	6	2	JR Thomson	run out (Murray)	21	21
AME Roberts	did not bat			DK Lillee	not out	16	19
Extras	(6 lb, 11 nb)	17		Extras	(2 b, 9 lb, 7 nb)	18	
Total	(8 wickets, 60 overs)	291		Total	(all out, 58.4 overs)	274	

Fall of wickets: 1-12 (Fredericks), 2-27 (Kallicharran), 3-50 (Greenidge), 4-199 (Lloyd), 5-206 (Kanhai), 6-209 (Richards), 7-261 (Boyce), 8-285 (Murray)

Fall of wickets: 1-25 (McCosker), 2-81 (Turner), 3-115 (GS Chappell), 4-162 (IM Chappell), 5-170 (Walters), 6-195 (Marsh), 7-221 (Gilmour), 8-231 (Edwards), 9-233 (Walker), 10-274 (Thomson, 58.4 ov)

AUSTRALIA	O	M	R	W	Wd	Nb	WEST INDIES	O	M	R	W	Wd	Nb
Lillee	12	1	55	1	-	-	Julien	12	0	58	0	-	-
Gilmour	12	2	48	5	-	-	Roberts	11	1	45	0	-	-
Thomson	12	1	44	2	-	-	Boyce	12	0	50	4	-	-
Walker	12	1	71	0	-	-	Holder	11.4	1	65	0	-	-
GS Chappell	7	0	33	0	-	-	Lloyd	12	1	38	1	-	-
Walters	5	0	23	0	-	-							

MOST RUNS

Player	Mat	Inns	NO	Runs	HS	Ave	BF	SR	100	50	0	4s	6s
GM Turner (NZ)	4	4	2	333	171*	166.5	486	68.51	2	0	0	33	2
DL Amiss (ENG)	4	4	0	243	137	60.75	288	84.37	1	1	0	28	0
Majid Khan (PAK)	3	3	0	209	84	69.66	277	75.45	0	3	0	26	1
KWR Fletcher (ENG)	4	3	0	207	131	69	299	69.23	1	1	0	17	1
A Turner (AUS)	5	5	0	201	101	40.2	259	77.6	1	0	0	17	1
AI Kallicharran (WI)	5	5	1	197	78	49.25	255	77.25	0	2	0	26	2
R Edwards (AUS)	5	4	1	166	80*	55.33	208	79.8	0	2	1	14	0
CH Lloyd (WI)	5	3	0	158	102	52.66	151	104.63	1	1	0	20	2
Zaheer Abbas (PAK)	3	3	0	136	97	45.33	155	87.74	0	1	0	16	1
GS Chappell (AUS)	5	5	0	129	50	25.8	171	75.43	0	1	0	13	1
KD Walters (AUS)	5	5	1	123	59	30.75	191	64.39	0	1	0	12	0
IM Chappell (AUS)	5	5	0	121	62	24.2	212	57.07	0	1	0	12	0
RB McCosker (AUS)	5	5	0	120	73	24	264	45.45	0	1	1	5	0
RC Fredericks (WI)	5	5	0	116	58	23.2	181	64.08	0	1	0	11	0
SM Gavaskar (INDIA)	3	3	2	113	65*	113	274	41.24	0	1	0	12	0
MH Denness (ENG)	4	4	2	113	37*	56.5	149	75.83	0	0	0	5	2
RB Kanhai (WI)	5	4	2	109	55	54.5	198	55.05	0	1	0	14	0
DL Murray (WI)	5	3	2	105	61*	105	136	77.2	0	1	0	9	2
Wasim Raja (PAK)	3	3	0	91	58	30.33	120	75.83	0	1	0	10	0
JFM Morrison (NZ)	4	4	0	91	55	22.75	182	50	0	1	0	8	1
FC Hayes (ENG)	3	3	0	90	52	30	136	66.17	0	1	0	12	2
Mushtaq Mohammad (PAK)	3	3	0	89	55	29.66	164	54.26	0	1	0	5	0
CM Old (ENG)	4	4	2	89	51*	44.5	65	136.92	0	1	1	7	3
CG Greenidge (WI)	4	4	0	88	55	22	180	48.88	0	1	0	13	1
Sadiq Mohammad (PAK)	3	3	0	85	74	28.33	123	69.1	0	1	0	13	1

MOST WICKETS

Player	Mat	Inns	Overs	Mdns	Runs	Wkts	BBI	Ave	Econ	SR	4	5
GJ Gilmour (AUS)	2	2	24	8	62	11	6/14	5.63	2.58	13	0	2
BD Julien (WI)	5	5	60	11	177	10	4/20	17.7	2.95	36	2	0
KD Boyce (WI)	5	5	52	3	185	10	4/50	18.5	3.55	31.2	1	0
DR Hadlee (NZ)	4	4	46	5	162	8	3/21	20.25	3.52	34.5	0	0
AME Roberts (WI)	5	5	56.4	11	165	8	3/39	20.62	2.91	42.5	0	0
DK Lillee (AUS)	5	5	53	6	223	8	5/34	27.87	4.2	39.7	0	1
CM Old (ENG)	4	4	32.3	8	86	7	3/29	12.28	2.64	27.8	0	0
JA Snow (ENG)	3	3	36	8	65	6	4/11	10.83	1.8	36	1	0
AW Greig (ENG)	4	3	31	2	89	6	4/45	14.83	2.87	31	1	0
S Abid Ali (INDIA)	3	3	36	7	115	6	2/22	19.16	3.19	36	0	0
RO Collinge (NZ)	4	4	48	13	137	6	3/28	22.83	2.85	48	0	0
MHN Walker (AUS)	5	5	57.2	10	210	6	3/22	35	3.66	57.3	0	0
Imran Khan (PAK)	2	2	17.1	3	59	5	3/15	11.8	3.43	20.6	0	0
P Lever (ENG)	4	4	36	3	92	5	3/32	18.4	2.55	43.2	0	0
Naseer Malik (PAK)	3	3	30	5	98	5	2/37	19.6	3.26	36	0	0
Sarfraz Nawaz (PAK)	2	2	24	1	107	5	4/44	21.4	4.45	28.8	1	0
S Madan Lal (INDIA)	3	3	33.2	4	141	5	3/15	28.2	4.23	40	0	0
HJ Howarth (NZ)	4	4	40	5	148	5	3/29	29.6	3.7	48	0	0
VA Holder (WI)	5	5	43.2	4	184	5	3/30	36.8	4.24	52	0	0
JR Thomson (AUS)	5	5	44	9	129	4	2/44	32.25	2.93	66	0	0
M Amarnath (INDIA)	3	3	30	3	139	4	2/39	34.75	4.63	45	0	0
DS de Silva (SL)	3	3	32	5	154	4	2/60	38.5	4.81	48	0	0
BJ McKechnie (NZ)	4	4	44	5	163	4	3/49	40.75	3.7	66	0	0
Zulfiqar Ali (EAf)	3	3	35	3	166	4	3/63	41.5	4.74	52.5	0	0
IVA Richards (WI)	5	2	10	0	39	3	2/18	13	3.9	20	0	0

HIGH SCORES

Player	Runs	Balls	4s	6s	SR	Team	Opposition	Ground
GM Turner	171*	201	16	2	85.07	New Zealand	v East Africa	Birmingham
DL Amiss	137	147	18	0	93.19	England	v India	Lord's
KWR Fletcher	131	147	13	0	89.11	England	v New Zealand	Nottingham
GM Turner	114*	177	13	0	64.4	New Zealand	v India	Manchester
CH Lloyd	102	85	12	2	120	West Indies	v Australia	Lord's
A Turner	101	113	9	1	89.38	Australia	v Sri Lanka	The Oval
Zaheer Abbas	97	89	10	1	108.98	Pakistan	v Sri Lanka	Nottingham
DL Amiss	88	116	7	0	75.86	England	v East Africa	Birmingham
Majid Khan	84	93	9	1	90.32	Pakistan	v Sri Lanka	Nottingham
R Edwards	80*	94	6	0	85.1	Australia	v Pakistan	Leeds

BEST BOWLING

Player	Overs	Mdns	Runs	Wkts	Econ	Team	Opposition	Ground
GJ Gilmour	12	6	14	6	1.16	Australia	v England	Leeds
DK Lillee	12	2	34	5	2.83	Australia	v Pakistan	Leeds
GJ Gilmour	12	2	48	5	4	Australia	v West Indies	Lord's
JA Snow	12	6	11	4	0.91	England	v East Africa	Birmingham
BD Julien	12	3	20	4	1.66	West Indies	v Sri Lanka	Manchester
BD Julien	12	5	27	4	2.25	West Indies	v New Zealand	The Oval
Sarfraz Nawaz	12	1	44	4	3.66	Pakistan	v West Indies	Birmingham
AW Greig	12	0	45	4	3.75	England	v New Zealand	Nottingham
KD Boyce	12	0	50	4	4.16	West Indies	v Australia	Lord's
S Madan Lal	9.3	2	15	3	1.57	India	v East Africa	Leeds

1979

SAME AGAIN, PLEASE!

BY MATT THACKER

The inaugural ICC World Cup had been a success whichever way you looked at it. A step into the unknown had brought great cricket, great weather, great PR, not inconsiderable sponsorship and ticket revenue, and the broadening of cricket's base. So, come 1979, why change a winning formula?

That was the thinking anyway. The World Cup would take place in the same fortnight in June, at the same six venues, and with the same 60-over limit. It would feature the same big six teams plus two additional sides, who would be expected to take part but not to take the spoils. But cricket had undergone seismic changes in the previous four years and things could and would never be the same again.

It started with the advent of colour TV in Australia, just as the first ICC World Cup was about to get under way in England in 1975. Businessman Kerry Packer had taken charge of commercial network Channel Nine and wanted to include more sports broadcasts, including cricket, which was regaining popularity in Australia with the likes of Dennis Lillee, Jeff Thomson, and Greg and Ian Chappell to the fore. Packer bid for the rights to broadcast home Tests but was turned down, despite the Channel Nine offer dwarfing that of the incumbent's, national broadcaster ABC. Incensed, Packer started secretly contracting players from around the world to play a series of exhibition games.

The upshot was that the first season of World Series Cricket (WSC) took place in 1978–79 in Australia and became, after an initially underwhelming reaction, a huge success. This was largely down to one-day cricket, which had been popularised by the World Cup in 1975 but was still in its infancy. WSC ushered in innovations such as coloured clothing, white balls, fielding restrictions, batting helmets and day-night cricket, the first major instance of which was when 40,000 plus fans flocked into the Sydney Cricket Ground in November 1978. Packer had made cricket into entertainment and cricketers into well-paid stars, with increased fitness levels now part and parcel of the game. The so-called "Packer Circus" threatened to destroy the game's traditional set-up, with national cricket boards no longer in control of their own players. The modern age of cricket was being brought, kicking and screaming, into the world. Or in this case, the World Cup.

A truce was brokered between Packer and the Australian Cricket Board (ACB) in early 1979, just before the World Cup was due to start, resulting in Channel Nine gaining exclusive rights to promote the Australian game for the next decade. Australia's WSC players – including Lillee, Thomson, the Chappells, Rod Marsh, David Hookes – were ineligible for selection for the World Cup so the finalists from 1975, the powerhouses of world cricket through most of the game's existence, would be at a huge disadvantage. England too were without their WSC stars (Tony Greig, Alan Knott, Bob Woolmer, Derek Underwood, John Snow and Dennis Amiss) but the sheer weight of numbers of those involved from the Australian side – almost 30 players – made their absence more significant.

There was turmoil in the non-cricketing universe too. In England, the winter of 1978 had seen widespread strikes by public sector trades unions, leading to rubbish being piled up on the pavements and understaffed hospitals. Adding a literal chill to what was dubbed the "Winter of Discontent", blizzards swept across the country during the early months of the year, with snow falling in the north even as the tournament was getting under way in June. The downfall of the Labour government and the election of the UK's first female Prime Minister, Margaret Thatcher, in May left many in the country turning towards the World Cup to provide the antidote in the form of a glorious summer.

***

Since 1975, West Indies had been the dominant force in world cricket, and there were few who seriously doubted that they would regain their crown, with the vast majority of their squad having the additional advantage of being battle-hardened by WSC. True, the team had been thrashed 5–1 by Australia Down Under in a Test series just after the 1975 World Cup but that was the turning point, leading captain Clive Lloyd to deploy four devastating quicks, who tore apart all but the very best batting line-ups. Michael Holding, Colin Croft, Joel Garner and a teenage Malcolm Marshall had all made their international bows, joining Andy Roberts as destroyers-in-chief, and Viv Richards had emerged as the world's leading batsman.

As for the rest, England were a very different group from four years earlier, with only Chris Old surviving from the 1975 squad. This was very much the England

Test side that had triumphed 5–1 in Australia over the winter against a side shorn of its WSC players. Despite the presence of 38-year-old Geoff Boycott and 37-year-old skipper Mike Brearley, there was an air of relative youth about it – the middle order G-Force of David Gower, Graham Gooch and Mike Gatting were all in their mid-20s and a young Ian Botham had already started to make a name for himself. He was one of the four decade-defining all-rounders, along with Imran Khan, Kapil Dev and Richard Hadlee, who took part in the 1979 ICC Cricket World Cup.

Pakistan were a strong side. In Test matches, which was still the criteria for judging a team with one-day cricket a relative novelty, they had been blown away in a Test series in England the previous summer (Botham scoring a hundred and taking 8 for 34 in his seventh Test and his first at Lord's) but since then had beaten India at home, New Zealand away and drawn in Australia in a bad-tempered series. They could call on the firepower of Majid Khan, Zaheer Abbas and Javed Miandad with the bat, the all-round skills of Imran and the nous of Sarfraz Nawaz.

India had played just ten ODIs in their history, by far the fewest of any of the six major Test-playing nations (England had racked up 36 by this stage and Australia 22), but they had the batting talent of Sunil Gavaskar, Gundappa Viswanath and the young Dilip Vengsarkar, allied to the lullaby lure of Bishan Bedi's left-arm spin and the off-breaks of skipper Venkat.

The Antipodean assault on the World Cup, thanks to WSC, had been left light in firepower from Australia's point of view, with captain Kim Hughes leading a squad of players, very few of whom would have been in the selectors' thoughts had it not been for Packer's intervention. The gaps in the batting line-ups did lead to the inclusion of the 23-year-old Allan Border, who had debuted that winter, to start a World Cup career that would culminate in him holding the trophy aloft in the Calcutta night sky eight years later. As for the New Zealanders, the core of their squad was returning, with Hadlee now a world-class operator, supported by Lance Cairns and Ewen Chatfield, while run-scoring was still in the hands of Geoff Howarth and Glenn Turner, alongside new boys John Wright and Bruce Edgar.

In contrast to 1975, the final two sides were no longer invitees, but had to qualify for the tournament by reaching the final of the ICC Trophy, the first of its kind to be staged. This was played in the Midlands on club grounds between 22 May and 21 June, with three groups of five battling it out.

It all started at Pickwick CC in Birmingham with Singapore taking on Argentina in group A and winning by one wicket. Bermuda went on to top that group, edging out East Africa, 1975 World Cup participants, meaning that no African side would appear in the World Cup proper for the first and only time in the tournament's history. Group B was topped by Denmark, who bowled out Canada for 72 in the table-deciding clash, with both sides having defeated a fledgling Bangladesh team. In group C, Sri Lanka, Wales and USA had identical records, partly down to the fact that Sri Lanka refused to play Israel on political grounds, but the Lankans went through on run rate. The Netherlands, who would go on to appear in four World Cups, could win only one match.

The semi-finals took place on 6 June, just three days before the World Cup started, and so Sri Lanka, having disposed of Denmark at the Allied Breweries ground in Burton-on-Trent on the Wednesday, found themselves up against New Zealand at Trent Bridge on the Saturday while Canada, victors over Bermuda in a tight game at the Mitchells and Butler's ground in Birmingham, similarly had a two-day turnaround before their appointment with Pakistan at Headingley.

The day after the World Cup proper's own finalists were decided, with the Old Trafford and Oval semi-finals taking place on 20 June, Sri Lanka and Canada returned to finish the job, Sri Lanka – emboldened perhaps by their showing in the tournament – racking up 324 for 8, with Duleep Mendis outstanding, and restricting Canada to 264 for 5. Sri Lanka's rise to the top had begun. Three years later they would become an ICC Full Member and 16 years on, they would be world champions.

***

And so to the Prudential Cup itself, the sponsorship (£250,000 this time) having been retained from 1975, as it would be in 1983. With Packer having got what he (and most players) wanted, the World Cup was the calm after the World Series storm. As John Arlott put it in the newly launched *Wisden Cricket Monthly* magazine: "All at once the air over our cricket grounds is sweet; free from the smell of war." Calm perhaps, but hardly the sunlit fortnight of four years previous. In the bleak midsummer, several of the games leaked and dripped into reserve days – the conditions helping make this the lowest-scoring (25.5 runs per wicket) and slowest-scoring (3.54 runs per over) World Cup ever. There were only two centuries in the whole event, one on the first day by Greenidge against India, and one on the last, Richards' masterpiece against England at Lord's. In the 11 completed matches in the group stages – West Indies v Sri Lanka at The Oval was the first ever World Cup abandonment without a ball bowled, despite having two reserve days –,a total of 200 was breached just four times. It was not the weather, or the tournament, for spinners – they took only 18 of the 184 wickets to fall to bowlers, of which front-line spinners were responsible for just seven. In all other World Cups, spinners have taken at least 15 per cent of wickets.

Eight years after the first ODI came the opening day of this World Cup, featuring the 61st, 62nd, 63rd and 64th ODIs. As in 1975, all the teams played on the opening day, with the most eye-catching match-up being in group A, between the old enemies England and Australia at the Home of Cricket, Lord's. In front of a full house of 25,000, England elected to field first under leaden skies and Australia's 14 runs from the first 10 overs gave an indication of the way the tournament would go, seamers Bob Willis, Mike Hendrick, Botham and Old proving both parsimonious and threatening. Indeed, as in 1975, England's bowlers ended up with the lowest collective average (15.8 in 1975; 20.2 in 1979), and best economy rate (2.3 in 1975, 2.9 in 1979) of any side.

On top they may have been but this did not stop Brearley bringing on Boycott just before lunch to send down a few of his part-time, round-the-wicket trundlers. He continued after the break, reducing Australia from 97 for 1 to 111 for 3, inducing Andrew Hilditch to play on and Kim Hughes to spoon the ball up to an inrushing Hendrick. Calamity for the Aussies (and for all of those for whom a man bowling in his cap was anathema) and joy for England.

It was further downhill from there with Australia, having had five men run out in their previous World Cup match (the final in 1975), seeing four of their last five wickets go the same way this time round. The result – an underwhelming 159 for 9.

At 5 for 2, with Boycott (more wickets than runs in the match!) and Derek Randall gone, things did not look bright, but a sheet anchor 147-ball 44 from Brearley (shades of Gavaskar in 1975…) and a 50 from guardsman Gooch, playing in the first of his four World Cups, saw England home with over 10 overs to spare.

The other group A game on the opening day saw Pakistan pitted against Canada, over half of whose players were West Indian-born. Curiously batting first at Headingley after winning the toss, Canada edged up to 85 for 1 but Pakistan's bowlers were just too good, squeezing the life out of an innings which limped to 139 for 9, Majid's occasional off-spin conceding just 11 runs in 11 overs. Pakistan cruised to their target, losing just two wickets.

Group B saw the reigning champions West Indies take on India, who had won just one game in the 1975 World Cup and were to go one worse this time round. Viswanath's 75 was the only score above 15 as West Indies inserted India and unleashed their quarter of Roberts, Holding, Garner and Croft (Marshall did not get a game in the entire Word Cup), aiming to get the most out of the early moisture in the Edgbaston pitch. They all took wickets but Holding's 4 for 33 did most damage as he ripped out the top order. 190 was the target for openers Greenidge, in his tenth ODI, and Haynes, in his second. The latter had announced his ODI arrival earlier in the year with 148 on debut against Australia and the two had opened together in two Tests already but this was the first time they had walked to the crease together in an ODI. Inevitably, they put on a hundred, a feat they were to achieve 15 times in total.

To complete the quartet of curtain openers, New Zealand took on Sri Lanka at Trent Bridge and came away with the fourth facile win of the day. The Kiwis followed England and West Indies' template and won the toss and bowled, the game running along the same lines as the day's other matches, Sri Lanka struggling to 189 all out and New Zealand chasing that down with ease, losing just one wicket. Sri Lankan skipper Anura Tennekoon resisted for 59 but Hadlee and co were too canny. Turner, Wright and Howarth all found form, although Howarth pulled a hamstring that was to keep him out of action until the semi-final.

Group B was up again on the Wednesday, although incessant rain in London meant a three-day wash-out for West Indies and Sri Lanka. The pitch was slightly damp but the weather was better up in Leeds, where it looked like a straight shoot-out for a semi-final place between New Zealand and India. And for a fifth straight game, the team batting first struggled to a sub-par total, prefacing a straightforward run chase. It was Kiwi skipper Mark Burgess who enjoyed the luck of the toss again and his bowlers shared the wickets around, only Gavaskar's half-century causing them any real problems. In reply, Wright, Edgar and Turner calmly steered the ship home, Turner in the process lifting his World Cup average after six matches to a frankly ludicrous 229.5.

With Canada unlikely to pull any surprises, the next day saw another probable knock-out game between Pakistan and Australia. As it transpired, a sixth big win out of six games saw Australia exit the tournament, Pakistan's 286 for 7 proving way too many for the callow Aussies as the match went into a reserve day. Kim Hughes had followed the now expected strategy of putting in the opposition on a dank English day pock-marked by rain breaks, and things were going to plan for most of the innings until Javed Miandad and Asif Iqbal upped the ante, scoring at a run a ball, a rare feat in this tournament, in putting on 87. Sparky cameos from Wasim Raja and Imran saw Pakistan – their side packed with players who had one-day experience in county cricket – to their imposing total, with 47 runs walloped from the last five.

Pakistan opened with the off-spin of Majid and the steady slow-medium of skipper Asif Iqbal and the next day they dismantled the Aussie line-up despite Hilditch's 72. Australia, with two losses from two, were as good as gone.

That was confirmed as the other game in group A ended, well into the evening of the reserve day, England comprehensively beating Canada by eight wickets at Old Trafford, having bowled them out for just 45 in 40.3 overs, which would remain the lowest score in ODIs until West Indies dismissed Pakistan for 43 in 1993. Inexplicably, given the near-farcical conditions, Canada's captain Bryan Mauricette again elected to bat, only to have confirmed what most suspected, that the best English seamers in the worst English conditions can be pretty near unplayable. 10.3-3-11-4 from Willis, 8-4-5-1 from Hendrick, 10-5-8-4 from Old spelled carnage, only Franklyn Dennis reaching double figures before he was out hit wicket. A heavy storm looked like it was going to put paid to England's chances of knocking off the runs but they got on a little after 7pm, taking 13.5 overs to get home, if not dry.

So with each side having played just two games, the semi-finalists were already decided, barring New Zealand pulling off a huge upset and beating the mighty West Indies and Sri Lanka becoming the first ever Associate nation to beat a Full Member in an ODI.

Well, one out of two ain't bad.

In a game that started on Saturday and ended on Monday (no World Cup cricket on Sundays back then!) Sri Lanka fulfilled their part of the bargain, racking up 238 for 5 up at Old Trafford – with 50s from Sunil Wettimuny, Roy Dias and Duleep

Mendis, with 17-year-old Sudath Pasqual helping Mendis add 52 in seven overs. That proved too big an ask for India, who subsided to 191 all out. They did at least take five wickets, having managed just one in their first match and two in the second. Unfortunately for Sri Lanka they knew that they were unable to progress, with Trent Bridge having managed to get a full game in on the Saturday.

Mark Burgess had won his third successive toss and for the third time inserted the opposition. Although things never got out of control, West Indies were able to score steadily and an unbeaten 73 from 80 balls from skipper Lloyd ensured the defending champions would have plenty to bowl at. Having done his bit, Lloyd let his four quicks off the leash and they combined hostility with accuracy, keeping New Zealand – still missing Howarth – in check, the innings ending at 212 for 9.

In group A, Australia finished with a win at Edgbaston, bowling out Canada for 105 (despite Glenroy Sealy taking 16 off the first over, bowled by Rodney Hogg), Alan Hurst finishing the tournament and his ODI career with one of only two 5-fors in the event. Australia knocked off the runs three wickets down, their underwhelming tournament over, with 1979 being one of only three times in World Cup history that they have not at least got through the group stages.

The clash between England and Pakistan, realistically to avoid playing West Indies in the semi-final, was the first genuinely close game of the tournament. Asif Iqbal put England in and saw Brearley and Randall depart in the first couple of overs. It was a struggle throughout and at 118 for 8, it looked for all money as if the hosts would have to face the champions in the semis. But the Bobs, Taylor and Willis, nudged, nurdled and slashed their way to a 43-run partnership, with the team finishing on 165 for 9, which the past week suggested was almost par. At 27 without loss, the hosts' hopes were fading. At 34 for 6, with Hendrick rampant and Botham chipping in, the smiles were back on English faces. But Pakistan captain Asif scored the only half-century of the match and Wasim Raja, Imran and Wasim Bari, a more-than-capable No.10, all chipped in, leaving Pakistan needing 21 to win with two wickets and plenty of overs left. Cue another Brearley-Boycott masterstroke. The skipper whistled up his opening batsman, who jogged in to lure both Wasim Bari and Sikander Bakht into fatal errors, the last man brilliantly caught by Hendrick at mid-on to complete a man-of-the-match performance. The winning margin – just 14 runs.

So West Indies would take on Pakistan, and England would play New Zealand...

***

At a gloriously sunny Old Trafford, Mark Burgess made it four tosses from four, yet again enabling his bowlers to have first use of the pitch. Wayne Larkins, replacing Phil Edmonds, was brought in for an intimidating ODI debut but he and Boycott were soon gone. Brearley and Gooch steadied the ship and Derek Randall chipped in to get England up to a serviceable 221 for 8. At 104 for 2 with John Wright well set and run-machine Glenn Turner to come, New Zealand were firm favourites.

But England's seamers kept plugging away, their fielders were tigerish (the impish Randall's run out of Wright proving a turning point), Boycott was again effective, and the required run rate kept nudging up. Three of England's bowlers – Willis, Hendrick and Botham – were injured but they had just enough runs to hold on, Botham defending 14 off the last over, helped by fielding restrictions being a thing of the future. England had won their second tight match (in truth, the only two of the tournament) in five days and were in the final.

At The Oval, Pakistan inserted West Indies only to see Greenidge and Haynes rack up their second century partnership of the World Cup. That 132-run start was built on by Richards, Lloyd and Collis King – a sign of things to come – and West Indies had the highest score of the World Cup, 293 for 6. In a glorious 166-run partnership spanning 36 overs, it looked like Majid, in his last World Cup innings, and Zaheer Abbas had tamed the mighty Caribbean pace bowlers but at 176 for 1, Colin Croft induced Zaheer to edge through to Deryck Murray for 93, still the highest score in a Word Cup semi-final defeat. Croft then had Majid taken by Kallicharran and Javed lbw first ball, and Viv Richards ran through the lower middle order to see Pakistan dismissed for a round 250.

***

Lord's, 23 June 1979. England v West Indies, the final most wanted to see. Both sides having won every game they had played. Hosts versus champions. England's yeomen against West Indies' showmen. The day again dawned bright, with the match unsurprisingly a 25,000 sell-out, with hundreds more queuing outside in vain. The bad news for England was that Bob Willis was out, struck down by the knee injury that had recurred in the semi-final. Larkins retained his place, Edmonds was brought back and England would be relying on Boycott – a revelation with the ball in the tournament to date – and Gooch to make up the fifth bowler's allocation.

Brearley did what pretty much every captain did on winning the toss in a Lord's final and elected to field, hopeful the morning dew would aid his seam bowlers. Botham, Hendrick and Old did not let their captain down, and England's fielders, the livewires Randall and Gower prominent, made sure no easy runs were on offer. At 99 for 4, with captain Clive Lloyd, the 1975 match-winner, back in the pavilion following a brilliant caught and bowled by Old, things were looking good for the hosts.

Enter Collis King to join Viv Richards, who had started cautiously. Richards says that he offered his new batting partner some advice as he walked to the wicket, with lunch not too far off: "Take it easy. We have plenty of time." King, Richards remembers, had other ideas. "Smokey," he replied, "I ain't gonna let Geoffrey get this, man. In the league there would be no mercy, so why should this be any different?"

77 minutes of batting later King was caught on the edge by Randall at deep square. In that time he had put on 139 with Richards, his share a breath-taking 86 in just 66 balls, with 10 fours and three sixes. England's fifth bowler – a combination of Boycott, Gooch and Larkins – had gone for 86 wicket-less runs in 12 overs and

the match was disappearing. Brearley was later criticised for not bringing back his front-line bowlers back but Clive Lloyd reckoned: "I don't think any bowler would have bothered King, the mood he was in that day. By the time has was out, I knew the match was ours."

Once King had departed, the king turned on the style. England can point to the scorecard and say the last three batsmen all made ducks but that did not stem the flow of runs from the other end. Those remaining batsmen scored five of the final 48 runs as Richards treated the bowlers with disdain, "as if they were net bowlers" according to Tony Cozier, the crowning moment being the last ball of the innings, delivered by Hendrick and deposited some distance over the square leg boundary into the Mound Stand from outside off stump. "I had sussed with long off and long on back that it would be fullish to allow me one or two," Richards said. "It was the correct ball, much fuller but slightly off the line and I stepped to the off side and flicked it." 286 for 9. In 1979, a score of Himalayan proportions.

The journey of a thousand miles begins with a single step. And Everest is only conquered by setting up basecamp. It is not known whether Mike Brearley, famously possessing "a degree in people" according to Australian quick Rodney Hogg, tried to rally his shell-shocked troops by making these points during the innings break but he and Boycott certainly adopted a softly, softly approach. In brilliant sunshine and on a Lord's track made for batting, the openers blunted the supreme West Indian quicks, understandably opting for survival rather than run-scoring – eight runs came off the first six overs and it was not until the seventeenth that Boycott made it into double figures.

If Brearley was considered to be the best tactical brain in the game, it was his opposite number Clive Lloyd who, inadvertently or not, provided a masterstroke. Tea had come after 25 overs with the score on 79 for 0, and the 100 was brought up seven overs later. With the field set back, Brearley and Boycott were pushing Richards for singles when the Yorkshireman ran down the pitch to try and hit over the top. He succeeded only in finding mid-on where the West Indian captain, who had already put down Brearley off Croft early in the piece, dropped a sitter. "A lot of people suggested I put it down purposefully just to keep him in. It's not true, but it wouldn't have been a bad tactic," said Lloyd.

37 overs ticked by and still no wicket had fallen. But the score had reached only 129. 22 overs left, 158 needed. These days, that equation would favour the batting side, with fielding restrictions in place, and the fact that those overs would not be bowled by four of the greatest fast bowlers ever to play the game.

Holding returned to have Brearley caught by King on the square leg boundary and Boycott mishooking to midwicket. Randall and Gooch desperately tried to up the rate and for a while their counter-punch was successful as the score climbed to 183 for 2 in the 47th over. Eight an over needed, eight wickets left. As it transpired, those last eight wickets added 11 runs in the next four overs, the 6ft 8 Joel Garner taking 5 for 4 in 11 balls, his spearing, searing yorkers coming from over the top of the sightscreen and proving more than a match for England's middle and lower order. Going one better than the West Indies, the last four men dismissed made ducks, making a grand total of eight in the match. Garner's 5 for 38, the tournament's second 5-for, are still the best bowling figures in a World Cup final.

Clive Lloyd, as in 1975, received the winners' cheque on the Lord's balcony – £10,000 compared to £4,000 for England – with Viv Richards pocketing £300 for his man of the match performance. Across the 14 games, attendances were down on four years earlier – 132,000 compared to some 160,000 – due to the bad weather but there was still a £350,000 surplus to distribute to ICC Full and Associate Members. And, after a meeting at the completion of the tournament, it was announced that the ICC World Cup would become a quadrennial event, with the next edition also taking place in England. Roll on 1983.

1979

RESULTS AND STATISTICS

GROUP A TABLE

		P	W	L	A	Pts	RR
1	England	3	3	0	0	12	3.066
2	Pakistan	3	2	1	0	8	3.695
3	Australia	3	1	2	0	4	3.227
4	Canada	3	0	3	0	0	2.159

GROUP B TABLE

		P	W	L	A	Pts	RR
1	West Indies	3	2	0	1	10	3.928
2	New Zealand	3	2	1	0	8	3.553
3	Sri Lanka	3	1	1	1	6	3.655
4	India	3	0	3	0	0	3.45

ENGLAND V NEW ZEALAND

PRUDENTIAL WORLD CUP 1979 (SEMI-FINAL)

Venue: Old Trafford, Manchester
Date: 20th June 1979
Toss: New Zealand
Result: England won by 9 runs
Umpires: JG Langridge, KE Palmer
Man of the Match: GA Gooch

ENGLAND		R	b	NEW ZEALAND		R	b
*JM Brearley	c Lees b Coney	53	115	JG Wright	run out	69	137
G Boycott	c Howarth b Hadlee	2	14	BA Edgar	lbw b Old	17	38
W Larkins	c Coney b McKechnie	7	37	GP Howarth	lbw b Boycott	7	12
GA Gooch	b McKechnie	71	84	JV Coney	lbw b Hendrick	11	39
DI Gower	run out	1	1	GM Turner	lbw b Willis	30	51
IT Botham	lbw b Cairns	21	30	*MG Burgess	run out	10	13
DW Randall	not out	42	50	RJ Hadlee	b Botham	15	32
CM Old	c Lees b Troup	0	2	+WK Lees	b Hendrick	23	20
+RW Taylor	run out	12	25	BL Cairns	c Brearley b Hendrick	14	6
RGD Willis	not out	1	2	BJ McKechnie	not out	4	9
M Hendrick	did not bat			GB Troup	not out	3	3
Extras	(8 lb, 3 w)	11		Extras	(5 b, 4 w)	9	
Total	(8 wickets, 60 overs)	221		Total	(9 wickets, 60 overs)	212	

Fall of wickets: 1-13 (Boycott), 2-38 (Larkins), 3-96 (Brearley), 4-98 (Gower), 5-145 (Botham), 6-177 (Gooch), 7-178 (Old), 8-219 (Taylor)

Fall of wickets: 1-47 (Edgar), 2-58 (Howarth), 3-104 (Coney), 4-112 (Wright), 5-132 (Burgess), 6-162 (Turner), 7-180 (Hadlee), 8-195 (Cairns), 9-208 (Lees)

NEW ZEALAND	O	M	R	W	Wd	Nb	ENGLAND	O	M	R	W	Wd	Nb
Hadlee	12	4	32	1	-	-	Botham	12	3	42	1	-	-
Troup	12	1	38	1	-	-	Hendrick	12	0	55	3	-	-
Cairns	12	2	47	1	-	-	Old	12	1	33	1	-	-
Coney	12	0	47	1	-	-	Boycott	9	1	24	1	-	-
McKechnie	12	1	46	2	-	-	Gooch	3	1	8	0	-	-
							Willis	12	1	41	1	-	-

PAKISTAN V WEST INDIES
PRUDENTIAL WORLD CUP 1979 (SEMI-FINAL)

Venue: Kennington Oval, Kennington
Date: 20th June 1979
Toss: Pakistan
Result: West Indies won by 43 runs
Umpires: WL Budd, DJ Constant
Man of the Match: CG Greenidge

WEST INDIES		R	b	PAKISTAN		R	b
CG Greenidge	c Wasim Bari b Asif Iqbal	73	107	Majid Khan	c Kallicharran b Croft	81	124
DL Haynes	c and b Asif Iqbal	65	115	Sadiq Mohammad	c Murray b Holding	2	7
IVA Richards	b Asif Iqbal	42	62	Zaheer Abbas	c Murray b Croft	93	122
*CH Lloyd	c Mudassar b Asif Iqbal	37	38	Haroon Rasheed	run out	15	22
CL King	c sub (Wasim Raja) b Sarfraz Nawaz	34	25	Javed Miandad	lbw b Croft	0	1
AI Kallicharran	b Imran Khan	11	14	*Asif Iqbal	c Holding b Richards	17	20
AME Roberts	not out	7	4	Mudassar Nazar	c Kallicharran b Richards	2	9
J Garner	not out	1	1	Imran Khan	c and b Richards	6	4
+DL Murray	did not bat			Sarfraz Nawaz	c Haynes b Roberts	12	15
MA Holding	did not bat			+Wasim Bari	c Murray b Roberts	9	12
CEH Croft	did not bat			Sikander Bakht	not out	1	4
Extras	(1 b, 17 lb, 4 nb, 1 w)	23		Extras	(9 lb, 1 nb, 2 w)	12	
Total	(6 wickets, 60 overs)	293		Total	(all out, 56.2 overs)	250	

Fall of wickets: 1-132 (Greenidge), 2-165 (Haynes), 3-233 (Richards), 4-236 (Lloyd), 5-285 (Kallicharran), 6-285 (King)

Fall of wickets: 1-10 (Sadiq Mohammad), 2-176 (Zaheer Abbas), 3-187 (Majid Khan), 4-187 (Javed Miandad), 5-208 (Haroon Rasheed), 6-220 (Mudassar Nazar), 7-221 (Asif Iqbal), 8-228 (Imran Khan), 9-246 (Wasim Bari), 10-250 (Sarfraz Nawaz)

PAKISTAN	O	M	R	W	Wd	Nb	WEST INDIES	O	M	R	W	Wd	Nb
Imran Khan	9	1	43	1	-	-	Roberts	9.2	2	41	2	-	-
Sarfraz Nawaz	12	1	71	1	-	-	Holding	9	1	28	1	-	-
Sikander Bakht	6	1	24	0	-	-	Croft	11	0	29	3	-	-
Mudassar Nazar	10	0	50	0	-	-	Garner	12	1	47	0	-	-
Majid Khan	12	2	26	0	-	-	King	7	0	41	0	-	-
Asif Iqbal	11	0	56	4	-	-	Richards	8	0	52	3	-	-

ENGLAND V WEST INDIES

PRUDENTIAL WORLD CUP 1979 (FINAL)

Venue: Lord's Cricket Ground, St John's Wood
Date: 23rd June 1979
Toss: England
Result: West Indies won by 92 runs
Umpires: HD Bird, BJ Meyer
Man of the Match: IVA Richards

WEST INDIES		R	b	ENGLAND		R	b
CG Greenidge	run out (Randall)	9	31	*JM Brearley	c King b Holding	64	130
DL Haynes	c Hendrick b Old	20	27	G Boycott	c Kallicharran b Holding	57	105
IVA Richards	not out	138	157	DW Randall	b Croft	15	22
AI Kallicharran	b Hendrick	4	17	GA Gooch	b Garner	32	28
*CH Lloyd	c and b Old	13	33	DI Gower	b Garner	0	4
CL King	c Randall b Edmonds	86	66	IT Botham	c Richards b Croft	4	3
+DL Murray	c Gower b Edmonds	5	9	W Larkins	b Garner	0	1
AME Roberts	c Brearley b Hendrick	0	7	PH Edmonds	not out	5	8
J Garner	c Taylor b Botham	0	5	CM Old	b Garner	0	2
MA Holding	b Botham	0	6	+RW Taylor	c Murray b Garner	0	1
CEH Croft	not out	0	2	M Hendrick	b Croft	0	5
Extras	(1 b, 10 lb)	11		Extras	(12 lb, 3 nb, 2 w)	17	
Total	(9 wickets, innings closed, 60 overs)	286		Total	(all out, 51 overs)	194	

Fall of wickets: 1-22 (Greenidge), 2-36 (Haynes), 3-55 (Kallicharran), 4-99 (Lloyd), 5-238 (King), 6-252 (Murray), 7-258 (Roberts), 8-260 (Garner), 9-272 (Holding)

Fall of wickets: 1-129 (Brearley), 2-135 (Boycott), 3-183 (Randall), 4-183 (Gooch), 5-186 (Gower), 6-186 (Larkins), 7-192 (Botham), 8-192 (Old), 9-194 (Taylor), 10-194 (Hendrick, 51 ov)

ENGLAND	O	M	R	W	Wd	Nb	WEST INDIES	O	M	R	W	Wd	Nb
Botham	12	2	44	2	-	-	Roberts	9	2	33	0	-	-
Hendrick	12	2	50	2	-	-	Holding	8	1	16	2	-	-
Old	12	0	55	2	-	-	Croft	10	1	42	3	-	-
Boycott	6	0	38	0	-	-	Garner	11	0	38	5	-	-
Edmonds	12	2	40	2	-	-	Richards	10	0	35	0	-	-
Gooch	4	0	27	0	-	-	King	3	0	13	0	-	-
Larkins	2	0	21	0	-	-							

MOST RUNS

Player	Mat	Inns	NO	Runs	HS	Ave	BF	SR	100	50	0	4s	6s
CG Greenidge (WI)	4	4	1	253	106*	84.33	406	62.31	1	2	0	17	3
IVA Richards (WI)	4	4	2	217	138*	108.5	293	74.06	1	0	0	13	4
GA Gooch (ENG)	5	5	1	210	71	52.5	329	63.82	0	2	0	18	4
GM Turner (NZ)	4	4	2	176	83*	88	314	56.05	0	1	0	12	0
JG Wright (NZ)	4	4	0	166	69	41.5	332	50	0	1	0	16	0
JM Brearley (ENG)	5	5	0	161	64	32.2	404	39.85	0	2	2	12	0
Majid Khan (PAK)	4	4	0	150	81	37.5	247	60.72	0	2	0	15	1
Zaheer Abbas (PAK)	4	4	0	148	93	37	224	66.07	0	1	0	13	2
DL Haynes (WI)	4	4	0	144	65	36	261	55.17	0	1	0	9	1
AMJ Hilditch (AUS)	3	3	0	143	72	47.66	267	53.55	0	1	0	9	0
CL King (WI)	4	3	0	132	86	44	109	121.1	0	1	0	13	3
Asif Iqbal (PAK)	4	3	0	129	61	43	181	71.27	0	2	0	13	0
CH Lloyd (WI)	4	3	1	123	73*	61.5	151	81.45	0	1	0	9	0
BA Edgar (NZ)	3	3	1	113	84*	56.5	228	49.56	0	1	0	9	0
GR Viswanath (INDIA)	3	3	0	106	75	35.33	206	51.45	0	1	0	7	0
Sadiq Mohammad (PAK)	4	4	1	104	57*	34.66	229	45.41	0	1	0	10	0
G Boycott (ENG)	5	5	1	92	57	23	214	42.99	0	1	0	5	0
SM Gavaskar (INDIA)	3	3	0	89	55	29.66	205	43.41	0	1	0	8	0
SRD Wettimuny (SL)	2	2	0	83	67	41.5	140	59.28	0	1	0	9	0
LRD Mendis (SL)	2	2	0	78	64	39	84	92.85	0	1	0	3	3
RL Dias (SL)	2	2	0	75	50	37.5	134	55.97	0	1	0	4	0
GR Sealy (CAN)	3	3	0	73	45	24.33	149	48.99	0	0	0	9	0
GP Howarth (NZ)	2	2	1	70	63*	70	87	80.45	0	1	0	9	1
Haroon Rasheed (PAK)	4	4	1	69	37*	23	135	51.11	0	0	0	4	0
IT Botham (ENG)	5	4	1	65	22	21.66	95	68.42	0	0	0	5	1

MOST WICKETS

Player	Mat	Inns	Overs	Mdns	Runs	Wkts	BBI	Ave	Econ	SR	4	5
M Hendrick (ENG)	5	5	56	14	149	10	4/15	14.9	2.66	33.6	1	0
BJ McKechnie (NZ)	4	4	45.5	4	141	9	3/24	15.66	3.07	30.5	0	0
Asif Iqbal (PAK)	4	4	47	5	157	9	4/56	17.44	3.34	31.3	1	0
CM Old (ENG)	5	5	58	10	157	9	4/8	17.44	2.7	38.6	1	0
MA Holding (WI)	4	4	41	5	106	8	4/33	13.25	2.58	30.7	1	0
CEH Croft (WI)	4	4	43	3	140	8	3/29	17.5	3.25	32.2	0	0
J Garner (WI)	4	4	47	2	172	8	5/38	21.5	3.65	35.2	0	1
Sikander Bakht (PAK)	4	4	41	10	108	7	3/32	15.42	2.63	35.1	0	0
RGD Willis (ENG)	4	4	44.3	8	109	7	4/11	15.57	2.44	38.1	1	0
Majid Khan (PAK)	4	4	47	8	117	7	3/27	16.71	2.48	40.2	0	0
AG Hurst (AUS)	3	3	32	6	119	7	5/21	17	3.71	27.4	0	1
AME Roberts (WI)	4	4	39.3	6	149	7	3/43	21.28	3.77	33.8	0	0
BL Cairns (NZ)	4	4	47.5	4	176	7	3/36	25.14	3.67	41	0	0
IT Botham (ENG)	5	5	53	13	168	6	2/38	28	3.16	53	0	0
G Boycott (ENG)	5	5	27	1	94	5	2/14	18.8	3.48	32.4	0	0
GJ Cosier (AUS)	3	3	27.2	4	95	5	3/54	19	3.47	32.8	0	0
RJ Hadlee (NZ)	4	4	45	11	117	5	2/20	23.4	2.6	54	0	0
Imran Khan (PAK)	4	4	42.1	7	123	5	2/29	24.6	2.91	50.6	0	0
Sarfraz Nawaz (PAK)	2	2	22	2	97	4	3/26	24.25	4.4	33	0	0
GB Troup (NZ)	3	3	32	3	104	4	2/36	26	3.25	48	0	0
M Amarnath (INDIA)	3	3	31.3	4	114	4	3/40	28.5	3.61	47.2	0	0
GD Porter (AUS)	2	2	18	5	33	4	2/13	11	1.83	36	0	0
LW Stott (NZ)	1	1	12	1	48	4	3/48	16	4	24	0	0
ARM Opatha (SL)	2	2	17.1	1	62	4	3/31	20.66	3.61	34.3	0	0
JN Valentine (CAN)	3	3	19	5	66	4	1/18	22	3.47	38	0	0

HIGH SCORES

Player	Runs	Balls	4s	6s	SR	Team	Opposition	Ground
IVA Richards	138*	157	11	3	87.89	West Indies	v England	Lord's
CG Greenidge	106*	173	9	1	61.27	West Indies	v India	Birmingham
Zaheer Abbas	93	122	8	1	76.22	Pakistan	v West Indies	The Oval
CL King	86	66	10	3	130.3	West Indies	v England	Lord's
BA Edgar	84*	167	8	0	50.29	New Zealand	v India	Leeds
GM Turner	83*	143	4	0	58.04	New Zealand	v Sri Lanka	Nottingham
Majid Khan	81	124	7	0	65.32	Pakistan	v West Indies	The Oval
GR Viswanath	75	134	7	0	55.97	India	v West Indies	Birmingham
CH Lloyd	73*	80	4	0	91.25	West Indies	v New Zealand	Nottingham
CG Greenidge	73	107	5	1	68.22	West Indies	v Pakistan	The Oval

BEST BOWLING

Player	Overs	Mdns	Runs	Wkts	Econ	Team	Opposition	Ground
AG Hurst	10	3	21	5	2.1	Australia	v Canada	Birmingham
J Garner	11	0	38	5	3.45	West Indies	v England	Lord's
CM Old	10	5	8	4	0.8	England	v Canada	Manchester
RGD Willis	10.3	3	11	4	1.04	England	v Canada	Manchester
M Hendrick	12	6	15	4	1.25	England	v Pakistan	Leeds
MA Holding	12	2	33	4	2.75	West Indies	v India	Birmingham
Asif Iqbal	11	0	56	4	5.09	Pakistan	v West Indies	The Oval
BJ McKechnie	12	1	24	3	2	New Zealand	v India	Leeds
BJ McKechnie	10.5	2	25	3	2.3	New Zealand	v Sri Lanka	Nottingham
Sarfraz Nawaz	10	1	26	3	2.6	Pakistan	v Canada	Leeds

1983

THE YEAR EVERYTHING CHANGED

BY SURESH MENON

The Indian dressing room, having run out of champagne bottles – which players generously kept handing down to the fans below from the Lord's balcony – decided to hand out milk bottles instead. That image from the 1983 World Cup final – surreal, improbable, borderline lunatic – summed up India's own performance. As minnows in the shorter form of the game, they were expected only to politely make up the numbers. It meant that, as with the two World Cups before, there would be an even eight teams in the fray, with Zimbabwe sharing minnow space with India. Indeed, between the 1979 and 1983 World Cups, India had the worst win–loss ratio of the six teams who had played more than 20 ODIs (won 10, lost 17).

Leading them was a 24-year-old from the cricketing boondocks of Haryana, a man whose broad smile was only matched by his all-consuming self-confidence. This latter he had so much of that he could afford to give away large chunks to his teammates, nearly all of whom had, in their minds, come to England for a holiday rather than to do anything so serious as turning the cricket world upside down. When Kapil Dev (for it was he) told his team: "We can win", it sent shock waves through a happy, unimaginative bunch. Surely this wasn't the plan?

"When Kapil Dev said we must win, we thought he had gone mad," recalled opening batsman Krishnamachari Srikkanth. "Beat the West Indies? With their batsmen and four fast bowlers whose names we don't want to remember? And this man says we will win?" The captain's initial efforts at geeing up the team were met with incredulity and laughter rather than a matching: "We can do it skip!"

Yet, at the end of it, Kapil had converted a team of non-believers into disciples who would follow him anywhere, accept anything he said, and even (possibly) take a bullet for him. The World Cup was as much the triumph of a team that, as the tournament grew, began to believe in itself as of its captain who had had nothing to base his confidence on except a vague belief that his boys would come good when it mattered.

In all, India's five seamers took 63 of the Indian attack's 68 wickets in the tournament (Roger Binny 18, Madan Lal 17, Kapil Dev 12, Mohinder Amarnath and Balwinder Sandhu 8 each). They all averaged at least ten runs per wicket less than their career averages heading into the tournament. Men transformed. The most striking example was Mohinder Amarnath, who took 2 for 27 in 12 overs in the semi-final against England, and 3 for 12 in 7 overs against West Indies in the final. He did not take another wicket in his next 10 ODIs over 20 months, and went for more than five runs per over. In a three-match series against West Indies later in 1983, he took 0 for 143 in 20.5 overs.

"Nobody in the Board of Control for Cricket in India, or anywhere else in the country, expected us to win even a single game. So what we achieved was nothing short of a miracle," said Man Singh, India's manager in the tournament.

"Before I left Hyderabad, my father made his workers in our shop clear out a cabinet, saying, 'My son will return with the Cup,'" Man said. "He was probably the only one thinking so!"

Surprisingly, none of the members of that 1983 team thought fit to write a book about the incredible triumph. There is no definitive history. Bollywood has recently woken up to the dramatic possibilities, and a movie is scheduled to appear later this year. Perhaps it has taken that dream factory all these years to acknowledge that dreams do come true even if, frankly, that was not the dream most fans dreamt when the team left for England.

All this seems to work to the advantage of the participants. Every year for many years, they have been expected to re-live the success at social gatherings, official functions, media sessions, and every year they were expected to say something new. Thus did the anecdotes grow, unencumbered by the pressure of having to be true. "Occasionally I made up stories to keep the media happy," a player once told me. It was understandable.

Madan Lal, who bowled the first ball at the first World Cup in 1975, and then claimed the crucial wicket of Viv Richards in the '83 final, was probably speaking for his teammates when he said: "Every four years I become young again."

For another 28 years – till Mahendra Singh Dhoni's team repeated the feat in 2011 – Kapil's boys were the only Indians to have won the World Cup, and there was a responsibility to fix it in history with the kind of repeatable, interesting stories that made the occasion memorable, and pinned it in our memories.

Every World Cup year, we would be honoured with the stories, mostly reruns but occasionally fresh and unverifiable. It was all part of the game. Nobody complained. Dhoni's win meant that some of the fringe players of 1983 dropped out of public consciousness; but Kapil Dev himself continued to be the most sought after historian of that tournament. After all, captaincy apart, he had authored two memorable chapters himself – the unbeaten 175 against Zimbabwe and the Richards' catch.

In some ways, India's 1983 World Cup triumph has become like the Taj Mahal. There is nothing more to be said about it. It is there, it happened, it inspired, it changed Indian cricket, it disrupted the world order, it shifted the hub of the game towards India. It would be another quarter century before another maiden World Cup triumph – at the T20 – would give rise to the IPL and make India the most coveted centre to play cricket in, but that evening at Lord's in June ensured that neither cricket nor India would ever be the same again.

Sporting triumphs hinge on events that could have gone either way. There was *that* catch by Kapil Dev running, turning and receiving the ball safely over his shoulder that cut a Viv Richards innings in its prime. "Had I been fielding at mid-wicket instead of Kapil, we would never have won the World Cup," teammate Sandip Patil said later.

"I saw Kapil coming across, Yashpal Sharma was running in from fine leg and there was a guy running in from the crowd. I feared a collision and turned my back on the scene. Then I heard shouts of: 'Well done, great catch!' Such a jittery moment. I fast-forward that scene whenever I watch the game," says Kirti Azad, one of India's bits-and-pieces all-rounders who played significant roles in the tournament.

There was Mohinder Amarnath, gentle, smiling, his pace gentle and smiling too, who might have been taken apart by the mighty batting line-up that saw the West Indies win the two previous Cups. But not on that day when the meek inherited the earth, and he himself won man of the match.

He bowled at a pace which suggested he could run after the ball and retrieve it if he didn't like where it was going. In fact Jeff Dujon probably committed batting suicide out of boredom, waiting and waiting for the ball to arrive. He let it go, or prepared to, but it hung on to take the edge of the bat and hit the stumps.

So deeply embedded in India's collective consciousness are the match details and the surrounding anecdotes of that final that even those who were not born in 1983 might believe they were present that day at Lord's when India turned from lambs to tigers in a few short hours.

***

1983 might have been just another unmemorable year for India. The monsoons were good and the government, in familiar fashion, took credit for it. Unmemorable, but for that one event that changed sport, changed cricket, and changed the way middle-class Indians saw themselves. India needed something to make them feel good about themselves, some occasion that would unite a country of three-quarters of a billion in celebration. The win at Lord's provided that opportunity.

In the half-century since India had made their Test debut, the maharajahs and the nawabs had gone, to be replaced by college-educated Brahmins, the backbone of the middle class. But already the next phase was beginning to reveal itself. The inspirational captain of the World Cup-winning team, Kapil Dev, was neither college-educated nor Brahmin. A generation or so later, Mahatma Gandhi's India, the one that lives in the villages, would push into the background first Prime Minister Jawaharlal Nehru's India of the cities, and international players would emerge from Najafgarh, Rae Bareilly, Bharuch, Palarivattom, Aligarh, Jalandhar and Ranchi. Cricketing boondocks all.

Before the '83 World Cup, India had played only 40 one-day internationals in the decade or so that the format had been around. They refused to see the shorter game as a legitimate version of cricket, behaving as if it was a pimple on the face of real cricket, one that would disappear quickly.

Victory, as many teams have discovered is a great solvent that dissolves all disappointments and gets rid of prejudices.

On 29 March, with the World Cup 72 days away, India beat twice world champions West Indies in Berbice, Guyana. Gavaskar made his first 50 in 52 balls before falling for 90. Kapil Dev made 72 off 38 balls and India amassed 282 for 5 in 47 overs. Madan Lal dismissed Viv Richards for 64 – a feat which he believed gave him the drop on the great batsman.

In the final a few months later, Madan Lal pleaded with his captain to give him another over after Richards had mauled him in the previous one. He felt he could get Richards again. It seemed foolhardy, and Kapil confessed later that in allowing Madan Lal to bowl, he had gone against his own instincts. Sometimes captaincy is about recognising when to ignore the instincts that have served you well before!

***

India began their World Cup campaign by defeating the West Indies (after having lost three of the four practice matches), so clearly Berbice was no fluke. While the team was creating upsets in England, the fans back home were transfixed in their living rooms, before shop windows, in offices, clubs and anywhere a television could be accommodated. Colour TV had come to India the previous year with the Asian Games in New Delhi. Suddenly it all came together – live telecast from distant fields, an audience hungry for action, a significant victory, and the awareness of the marketing possibilities – and the first steps towards India's domination of world cricket were taken.

Talented players were soon assured of getting into the millionaires' club. Parents didn't think any longer that academics alone mattered; sport, especially cricket, had become a viable career option too.

Among those who had tuned in to the telecast was future India captain Rahul Dravid, then ten years old. "I remember watching that final in Bangalore," he recalled. "That win inspired a lot of young kids to take to the game." Among the young kids were Sachin Tendulkar, Sourav Ganguly, Anil Kumble and VVS Laxman – the generation that gave the golden era of Indian cricket its name.

25 June is an important date in Indian cricket history. On that day they made their Test debut at Lord's in 1932. England were reduced to 19 for three, setting Neville Cardus off on that much-quoted flight of fancy: "In my mind's eye, I saw the news flashing over the air to far-flung places in India, Punjab and Karachi… to dusky men in the hills, to the bazaars of the East, to Gandhi himself and to Gunga Din." Evocative, if politically incorrect today.

Fifty-one years later on the same day, India became a modern cricketing nation.

A team that had looked down upon the one-day game (still played then over 60 overs in whites and with a red ball) either because they were not very good at it or because that was the way "real" cricketers reacted to something they felt was artificial, suddenly discovered that they were very good at it. Love followed success, and a nation took to the format as if it had been just waiting for a sign before doing so.

***

It might be an exaggeration to say that the Indian team went to England to bury one-day cricket – they had won only a single match, against East Africa, in the two previous World Cups – but it is no exaggeration to say that it returned praising it. In 1975, Sunil Gavaskar took 174 deliveries over his 36 not out in the inaugural match. Eight years later, Kapil Dev made 175 not out in 138 deliveries. Nothing so starkly demonstrated the change in India's mindset as that comparison.

A mindset that was doubly distorted. "We saw the one-day game merely as an extension of Test cricket," India's first ODI captain Ajit Wadekar once said. As if that wasn't bad enough, in the first decade of the format: "We didn't take the game seriously," he said. The "we" included players, fans, media. It was a rare show of unanimity among a people characterised by the Nobel-winning economist Amartaya Sen, as "argumentative Indians." Bring three Indians together, went the joke in the country "and you have four opinions already."

For the inaugural World Cup, India stuck to the formula they knew best: an attack led by spinners, batting led by their Test stalwarts, neither lot particularly agile fielders. To captain, they picked Srinivas Venkatraghavan, the off-spinner who was one of the few good men in close-catching positions, and above all, had some experience in the format during his stint with Derbyshire.

Venkat was a shrewd thinker on the game and later a successful international umpire. But on that first World Cup trip he had to deal with the inexperience of his team as India had only previously played two ODIs.

Four years later, it was another World Cup, but the same India. The first match against the West Indies was only their 11th in the format. Nothing had changed. India still looked down on the bastard child of "real" cricket, still had a team which regarded it as punishment to play it, and still had the same captain.

This time they lost all their matches, including the one to Sri Lanka, then not yet a Full Member of the ICC. Indians scored just two fifties, Gavaskar making one of them. The other was Gundappa Viswanath's 75 in the first game. It would be another four years before an Indian would score the first century in the format; that was another distinction Kapil Dev earned with that magical 175 not out.

At Old Trafford in '83, India began the World Cup beating the West Indies for the second time in three matches. You could see in that a harbinger, but only in hindsight. At the moment, as wicket-keeper Syed Kirmani recalled, there was excitement in the team but no long-term hope. Considering India's record till then, it was a momentous win by 34 runs built on the batting of Yashpal Sharma (89) and the medium pace of Roger Binny (3 for 48). The West Indies' last wicket pair of Andy Roberts and Joel Garner added 71, and had the West Indies won the final, that might have been seen as a sign. In sport, it is the easiest thing to detect patterns after the event; the difficulty is in recognising them from the other end.

India next beat Zimbabwe by five wickets, Kirmani becoming the first keeper to have five victims in a World Cup match. For pattern-seekers, there was the success of the medium pacers, all four of whom picked up wickets while conceding fewer than 30 runs each. Two wins in two matches had already broken a pattern for India in the World Cup, but the next outing restored everything to factory setting. India folded for 158 replying to Australia's 320 (Trevor Chappell 110) with only Kapil Dev reaching 40. The West Indies, in the return game, seemed to confirm this with a 66-run win. Richards made a century, Michael Holding claimed three wickets, and Mohinder Amarnath (80) and Binny (3 for 71) apart, there was little to cheer for the Indians.

And then came Zimbabwe, who pushed India to the edge. India were quickly 9 for four and 17 for five. Both openers, Gavaskar and Srikkanth, had fallen for nought, the middle order had been carved out by medium pacers Peter Rawson and Kevin Curran, and that looked like the end.

But clearly skipper Kapil Dev was viewing it through a different set of lenses. He began cautiously, with singles and twos, but then started striking hard and often. His unbeaten 175 established a record for the World Cup. More, it took the team to a plane from which it never descended, a stepping stone to bigger and better things.

"He didn't loft the ball till he had got into the 80s," recalled Gavaskar, who considers it the finest one-day innings he has seen. Every memorable finish needs an iconic event, and Kapil had provided one.

Binny helped Kapil add 60 for the sixth wicket, then Madan Lal made 17 in a partnership worth 62 for the eighth, after which Kirmani came in. The wicket-keeper made the second highest score, 24, as Kapil opened up to finish with six sixes and 16 boundaries in 138 balls. The pair added 126 for the ninth wicket, easily the game-turning partnership and a record that stood for 27 years. "He told me just to make sure we played the full 60 overs," recalled Kirmani.

"I took my time settling down," said Kapil Dev, "I was angry when I returned at lunch. The players avoided me. I had to fetch my own lunch. This was deliberate, I think. They wanted me to remain in solitude and perhaps unleash my anger on the field rather than in the dressing room."

That single innings did more for Indian cricket than anything else up to that time. It showed the captain's confidence wasn't misplaced, and his encouraging words in the dressing room gained credibility as a result. For the first time since India left their home shores they realised they could afford to dream of a semi-final berth – anything beyond was still fantasy.

The 31-run win also put them in the right mood for the return match against Australia. India's 247 against them included contributions that were decent rather than spectacular, Gavaskar alone falling (he had a poor tournament, and was even dropped for two matches before regaining his place for the Zimbabwe match) for a single-digit figure among the top ten batsmen. Madan Lal (4 for 20) and Binny (4 for 29) kept Australia down to 129, much to the dismay of the British media, which had been preparing for an Australia-England semi-final.

The *Guardian* captured the mood with: "India, and not Australia will face England at Old Trafford. It will be a match of altogether less resonance and less difficulty for England."

England had come through Group A with little trouble. They had hit 300 plus scores against both New Zealand and Sri Lanka with hundreds from Lamb and Gower, who would end the tournament as leading run-scorer. They then came unstuck at Edgbaston in a tight return match against New Zealand, for whom Jeremy Coney starred with bat and ball, but two crushing victories over Pakistan and a similarly one-sided encounter against Sri Lanka meant they topped the group with five wins from six.

The new format of each side playing the others in the group twice meant that Pakistan, despite those two big losses to the hosts, could still qualify, although with New Zealand needing to win just one of their last two games, this appeared unlikely. But Sri Lanka bundled out the Kiwis at Derby for 181, Asantha de Mel returning 5 for 32, and leg-spinner Somachandra De Silva weighing in with the remarkable figures of 12-5-11-2. Despite a wobble towards the end, Sri Lanka got over the line, meaning Pakistan could draw level with New Zealand on points and bring run rate into the equation if they beat the in the final group game.

At Trent Bridge Pakistan batted first and racked up 261 for 3, an unbeaten hundred for Zaheer and 79 at better than a run a ball from Imran the key contributions. When the Kiwis batted, Pakistan kept chipping away and in the end Jeremy Coney was run out for 51 off the first ball of the final over, with his side still 11 runs short. So Pakistan joined England in the semi-finals, where they would take on West Indies at The Oval, just as they had done four years earlier.

Almost inevitably, West Indies crushed Pakistan at The Oval, none of the four quicks going for much more than two an over as Pakistan posted an underwhelming 184 for 8 in their full 60 overs. Richards saw the West Indies home, his unbeaten 80 coming from 96 balls.

Before India's semi-final with England, despite the disparaging nature of some of the press comment, Indians were getting noticed too. The term Kapil's Devils was used with some affection, and a journalist dug up the fact that Binny's great grandfather was a Scotsman. It seemed both a way of placing his success in perspective and taking a portion of the credit for it on behalf of Britain. Clearly, the Indian one-day team had finally arrived.

When England, batting first, were 150 for four, the Indian dream seemed to be fizzling out. India, having already lost all their five matches against the hosts, were heading for the sixth defeat when Yashpal Sharma ran out Allan Lamb, and Amarnath dismissed Mike Gatting. Ian Botham was bowled by Kirti Azad, who had come in as a relief bowler but bowled his full quota of 12 overs. England lost their last seven wickets for 72, the key bowlers being Azad and Amarnath who together had figures of 24-2-55-3.

Amarnath (46), Yashpal (61) and Kapil Dev (51 not out) ensured there would be no panic as India won by six wickets to extend their fantasy and leave the country in a state of excitement and anticipation it had never experienced before at a World Cup.

Television, which had a lot to do with this, saw fans in India miss two of the key moments. Kapil Dev's knock against Zimbabwe was not telecast because the BBC was on strike at the time, and no one who wasn't at Tunbridge Wells that day actually saw that innings. Yet, so powerful has been the picture presented by the few who were there and the lot who played that many believe they actually saw the game on television, and can recall incidents from it. Sometimes false memory can be more lasting than the real thing because like in a kaleidoscope, it keeps changing patterns as it absorbs new information.

The other key moment denied viewers in India was Kapil's catch that dismissed Richards in the final. At this key psychological moment there appeared on the screen the words: "Sorry for the Interruption", which was a Doordarshan (national broadcaster) regular when it lost the picture briefly. But it has been replayed any number of times and, thanks to YouTube, can be seen today with little effort.

The final was a day game – they were all day games then – and I knew I could watch the first half as it should be watched: with friends, and with the proper snacks and drinks. For the superstitious among us – and in a World Cup final every viewer with a team to support is superstitious – there are rules to be followed. Do not move, or continue to sit in a particular chair, or ensure that whoever was outside the room when a West Indies wicket fell remained outside in order to get another wicket to fall. All standard stuff.

We couldn't bat or bowl for India, but we could control our bladders and exaggerate the moves we were making when something positive had happened the last time we had done something like this.

Fans often missed large chunks of the game because they happened to be in the wrong place at the right time or vice versa, but that was the sacrifice they were willing to make. Such contributions to a team's success are never acknowledged, but no one minds that. There is something pure about such sacrifices.

The first ten in India's line-up had all made first class centuries, yet their total of 183 didn't reflect that. Still, I left for work on the graveyard shift at the newspaper I was working for then, thinking they had done well to get this far. I drove past a movie theatre that had at some point screened *Man of La Mancha*. A portion of the movie poster (from a few years earlier) with its tag line was still visible: *Dream the impossible dream*. It referred to Quixote and his dream, a statement rather than an appeal, but as coincidences and messages from the future go, this was an old Peter O'Toole movie gaining unexpected relevance. Perhaps there was a chance for India after all if they dared to dream the impossible dream, just as (one learnt later), Kapil Dev continued to do.

I asked Kirmani recently when he felt India could win the tournament. Was it when they beat Zimbabwe a second time? No, he said, after Zimbabwe we were just a tad more confident about the Australia match coming up. The semi-finals were still far away.

Importantly, India did not rest on their laurels. Indian sportsmen of that and earlier generations had been famous for lacking the killer instinct. Doing slightly better than previously, qualifying for the Olympics rather than trying to win anything there, scoring a consolation goal in soccer, taking out a top ten player once in a while in tennis – such were the limits of ambitions.

For a team that had done precious little earlier, getting to the semi-final of the World Cup would have been climbing a hill that hadn't even existed before. In Test cricket, honourable draws rather than aggressive attempts to win had been the hallmark of the Indian approach. It was 25 years before India won their first-ever Test, and another 16 before they won their first abroad. The 1971 series win in England had been followed by a 3-0 massacre on the next tour three years later; for 15 years India did not win a series in England.

Indian sportsmen came across as a bunch too easily satisfied. The important psychological impact of the '83 win was a change in the mindset of the Indian sportsman – not just the cricketer – who began to accept the wholly risible notion till then that perhaps he could actually win at the international level.

"We have beaten them before, we can beat them again," the captain's cry at the break at Lord's was a clarion call the team responded to because of the way the tournament had turned out.

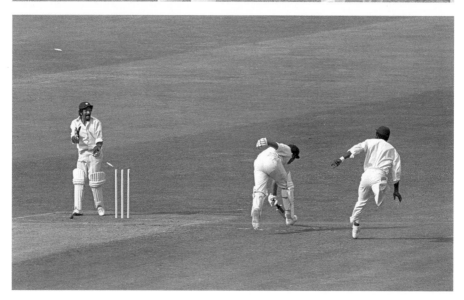

Top: Queen Elizabeth and Prince Philip meet the teams at Buckingham Palace on 6 June.
Middle: Dennis Lillee pats Gary Gilmour on the back after his semi-final demolition of England.
Bottom: Viv Richards effects one of his three run outs in the final.

Top: In the final, Roy Fredericks swivels to pull Dennis Lillee for six but cannot avoid treading on his stumps.

Bottom: Clive Lloyd lifts the inaugural trophy.
Right: Lloyd in magisterial form in the final, where he hit an 85-ball 102.

Top: The eight competing teams assemble on the Lord's outfield on 8 June, at the start of the tournament.

Bottom: Geoff Boycott, a surprise destroyer with the ball for England, has Geoff Howarth lbw in the semi-final.

Top: Sri Lanka captain Anura Tennekoon with the ICC Trophy after they beat Canada at New Road, Worcester on 21 June.

Bottom: Viv Richards flays one through the off side in his stunning century against England in the final.

Top: Collis King during his 66-ball 86, part of a 139-run partnership with Richards in the final that buried English hopes.
Bottom: Unused squad member Malcolm Marshall lifts the trophy, flanked by England captain Mike Brearley, Ian Botham, Bob Taylor, Graham Gooch, Mike Hendrick and Chris Old, along with man of the match Viv Richards.

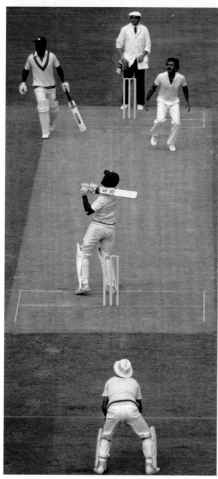

Top: Kris Srikkanth has the audacity to smash Andy Roberts square for four in the final.
Bottom left: Viv Richards, cruising on 33 in the final, mishits Madan Lal to the leg side, where

Kapil Dev completed a brilliant catch to start West Indies' slide.
Bottom right: David Gower was the tournament's leading run scorer with 384.

Top: Crowds invade the Lord's pitch to see Kapil Dev lift the trophy after his side pull off a shock 43-run victory over West Indies.

Bottom: Kapil, alongside man of the match Mohinder Amarnath, raises the trophy on a day that changed the game for ever.

183 seemed to be the ideal score to defeat the mighty West Indies. Twenty runs fewer or 50 runs more, and the world champions would have sauntered through. Had India made 250, their batsmen would have focused better, and not left it to the next in line to complete the job.

Gordon Greenidge, prince among opening batsmen, decided not to play a Balwinder Sandhu delivery that came up the hill and knocked back the off stump. Another consolation prize, I thought, in a sporting system that was used to consolation prizes while the main ones went elsewhere.

And then it began. The procession. Clive Lloyd caught off Binny, Haynes and Gomes and Bacchus walking in and out rudderless. Was it hubris or the efficiency of the medium pacers? Perhaps the latter caused the former (as did that 183). In the midst of all this, the Kapil Dev catch and the end of Richards.

At 119 for six, the odds were still with the West Indies. And then Dujon was bowled. The panic was complete. The look on the faces of the world champions said it all. Suddenly Indians were all over the place. It had been a tense game even if the cricket itself hadn't been of the highest quality. That Srikkanth's 38 was the highest score of the match told its own story. But the Indians held their catches, played better under pressure against a team which had not known such pressure before and seemed uncertain about how to react.

"There has been a great improvement in fielding since my days," announced Farokh Engineer, who had kept wickets for India in 1975. As far as understatements go, that one went a great distance.

The essence of the West Indies disappointment was articulated by the late Malcolm Marshall who was quoted as saying: "I was so sure about the outcome that I even ordered a new BMW car in the misguided belief that I could pay for it out of my winnings. Cricket has a nasty habit of punishing those who come to believe in their infallibility."

Last year Sandip Patil revealed that he had played the World Cup with a broken rib he sustained while playing an Indian medium pacer at home. Srikkanth talked about missing his honeymoon (he was booked to fly to the US with his new bride after the World Cup) because the team was asked to return to India to meet the Prime Minister. "Every time I speak about it, I remember something new," said Kapil Dev.

And so the stories continue, some teased out of their hiding places in the memory after three decades, others made up to satisfy the demands of a constantly inquiring public. From being unique, the 1983 triumph is now "the first", thanks to the repeat in 2011. But as it recedes further into history, it also picks up a veneer of otherness, a special position reserved for classics, its stories further steeled against falsifiability. Many stories are exaggerated by a generation of fans too who "were there" in spirit if not physically.

Did the players really distribute milk bottles when they ran out of champagne? It is a story one would like to believe if only because it tied up the strange and the fantastic so neatly and was just crazy enough to be true.

1983

RESULTS AND STATISTICS

GROUP A TABLE

		P	W	L	Pts	RR
1	England	6	5	1	20	4.671
2	Pakistan	6	3	3	12	4.014
3	New Zealand	6	3	3	12	3.927
4	Sri Lanka	6	1	5	4	3.752

GROUP B TABLE

		P	W	L	Pts	RR
1	West Indies	6	5	1	20	4.308
2	India	6	4	2	16	3.87
3	Australia	6	2	4	8	3.808
4	Zimbabwe	6	1	5	4	3.492

ENGLAND V INDIA

PRUDENTIAL WORLD CUP 1983 (SEMI-FINAL)

Venue: Old Trafford, Manchester
Date: 22nd June 1983
Toss: England
Result: India won by 6 wickets
Umpires: DGL Evans, DO Oslear
Man of the Match: M Amarnath

ENGLAND		R	b	INDIA		R	b
G Fowler	b Binny	33	59	SM Gavaskar	c Gould b Allott	25	41
CJ Tavaré	c Kirmani b Binny	32	51	K Srikkanth	c Willis b Botham	19	44
DI Gower	c Kirmani b Amarnath	17	30	M Amarnath	run out (Allott->Botham)	46	92
AJ Lamb	run out (Yashpal Sharma)	29	58	Yashpal Sharma	c Allott b Willis	61	115
MW Gatting	b Amarnath	18	46	SM Patil	not out	51	32
IT Botham	b Azad	6	26	*Kapil Dev	not out	1	6
+IJ Gould	run out (Kirmani)	13	36	KBJ Azad	did not bat		
VJ Marks	b Kapil Dev	8	18	RMH Binny	did not bat		
GR Dilley	not out	20	26	Madan Lal	did not bat		
PJW Allott	c Patil b Kapil Dev	8	14	+SMH Kirmani	did not bat		
*RGD Willis	b Kapil Dev	0	2	BS Sandhu	did not bat		
Extras	(1 b, 17 lb, 4 nb, 7 w)	29		Extras	(5 b, 6 lb, 2 nb, 1 w)	14	
Total	(all out, 60 overs)	213		Total	(4 wickets, 54.4 overs)	217	

Fall of wickets: 1-69 (Tavaré), 2-84 (Fowler), 3-107 (Gower), 4-141 (Lamb), 5-150 (Gatting), 6-160 (Botham), 7-175 (Gould), 8-177 (Marks), 9-202 (Allott), 10-213 (Willis, 60 ov)

Fall of wickets: 1-46 (Srikkanth), 2-50 (Gavaskar), 3-142 (Amarnath), 4-205 (Yashpal Sharma)

INDIA	O	M	R	W	Wd	Nb	ENGLAND	O	M	R	W	Wd	Nb
Kapil Dev	11	1	35	3	-	-	Willis	10.4	2	42	1	-	-
Sandhu	8	1	36	0	-	-	Dilley	11	0	43	0	-	-
Binny	12	1	43	2	-	-	Allott	10	3	40	1	-	-
Madan Lal	5	0	15	0	-	-	Botham	11	4	40	1	-	-
Azad	12	1	28	1	-	-	Marks	12	1	38	0	-	-
Amarnath	12	1	27	2	-	-							

PAKISTAN V WEST INDIES

PRUDENTIAL WORLD CUP 1983 (SEMI-FINAL)

Venue: Kennington Oval, Kennington
Date: 22nd June 1983
Toss: West Indies
Result: West Indies won by 8 wickets
Umpires: DJ Constant, AGT Whitehead
Man of the Match: IVA Richards

PAKISTAN		R	b	WEST INDIES		R	b
Mohsin Khan	b Roberts	70	176	CG Greenidge	lbw b Rashid Khan	17	38
Mudassar Nazar	c and b Garner	11	39	DL Haynes	b Abdul Qadir	29	58
Ijaz Faqih	c Dujon b Holding	5	19	IVA Richards	not out	80	96
Zaheer Abbas	b Gomes	30	38	HA Gomes	not out	50	100
*Imran Khan	c Dujon b Marshall	17	41	*CH Lloyd	did not bat		
Wasim Raja	lbw b Marshall	0	3	SFAF Bacchus	did not bat		
Shahid Mahboob	c Richards b Marshall	6	10	+PJL Dujon	did not bat		
Sarfraz Nawaz	c Holding b Roberts	3	12	MD Marshall	did not bat		
Abdul Qadir	not out	10	21	AME Roberts	did not bat		
+Wasim Bari	not out	4	7	J Garner	did not bat		
Rashid Khan	did not bat			MA Holding	did not bat		
Extras	(6 b, 13 lb, 5 nb, 4 w)	28		Extras	(2 b, 6 lb, 4 w)	12	
Total	(8 wickets, 60 overs)	184		Total	(2 wickets, 48.4 overs)	188	

Fall of wickets: 1-23 (Mudassar Nazar), 2-34 (Ijaz Faqih), 3-88 (Zaheer Abbas), 4-139 (Imran Khan), 5-139 (Wasim Raja), 6-159 (Shahid Mahboob), 7-164 (Sarfraz Nawaz), 8-171 (Mohsin Khan)

Fall of wickets: 1-34 (Greenidge), 2-56 (Haynes)

WEST INDIES	O	M	R	W	Wd	Nb	PAKISTAN	O	M	R	W	Wd	Nb
Roberts	12	3	25	2	-	-	Rashid Khan	12	2	32	1	-	-
Garner	12	1	31	1	-	-	Sarfraz Nawaz	8	0	23	0	-	-
Marshall	12	2	28	3	-	-	Abdul Qadir	11	1	42	1	-	-
Holding	12	1	25	1	-	-	Shahid Mahboob	11	1	43	0	-	-
Gomes	7	0	29	1	-	-	Wasim Raja	1	0	9	0	-	-
Richards	5	0	18	0	-	-	Zaheer Abbas	4.4	1	24	0	-	-
							Mohsin Khan	1	0	3	0	-	-

INDIA V WEST INDIES

PRUDENTIAL WORLD CUP 1983 (FINAL)

Venue: Lord's Cricket Ground, St John's Wood
Date: 25th June 1983
Toss: West Indies
Result: India won by 43 runs
Umpires: HD Bird, BJ Meyer
Man of the Match: M Amarnath

INDIA		R	b	WEST INDIES		R	b
SM Gavaskar	c Dujon b Roberts	2	12	CG Greenidge	b Sandhu	1	12
K Srikkanth	lbw b Marshall	38	57	DL Haynes	c Binny b Madan Lal	13	33
M Amarnath	b Holding	26	80	IVA Richards	c Kapil Dev b Madan Lal	33	28
Yashpal Sharma	c sub (JT Willoughby) b Gomes	11	32	*CH Lloyd	c Kapil Dev b Binny	8	17
SM Patil	c Gomes b Garner	27	29	HA Gomes	c Gavaskar b Madan Lal	5	16
*Kapil Dev	c Holding b Gomes	15	8	SFAF Bacchus	c Kirmani b Sandhu	8	25
KBJ Azad	c Garner b Roberts	0	3	+PJL Dujon	b Amarnath	25	73
RMH Binny	c Garner b Roberts	2	8	MD Marshall	c Gavaskar b Amarnath	18	51
Madan Lal	b Marshall	17	27	AME Roberts	lbw b Kapil Dev	4	14
+SMH Kirmani	b Holding	14	43	J Garner	not out	5	19
BS Sandhu	not out	11	30	MA Holding	lbw b Amarnath	6	24
Extras	(5 b, 5 lb, 1 nb, 9 w)	20		Extras	(4 lb, 10 w)	14	
Total	(all out, 54.4 overs)	183		Total	(all out, 52 overs)	140	

Fall of wickets: 1-2 (Gavaskar), 2-59 (Srikkanth), 3-90 (Amarnath), 4-92 (Yashpal Sharma), 5-110 (Kapil Dev), 6-111 (Azad), 7-130 (Binny), 8-153 (Patil), 9-161 (Madan Lal), 10-183 (Kirmani)

Fall of wickets: 1-5 (Greenidge), 2-50 (Haynes), 3-57 (Richards), 4-66 (Gomes), 5-66 (Lloyd), 6-76 (Bacchus), 7-119 (Dujon), 8-124 (Marshall), 9-126 (Roberts), 10-140 (Holding)

WEST INDIES	O	M	R	W	Wd	Nb	INDIA	O	M	R	W	Wd	Nb
Roberts	10	3	32	3	-	-	Kapil Dev	11	4	21	1	-	-
Garner	12	4	24	1	-	-	Sandhu	9	1	32	2	-	-
Marshall	11	1	24	2	-	-	Madan Lal	12	2	31	3	-	-
Holding	9.4	2	26	2	-	-	Binny	10	1	23	1	-	-
Gomes	11	1	49	2	-	-	Amarnath	7	0	12	3	-	-
Richards	1	0	8	0	-	-	Azad	3	0	7	0	-	-

MOST RUNS

Player	Mat	Inns	NO	Runs	HS	Ave	BF	SR	100	50	0	4s	6s
DI Gower (ENG)	7	7	2	384	130	76.8	452	84.95	1	1	0	33	2
IVA Richards (WI)	8	7	2	367	119	73.4	452	81.19	1	2	0	28	0
G Fowler (ENG)	7	7	2	360	81*	72	573	62.82	0	4	0	26	1
Zaheer Abbas (PAK)	7	7	2	313	103*	62.6	383	81.72	1	2	2	17	1
N Kapil Dev (INDIA)	8	8	3	303	175*	60.6	278	108.99	1	0	0	17	1
Imran Khan (PAK)	7	7	3	283	102*	70.75	370	76.48	1	2	0	26	2
AJ Lamb (ENG)	7	6	2	278	102	69.5	347	80.11	1	1	0	14	0
HA Gomes (WI)	8	7	3	258	78	64.5	461	55.96	0	3	0	20	2
CG Greenidge (WI)	7	7	1	250	105*	41.66	413	60.53	1	1	0	16	1
DL Haynes (WI)	8	8	1	240	88*	34.28	429	55.94	0	1	0	13	1
Yashpal Sharma (IND)	8	8	1	240	89	34.28	375	64	0	2	0	12	0
M Amarnath (INDIA)	8	8	0	237	80	29.62	507	46.74	0	1	0	12	0
GP Howarth (NZ)	6	6	0	224	76	37.33	336	66.66	0	2	0	5	0
Mohsin Khan (PAK)	7	7	0	223	82	31.85	505	44.15	0	2	1	11	0
Javed Miandad (PAK)	6	6	0	220	72	36.66	298	73.82	0	2	0	12	0
SM Patil (INDIA)	8	8	1	216	51*	30.85	240	90	0	2	1	5	2
KM Curran (ZIM)	6	6	0	212	73	35.33	315	67.3	0	2	0	14	0
CJ Tavare (ENG)	7	7	0	212	58	30.28	432	49.07	0	1	0	9	2
MD Crowe (NZ)	6	6	0	202	97	33.66	316	63.92	0	1	1	10	0
JV Coney (NZ)	6	6	2	197	66*	49.25	352	55.96	0	2	0	8	1
DAG Fletcher (ZIM)	6	6	2	191	71*	47.75	289	66.08	0	2	0	12	2
GN Yallop (AUS)	6	6	2	187	66*	46.75	262	71.37	0	2	0	5	0
DSBP Kuruppu (SL)	6	6	0	182	72	30.33	356	51.12	0	2	0	7	3
DL Houghton (ZIM)	6	6	0	176	84	29.33	286	61.53	0	2	2	13	1
KJ Hughes (AUS)	5	5	0	170	69	34	289	58.82	0	2	1	13	1

MOST WICKETS

Player	Mat	Inns	Overs	Mdns	Runs	Wkts	BBI	Ave	Econ	SR	4	5
RMH Binny (INDIA)	8	8	88	9	336	18	4/29	18.66	3.81	29.3	1	0
ALF de Mel (SL)	6	6	66	13	265	17	5/32	15.58	4.01	23.2	0	2
S Madan Lal (INDIA)	8	8	83	8	285	17	4/20	16.76	3.43	29.2	1	0
RJ Hadlee (NZ)	6	6	65.1	17	180	14	5/25	12.85	2.76	27.9	0	1
VJ Marks (ENG)	7	7	78	9	246	13	5/39	18.92	3.15	36	0	1
MD Marshall (WI)	6	6	70	10	175	12	3/28	14.58	2.5	35	0	0
MA Holding (WI)	7	7	74.5	11	235	12	3/40	19.58	3.14	37.4	0	0
N Kapil Dev (INDIA)	8	8	84	13	245	12	5/43	20.41	2.91	42	0	1
Abdul Qadir (PAK)	6	6	67.4	6	264	12	5/44	22	3.9	33.8	1	1
RGD Willis (ENG)	7	7	73.4	19	206	11	4/42	18.72	2.79	40.1	1	0
AME Roberts (WI)	7	7	74	12	238	11	3/32	21.63	3.21	40.3	0	0
JV Coney (NZ)	6	6	58	7	183	9	3/28	20.33	3.15	38.6	0	0
RM Hogg (AUS)	6	6	67	8	220	9	3/40	24.44	3.28	44.6	0	0
HA Gomes (WI)	8	8	74	4	304	9	2/46	33.77	4.1	49.3	0	0
KH MacLeay (AUS)	4	4	44.5	6	163	8	6/39	20.37	3.63	33.6	0	1
M Amarnath (INDIA)	8	6	49	2	178	8	3/12	22.25	3.63	36.7	0	0
WW Davis (WI)	5	5	54.3	6	206	8	7/51	25.75	3.77	40.8	0	1
PWE Rawson (ZIM)	6	6	62.1	10	239	8	3/47	29.87	3.84	46.6	0	0
EJ Chatfield (NZ)	6	6	70.2	8	249	8	2/24	31.12	3.54	52.7	0	0
Rashid Khan (PAK)	7	7	71	11	266	8	3/47	33.25	3.74	53.2	0	0
RJ Ratnayake (SL)	6	6	64	6	274	8	2/18	34.25	4.28	48	0	0
IT Botham (ENG)	7	7	80	13	288	8	2/12	36	3.6	60	0	0
BS Sandhu (INDIA)	8	8	83	10	297	8	2/26	37.12	3.57	62.2	0	0
PJW Allott (ENG)	7	7	80.3	10	335	8	3/41	41.87	4.16	60.3	0	0
DAG Fletcher (ZIM)	6	6	50.1	5	221	7	4/42	31.57	4.4	43	1	0

HIGH SCORES

Player	Runs	Balls	4s	6s	SR	Team	Opposition	Ground
N Kapil Dev	175*	138	16	6	126.81	India	v Zimbabwe	Tunbridge Wells
DI Gower	130	120	12	5	108.33	England	v Sri Lanka	Taunton
IVA Richards	119	146	6	1	81.5	West Indies	v India	The Oval
TM Chappell	110	131	11	0	83.96	Australia	v India	Nottingham
CG Greenidge	105*	147	5	1	71.42	West Indies	v Zimbabwe	Worcester
Zaheer Abbas	103*	121	6	0	85.12	Pakistan	v New Zealand	Nottingham
Imran Khan	102*	133	11	0	76.69	Pakistan	v Sri Lanka	Leeds
AJ Lamb	102	105	12	2	97.14	England	v New Zealand	The Oval
MD Crowe	97	118	8	0	82.2	New Zealand	v England	The Oval
IVA Richards	95*	117	9	3	81.19	West Indies	v Australia	Lord's

BEST BOWLING

Player	Overs	Mdns	Runs	Wkts	Econ	Team	Opposition	Ground
WW Davis	10.3	0	51	7	4.85	West Indies	v Australia	Leeds
KH MacLeay	11.5	3	39	6	3.29	Australia	v India	Nottingham
RJ Hadlee	10.1	4	25	5	2.45	New Zealand	v Sri Lanka	Bristol
ALF de Mel	12	4	32	5	2.66	Sri Lanka	v New Zealand	Derby
VJ Marks	12	3	39	5	3.25	England	v Sri Lanka	Taunton
ALF de Mel	12	1	39	5	3.25	Sri Lanka	v Pakistan	Leeds
N Kapil Dev	12	2	43	5	3.58	India	v Australia	Nottingham
Abdul Qadir	12	1	44	5	3.66	Pakistan	v Sri Lanka	Leeds
S Madan Lal	8.2	3	20	4	2.4	India	v Australia	Chelmsford
Abdul Qadir	12	4	21	4	1.75	Pakistan	v New Zealand	Birmingham

1987

BREAKING FREE

BY SCOTT OLIVER

The fourth ICC World Cup in 1987, in India and Pakistan, marked the onset of the tournament's adolescence, a glimpse of how it – and ODI cricket more broadly, which was still a teenager – would come to look in its muscular, adventurous adulthood. It was the first World Cup to be played outside England, the first played over the now-standard 50 overs, the first with neutral umpires. It was also the last tournament played in white clothing, and the last with a red ball.

It was the tournament in which modern limited-overs cricket started to burst through the old, when its separation and divergence from the long-form game was jimmied a little bit wider, but also one in which the old rhythms of short-form cricket – or *young*, from another vantage point – were manifest (the opening game was, after all, just the 451st ODI ever played). Field-placings were cautious, batting platforms were built, and finger spinners often operated to 3/6 fields (since prohibited, of course), although they were countered with reverse-sweeps from the likes of Javed Miandad, Mike Gatting and Dave Houghton, with varying degrees of success. Signs, then, that the brightly coloured butterfly of grown-up ODI cricket would not be long in emerging from the crawling caterpillar of its youth.

Competing for glory were the seven Test nations – South Africa were still in the political and sporting wilderness, Bangladesh over a decade away – and the next one to join the club, Zimbabwe, who qualified by beating the Netherlands in the ICC Trophy final in England the previous July.

The Joint Management Committee allocated the matches to 21 cities across the two host countries – 14 in India and seven in Pakistan – which spread the glamour of a global event as widely as feasible, but also meant a fair amount of travelling: for instance, Sri Lanka played consecutive games in Peshawar, Kanpur, Faisalabad and Pune.

That the format – two groups of four playing each other twice as in 1983 – took three-quarters of the tournament's duration to reduce the teams by half might be considered an unavoidable design flaw, yet the pitches were generally true, the weather invariably fair, and the scores largely comparable to four years earlier, despite 10 overs per innings being pruned. Indeed, it is still the second highest-scoring World Cup in terms of runs per wicket (32.5; only 2015 has been higher, at 32.9) and also the fastest-scoring of the first eight tournaments (4.87 runs per over).

And the tournament certainly produced more than its fair share of unforgettable games – of 27 matches, 13 were won by margins of 35 runs or fewer, including nine by under 20 runs.

Pakistan got things started in Group B, beating Sri Lanka in Hyderabad, where Javed Miandad passed 50 for the ninth consecutive ODI en route to a 96-ball hundred and the Lankans' valiant chase of 267 fell 15 short. It was the closest they would come to victory in the tournament, as a talented group of batsmen – including, in Arjuna Ranatunga, Asanka Gurusinha and Aravinda de Silva, the three lynchpins of their final triumph against Australia in Lahore nine years later – were unable to compensate for an attack that lacked firepower or cutting edge, leaving them with little more than a puncher's chance.

After the intriguing curtain-up, the greatest show in cricket was given lift-off by its next three matches, a triptych of stone-cold ODI classics. The first, between Group B's other two sides, England and West Indies, took place in the stifling heat of Gujranwala, with the England team taking pillows on their 6.30am coach trip to the ground. Advised to hydrate on the eve of the match, Phil DeFreitas quickly tired of water and switched to Fanta, most of which failed to survive his opening spell before being regurgitated onto the outfield.

Viv Richards' men would have felt reasonably happy with a total of 243, even more so when an England team missing two stars in Ian Botham and David Gower – both of whom had opted out – entered the final 10 overs needing 91 to win with just four wickets intact. West Indies were missing their own superstars in Gordon Greenidge and Malcolm Marshall, the world's top-rated ODI bowler at the time, while Joel Garner, the yorker-bowling maestro of the previous decade, had retired earlier that year. It was thus left to two relatively callow Jamaicans, Courtney Walsh and Patrick Patterson, to close the game out.

Lying in wait was Allan Lamb, so often a thorn in the West Indies' side and a player with form when it came to last-over heroics. Earlier that year, under lights and in colours at the SCG, Lamb had begun the final over from Bruce Reid (9-3-26-1) on 59 not out from 97 balls and boundary-less, before plundering 18 from the next five balls, prompting a banner at the next game that mischievously enquired: "Can Bruce Reid please call Allan Lamb on 24624?" With 34 needed from three overs, he took 15 off Walsh, before a tight penultimate over from Patterson yielded just six, leaving 13 to get from the final over. It was achieved, miraculously, with three balls to spare, leaving a well-cooked Lamb to head for the dressing room where he sat being doused with cold water.

Walsh may have felt like a cold shower himself. Taken for 31 from his last nine legal deliveries, he copped most of the flak – *Wisden* described him as "hapless" – although in his defence he had been asked to bowl to an unusual and unforgiving field, with five on the leg side (including two mid-wickets in the circle) and only one of the four on the offside, long off, patrolling the boundary. This somewhat telegraphed his intentions, both in line and length. Consequently, Lamb repeatedly backed away at the last nanosecond, four times slashing to the vacant third man boundary as Walsh missed the blockhole (Foster's winning blow also went through there for four). When Walsh followed him, he over-corrected and speared four wides down the leg side, effectively sealing the game. It was a chastening if character-building experience, and would not be his only death-overs disembowelling of the tournament. As it turned out, the game ultimately proved the difference between England and West Indies qualifying.

Meanwhile, with no day/night matches and thus no staggered starts, the Group A opener between reigning champions India and eventual champions Australia in Madras was played simultaneously, with 14 of the players that took part in the tied Test at the same venue 12 months earlier involved again.

This was austerity-era Australia, being shepherded from the Chappell-Lillee-Marsh era to the glories of the 1990s and beyond by that grizzled pragmatist Allan Border, and few expected much of them, which may have worked to their advantage. They had arrived in Madras nine days before the game to acclimatise, and were put through their paces by the coach, Bobby Simpson, who sought to overcome a lack of obvious subcontinent game-breakers by instilling professionalism and seeking out marginal gains. "We tried to work hard to run the singles and twos", recalled Dean Jones. "We tried to make the opposition look ragged, and that worked." They even had their kitbags inscribed with the motto: *to lose patience is to lose the battle.* Indeed, Australia would score only 78 in boundaries in their total of 270, compared to India's 128, yet one of them would prove the game's most decisive and controversial moment.

Jones had skipped down to Maninder Singh and lofted him in the direction of Ravi Shastri at long off, who misjudged the flight and, backpedalling, failed to take the catch. Umpire Dickie Bird asked Shastri whether it had cleared the rope, and the fielder signalled four, as then did Bird. The Australians, however, were adamant it had gone for six – "by at least a metre", said Jones – and so, during the interval, representation was made to the Indian captain, Kapil Dev, who sportingly agreed to have the total bumped by two runs. His team would lose by a single.

India set about the target with alacrity, Sunil Gavaskar, perhaps freed up by his imminent retirement, scoring 37 from 32 balls, while Kris Srikkanth and the debutant Navjot Sidhu made 70s. At 207 for 2 there looked like being only one winner, but Craig McDermott, whose first four overs had gone for 31, bowled Sidhu with a cutter before running through the vaunted middle order of Dilip Vengsarkar, Mohammad Azharuddin and Shastri. Simon O'Donnell then deceived Kapil Dev, exposing the tail, and two run outs left India behind the eight-ball. However, the competition's strongest batting line-up had Manoj Prabhakar at No.10, a man who would go on to score a Test hundred, and he manoeuvred his team through to the final over needing just six to win, although he was not on strike. Two twos were scrambled by Maninder, last man out in the tied Test, before he lost his off stump to the 22-year-old Steve Waugh, who would make a habit of nerveless death bowling as the tournament went on.

The competition format allowed India plenty of latitude to turn the result around, but there were early signs that the burden of expectation for the hosts and reigning champions might prove cumbersome. The Australians, meanwhile, had settled into a pattern of play: bat first, with discipline, hustle and harry, then defend the total with razor-sharp fielding, clever use of cutters and only one frontline spinner, occasionally none (anomalously, given that seven of the nine most economical bowlers in the qualifying round would be spinners).

The other Group A opener paired the outsiders Zimbabwe and New Zealand in the humidity of the Indian Hyderabad, a game that would be remembered for one of the greatest innings in World Cup history, even if it was, ultimately, in vain. Before all that, New Zealand coach Glenn Turner, sensing some early morning moisture and the likelihood of seam movement, had informed Martin Snedden half an hour before play that he would be opening the batting for the first time in his career – not so much pinch-hitting as pinch-blocking. He made 64, with Martin Crowe adding a typically elegant 72 as the Kiwis closed on 242 for 7.

It wouldn't be entirely accurate to call the Zimbabweans reply a lone hand, although Dave Houghton did score 130 runs more than anyone else in the top eight. It wasn't until Ian Butchart joined Houghton at a forlorn 104 for 7 – this despite the New Zealand attack being severely weakened by the absence of Richard Hadlee, at the time second only to Marshall in the ICC ODI bowling rankings – that humiliation was avoided. This then morphed into competitive respectability and, before long, a 117-run partnership for the eighth wicket, at the time a record in ODIs, that had the Kiwis on the rack.

In the early stages of the re-build, Houghton had made liberal use of the reverse-sweep, much to the consternation of manager Don Arnott, whose son, Kevin, in the squad but not the side, was called upon to relay his father's concerns. "Every over Kev would come out with a bottle of water and say, 'Dad says, please stop playing the reverse-sweep'", recalled Houghton. "I'm not going to tell you what I told him to tell his dad." The trouble was, after a certain point, the water, like the advice, wasn't going in, so dehydrated had he become, having also earlier kept wicket for 50 overs. As the fatigue kicked in, Houghton started to hit out, passing three figures – which earned him a kiss from a jubilant spectator – and taking the Zimbabweans to within 22 of their target before falling to a stunning over-the-shoulder catch by Martin Crowe, running back toward the long-on boundary, having made a brilliant 142 from 137 balls, featuring 13 fours and seven sixes.

Next man in, Eddo Brandes, engrossed as everyone else by the innings-reviving partnership, hadn't moved for some time by the time Butchart was calling him through for a sharp single, and so not only was he run out without facing a ball, he also pulled a hamstring that kept him sidelined for two games. Despite 228 for 7 having become 228 for 9, the Zimbabweans stayed in the game until, with four needed from three balls, bowled by off-spinner Stephen Boock, non-striker John Traicos tore down the wicket for a run that the big-hitting Butchart, reckoning on a single blow to win it, hadn't computed, and with that the game was up.

The two sides would each lose to Australia and India in their next two games, leaving Group A looking cut and dried, especially after India then exacted some vengeance for Madras in the return fixture against Australia, winning by 56 runs in Delhi. It was the only time Australia chased during the tournament, and the only game they lost.

With New Zealand having beaten Zimbabwe a little more convincingly second time around, they needed to turn over the Australians in their fifth game to maintain the slim chance of qualification for the semi-finals. First time out, in Indore, in a 'Thirty30' game – the tournament's only reduced overs match, played on the reserve day against the backdrop of "Black Monday", when 45 per cent was wiped from the Hong Kong stock markets and the effects rippled around the world – they had gone down to their trans-Tasman rivals by just three runs, having needed seven off the final over with four wickets in hand. In Chandigarh, they would fall 17 runs short, bowled out with eight balls remaining as the hawkish Australians effected four run outs.

Meanwhile, India saw off Zimbabwe in Ahmedabad, although with Gavaskar taking 114 balls over his 50 they scored at just 4.6 runs per over in knocking off 191, and so headed into the final round of games – now a straight shoot-out to see who would top the group and avoid a semi-final in Lahore against the Pakistanis – with an overall run-rate of 5.18 to the Australians' 5.20. India, however, would have the considerable advantage of playing a day after Australia, who did well to score 266 in beating Zimbabwe by 70 runs on a capricious Cuttack pitch.

If Group A would ultimately end up being about the mathematical jockeying of run-rate calculations, Group B contained far more jeopardy, with three good sides understanding perfectly the maths of trying to squeeze into two semi-final berths.

England followed their opening game heist with defeat to Pakistan in Rawalpindi, a game they might easily have won. With Imran Khan too ill to bowl, England needed 34 off four overs with six wickets in hand, promptly lost half of them in one Abdul Qadir over and fell 18 short. The lack of real batting strength in the lower middle-order – in part a consequence of Mike Gatting's insistence on picking five specialist bowlers which, once Eddie Hemmings had been drafted in as second spinner to replace Derek Pringle, left them with three No.8s and no genuine No.6 or 7 – would prove England's Achilles heel when it mattered most.

West Indies took out their frustrations from Gujranwala on the Sri Lankans, racking up a mammoth 360 for 4 in Karachi, then the highest team score not only in World Cups but all ODI matches. Viv Richards, who came in on a hat-trick ball after Ravi Ratnayeke had dismissed Carlisle Best and Richie Richardson, broke the individual batting record, eclipsing Kapil Dev's previous mark of 175 as he bludgeoned 181 not out from just 125 balls, including 16 fours and 7 sixes, as Ratnayeke was taken for 44 from his final two overs and Asantha de Mel disappeared for 97 off his allotted ten. Desmond Haynes chipped in with 105, too, the first time a World Cup innings had contained two centurions.

A shell-shocked Sri Lanka limped to 169 for 4 in reply, while a revived West Indies knew that victory over Pakistan in their next match in Lahore would leave Group B evenly poised between the three heavyweight contenders. However, in the tournament's fourth classic in just nine matches, they would suffer another final-over heartbreak, and once again Courtney Walsh was at the heart of things – in both a bad and good way.

In the Test arena, Pakistan had been the one team to consistently challenge the dominant West Indies during the 1980s: they were the only visiting team to win a Test in the Caribbean that decade, and the only team to avoid defeat in a series in the Caribbean between 1974 and 1995. Imran Khan was not one to be cowed, whoever the opponent. Throw in home advantage, and they were marginal favourites.

By the time Imran had taken 4 for 37 to hustle out West Indies for 216, they looked dead certs, but Richards' men roared back and Pakistan were in trouble at 110 for 5 when wicket-keeper Salim Yousuf played a man-of-the-match-winning gem of 56 from 49 balls. However, having needed 21 from three overs with four wickets in hand, Pakistan arrived at the final over nine down and still 14 shy of victory, with Walsh bowling to a helmetless Abdul Qadir. Two singles were taken from the first two balls, then a two, at which point Qadir carved a six over long off, followed by another scurried two as the atmosphere in the Gaddafi Stadium reached feverish intensity. What followed has entered into legend.

After a chat with Roger Harper, who had jogged in from long off, Walsh galloped in to deliver the final ball, but instead stopped dead in his follow-through, by which time the No.11, Saleem Jaffar had advanced a few steps up the pitch. Walsh looked at him admonishingly, arms folded, but declined to run the batsman out – under the Laws at the time, if rarely under the etiquette, he was entitled to have broken the wicket and claimed a crucial win. Instead, the batsman scurried sheepishly back to the crease. For his act of sportsmanship, Walsh later received a medal from the Pakistani government as well as a hand-woven carpet from a local fan.

After all the commotion of the dry-run, Walsh did then bowl and, with Richards having brought all his men inside the circle, a low full toss was sliced away through backward point to give Pakistan a famous last-ball win. As pandemonium engulfed the stadium, Qadir was carried off on spectators' shoulders. Viv? He just lay back on the turf as the pitch invasion happened around him. With England having brushed aside Sri Lanka, West Indies, finalists in all three World Cups to that point, were in danger of an early exit. Pakistan were in the box seat, a position they consolidated with victory over England in Karachi, a game briefly interrupted when spectators threw stones on the outfield.

West Indies, meanwhile, were given a much more testing game by the Sri Lankans second time around. Restricted to 236 for 8, they eventually won by 25 runs, but not before an unbeaten 86 from Ranatunga had given the Lankans an outside chance. Duleep Mendis' men then lost by 113 to the Pakistanis in Faisalabad, for whom Saleem Malik made a maiden ODI hundred, all of which meant the West Indies game against England in Jaipur was, to all intents and purposes, sudden death: lose, and they would need the Sri Lankans to beat England in Pune; win, and follow up with victory over Pakistan, and it would come down to a run-rate shoot-out for second place.

As it was, England produced their most commanding display of the tournament, posting a formidable 269 for 4 thanks to the discipline of Graham Gooch, whose 92 from 137 balls earned him the first of three straight man of the match awards, and the indiscipline of the West Indian bowlers, who conceded 22 in wides and no balls as they went down by 34 runs.

It had been a tough 12 months for Gooch, who had opted out of the previous winter's victorious Ashes tour for the birth of his twins, then failed to regain his opening berth after six ducks in ten innings for Essex at the start of the year. "I had some issues with my technique, falling over a bit, and fell into a bit of disrepair. But I was in the MCC team for the Bicentenary game, because they picked the side at the start of the summer, for publicity reasons, and I suppose I got selected on my past record. Call it fate, but I got a hundred in that game, and it just clicked from there. I carried that form and confidence into the World Cup, and it was probably my best tournament."

The West Indies were heading home early, and a consolation victory over the hitherto unbeaten Pakistanis in Karachi did little to raise their spirits, although it may have put a slight dent in the hosts' confidence in advance of their semi-final in Lahore. England, meanwhile, steamrollered Sri Lanka and would be heading to Mumbai for the semis, where they would meet India, provided the latter could score at 5.25 runs per over in the final game of the qualifiers against New Zealand in Nagpur.

First, they restricted the Kiwis to 221 for 9, with Chetan Sharma completing the first ever ODI hat trick for India, and the first by anyone in a World Cup, with all three victims clean bowled with skiddy pace and late movement. The third victim, Ewen Chatfield, got in such a tangle that he was castled between his legs. The upshot was that India needed to knock off the runs in 42.2 overs to avoid a perilous trip to Lahore. They did it at a canter.

The dashing Srikkanth was in his element, and made 75 from 58 balls. But the real surprise was Gavaskar, whose stodgy innings against Zimbabwe was quickly forgotten in a blaze of bravura shot-making, including consecutive sixes then consecutive fours in Chatfield's second over as India raced to 39 from three overs and never looked back. The "Little Master" went on to record his first and only ODI hundred, from 85 balls, India reaching their target ten overs ahead of schedule and duly booking themselves in against England at the Wankhede.

Before that, however, Australia made their way to the Punjab to face the Pakistanis, with the hosts' former batting great Zaheer Abbas' assessment of them as "a bunch of club cricketers" no doubt pinned to the metaphorical dressing room wall, if not the literal. It may also have inadvertently pressurised his compatriots – how could you not beat a team of club players? – who produced their second shaky performance in a row to be dumped out in front of 30,000 heartbroken fans.

Not that Australia didn't have some luck. After Geoff Marsh had needlessly run himself out, Dean Jones, not yet off the mark, was fortunate to survive a vociferous lbw appeal after planting his front pad to an Abdul Qadir top-spinner. He then appeared well short when running a risky two to long leg (there was no TV umpire to adjudicate in 1987), the stumps being demolished by Javed Miandad, who had donned the gloves after Saleem Yousuf had taken one in the mouth from another Qadir fizzer that deflected off Jones' front pad. Jones was eventually bowled, cutting off-spinner Tauseef Ahmed, who finished his spell and headed off for a stitch in his hand, before Miandad pulled off a not entirely silken legside stumping to dismiss Boon for 65.

At 155 for 3, the unheralded Mike Veletta entered, and scored a vital 48 from 50 balls before Imran flattened his stumps, which he then did to Dyer and McDermott as Australia began the 50th over on 249 for 8, whereupon Steve Waugh opened his shoulders to take the already expensive Jaffar for 18 – the eventual margin of victory – and tilt the game decisively Australia's way. A chase of 268 was not impossible – it had been achieved once before in the World Cup – but the venue, the occasion, the stakes would not work in the Pakistanis' favour if they fell behind the game, as they did in stumbling to 38 for 3. A daunting chase suddenly appeared Himalayan.

Having announced he would retire at the end of the tournament, this was supposed to be Imran's final game in his home city, and in alliance with Javed Miandad – for so long the alpha and omega of Pakistani cricket, the prince and the prankster, the statesman and the streetfighter – the innings was rebuilt. But slowly. Imran was himself lucky not to be adjudged lbw first ball, lunging at Waugh's back-of-the-hand slower ball, although it would have taken a brave umpire to give it.

As the run-rate mounted and it became time to accelerate, Imran was dismissed by his opposite number, Border, under-edging an ungainly hack. Still, a cameo from Wasim Akram brought the equation to 105 off 80 balls, but he was yorked by McDermott, and once Bruce Reid had dismissed a teenage Ijaz Ahmed and then Miandad, the Pakistani race looked run. McDermott had Yousuf, Jaffar and Tauseef caught at the wicket to seal things and finish with 5 for 44, the tournament's sole five-wicket haul for its leading wicket-taker.

The Australians had made it through less with flamboyance than sleeves-rolled-up yakka, squeezing everything from a workmanlike side that played to its strengths. They may have lacked the stars of teams of yore or teams to come – although, to be sure, Border, Boon, McDermott and the young Steve Waugh were world-class performers – but they were already leading the way with their preparation. As an "absolutely ecstatic" Border said in his post-match interview: "There weren't too many people who gave us much of a chance to get through even this far", before immediately extinguishing the dreaminess with the warning, "we're going to be a very hard side to beat in that final". This was the ethos of his captaincy distilled to its absolute essence.

The following day they sat and watched the second semi-final, where England named an unchanged team once Neil Foster had passed a late fitness test on his troublesome knees, while India would be without Dilip Vengsarkar – who would end 1987 as the world's number one Test batsman – after he withdrew through illness.

The pitch was expected to be "a real turner made for the Indian spinners", recalls Tim Robinson, whose opening partner prepared accordingly: "The day before the game Gooch didn't have a net as such. He just had this little Indian lad throwing him balls and he swept every single one. That's all he did for an hour: swept. That's all he did the next day: swept and swept, and won us the game".

It was a masterful 115 from 136 balls from the tournament's leading run-scorer, although its genesis wasn't solely in the nets the day before. "In those days, there were no analysts," Gooch recalled. "But we watched all the matches on telly. We knew what we were going to get in terms of the pitch, knew they would play two left-arm spinners, so I practised sweeping. It was Alan Knott who taught me how to play the shot, how to manipulate the field, and it came down to where you positioned your front leg: if you kept it inside the ball, you could hit it squarer; if you put it in line, it would go where the general shot goes, just behind the umpire; and if you went outside the ball you could get it finer. I'd made up my mind. To score in the conventional way was very difficult, and Kapil Dev didn't really change the field that much, other than the angle of the deep-backward square. And it worked. The fielders on the offside hardly fielded a ball."

Abetted by some conservative (if conventional) fields, England's most adept player of spin, Mike Gatting, contributed a breezy 54 to a partnership of 117 in 19 overs with Gooch, and a late flurry from Allan Lamb took England to a challenging 254 for 6. DeFreitas then sent Gavaskar's off-stump cartwheeling in the third over, while the free-scoring Srikkanth and Sidhu were first becalmed, then dismissed by Foster. Nevertheless, with Azharuddin holding things together, India had manoeuvred themselves into a winnable position – 87 wanted from 16 overs with six wickets in hand – when Kapil Dev, having made a sprightly 30 from 22 balls, picked out Gatting at deep mid-wicket from a top-edged slog-sweep off Hemmings, arguably as unnecessary an act of boldness as that for which his opposite number would be pilloried at the end of the week.

Kiran More joined Azharuddin, and the equation came down to 51 off 9 overs, Emburey and Hemmings bowling to 3/6 fields. It was Hemmings, again, who broke the partnership, sliding one under Azhar's sweep en route to 4 for 21 from his final 34 balls as England, in the end, ran out comfortable winners and booked their flights to Calcutta, where they found the hotel room cards had the Indian players' names crossed out and theirs added in biro.

Like Pakistan, India were left to lick their wounds, the reward for reaching the semi-finals just £6,000 each. Widely expected to contest the final, the co-hosts had ended up not playing each other at all, with a hastily arranged third-place play-off falling through due to the financial demands of leading players from both camps. And so, with the old enemies' exiting, the final threw together the oldest of cricketing foes for an underdog scrap in front of an enormous Eden Gardens crowd. There would be a new name on the trophy.

England certainly fancied their chances. Already in 1987, en route to an unprecedented haul of three straight multilateral limited-overs titles, they had beaten Australia in the quadrangular Perth Challenge, beaten them 2-0 in the best-of-three finals of the triangular Benson & Hedges World Series, and, in conditions most like Calcutta, beaten them in the quadrangular Sharjah Cup. Nevertheless, Australia had been only that final-over Allan Lamb demolition at the SCG away from winning all four of the WSC qualifiers and besides, they weren't given to talking down their chances. Indeed, before the Mumbai semi-final, Border had said he'd prefer to play England, which was not only refreshingly candid but entirely logical. Meanwhile, the Australians' victory over Pakistan, coupled with England's over India, meant that the ostensibly neutral crowd of near 100,000 would be almost unanimously rooting for the boys in the Baggy Green.

Both sides were unchanged from the semis, although Mike Gatting admitted to a selection dilemma concerning which of his two Nottinghamshire openers would partner Gooch. In the end, Robinson would get a first-baller, while Chris Broad, who had hit Ashes hundreds in three straight Tests the previous winter and might have been considered to have the wood on the Australians, carried the drinks.

First blood went to Australia, Border's call at the toss allowing his team to bat first. If Gatting "wasn't too fussed" about chasing, he was certainly perturbed by an erratic opening ten overs from DeFreitas and Small, as the formidable combination of Boon and Marsh again gave their team a solid platform. Marsh was the only batsman to make two hundreds in the tournament, while Boon's scores were 49, 2, 87, 62, 14, 93, 65 and, here in the final, 75, which would win him man of the match. There wasn't a game in which neither one of them made a half-century, and partnerships of 110, 10, 17, 88, 25, 90, 73 and now 75 did so much to underpin the Australians' success.

Dean Jones played neatly, albeit with restraint, as the England spinners dragged things back in the middle overs to back up Foster, who at one stage had figures of 8-0-16-1. Nevertheless, after an important, if brief, cameo from McDermott, chucked in as a pinch-hitter at No.4, it was Veletta, with a 31-ball 45, his third consecutive 40-plus score, who turned a middling total into a challenging one, 65 runs coming in the final six overs as England's fielding buckled.

"It was the one match where we didn't bowl well in the first 10 overs", recalls Gatting, "and didn't get it right in the last six to eight overs. We got run ragged. They were turning ones into twos, and those were the extra 10 runs that they shouldn't have got. It was the worst game we played."

After McDermott had pinned Robinson in front at the start of England's chase, Gooch and Athey slowly rebuilt until the former also fell lbw, to Simon O'Donnell, Australia's best bowler on the day. Another partnership developed, 65 in 13 overs, with Gatting looking in fine touch, and England were cruising at 135 for 2 after 31 overs when Allan Border, running out of options, brought himself on. Then it happened.

Gatting, 41 from 44 balls, surveyed the field and decided he would reverse-sweep his opposite number's first delivery. "We all knew where he was going to bowl it," he recalls. "I knew where he was going to bowl it. He did. Everybody did. It was just that he bowled it even further down leg than I expected. I'd made up my mind. I just wanted to keep the momentum going. There was nobody behind square on the offside; it was a shot I'd been playing, so I played it. But because it was so wide, I had to fetch it from a long way, and didn't get enough bat on it to get it past my body. It hit my shoulder and just looped up, sadly. Had it not hit my shoulder, that would have been three or four, and I don't know what would have happened after that..."

For Border, dismissing the opposition captain was becoming something of a habit. He took six wickets in Australia's final four matches, all top six players, including three captains. He had bowled only three times in his previous 29 ODIs, over 20 months, and not taken a single wicket. After the 1987 final, he bowled only two overs in his next 13 ODIs.

So England would be left with what-ifs. As Scyld Berry wryly observed in *Wisden*, England's party had "arrived with a specialist in tropical diseases and a microwave oven but with only three batsmen capable of scoring at a run a ball". What might the team of Gooch, Lamb and Gatting have achieved with Gower and Botham alongside them?

Lamb again battled gamely, scoring 45 from 55 balls, but the required run-rate crept up and up as the crowd roared the Australians on. Downton and Emburey were exposed at No.6 and 7 respectively, although a late flourish from DeFreitas, launching McDermott for a vast six and two fours in the 48th over, gave England a sniff. However, with 19 needed from 12 balls, Steve Waugh, who had earlier bowled Lamb and run out Athey, conceded just two runs and had DeFreitas caught by Reid at long off. McDermott closed out the game without any further alarms, and the Australians had won by eight runs, leaving England to pick over the bones of their near-miss.

Eddie Hemmings was adamant that England had "lobbed it, totally lobbed it. The reverse sweep that Gatting played really well, he didn't play really well because he'd pre-empted it. He should have swept it, but back-flapped it onto his shoulder and got caught. We were walking it, totally walking it. A sad day." Robinson, meanwhile, was more measured, describing it as "the worst game we played, tactically. We had a couple of chances, and we blew it. You can't just point the figure at Gatt." For Gooch, the responsibility was collective: "On the day, we didn't get the big performance from one player that would have made the difference."

Of course, the old enemy's recriminations were no concern for the Australians, who cavorted long into the night, drinking not only the traditional few coldies but also the elixir of maiden World Cup glory. They would develop quite a taste for it.

1987

RESULTS AND STATISTICS

GROUP A TABLE

		P	W	L	Pts	RR
1	India	6	5	1	20	5.413
2	Australia	6	5	1	20	5.193
3	New Zealand	6	2	4	8	4.887
4	Zimbabwe	6	0	6	0	3.757

GROUP B TABLE

		P	W	L	Pts	RR
1	Pakistan	6	5	1	20	5.007
2	England	6	4	2	16	5.14
3	West Indies	6	3	3	12	5.16
4	Sri Lanka	6	0	6	0	4.041

PAKISTAN V AUSTRALIA

RELIANCE WORLD CUP 1987/88 (SEMI-FINAL)

Venue: Gaddafi Stadium, Lahore
Date: 4th November 1987
Toss: Australia
Result: Australia won by 18 runs
Umpires: HD Bird, DR Shepherd
Man of the Match: CJ McDermott

AUSTRALIA		R	b	PAKISTAN		R	b
GR Marsh	run out	31	57	Rameez Raja	run out	1	1
DC Boon	st +Javed Miandad b Saleem Malik	65	91	Mansoor Akhtar	b McDermott	9	19
DM Jones	b Tauseef Ahmed	38	45	Saleem Malik	c McDermott b Waugh	25	31
*AR Border	run out	18	22	Javed Miandad	b Reid	70	103
MRJ Veletta	b Imran Khan	48	50	*Imran Khan	c Dyer b Border	58	84
SR Waugh	not out	32	28	Wasim Akram	b McDermott	20	13
SP O'Donnell	run out	0	2	Ijaz Ahmed	c Jones b Reid	8	7
+GC Dyer	b Imran Khan	0	1	+Saleem Yousuf	c Dyer b McDermott	21	15
CJ McDermott	b Imran Khan	1	3	Abdul Qadir	not out	20	16
TBA May	not out	0	2	Saleem Jaffar	c Dyer b McDermott	0	2
BA Reid	did not bat			Tauseef Ahmed	c Dyer b McDermott	1	3
Extras	(1 b, 19 lb, 1 nb, 13 w)	34		Extras	(6 lb, 10 w)	16	
Total	(8 wickets, 50 overs)	267		Total	(all out, 49 overs)	249	

Fall of wickets: 1-73 (Marsh), 2-155 (Boon), 3-155 (Jones), 4-215 (Border), 5-236 (Veletta), 6-236 (O'Donnell), 7-241 (Dyer), 8-249 (McDermott).

Fall of wickets: 1-2 (Rameez Raja), 2-37 (Mansoor Akhtar), 3-38 (Saleem Malik), 4-150 (Imran Khan), 5-177 (Wasim Akram), 6-192 (Ijaz Ahmed), 7-212 (Javed Miandad), 8-236 (Saleem Yousuf), 9-247 (Saleem Jaffar), 10-249 (Tauseef Ahmed).

PAKISTAN	O	M	R	W	Wd	Nb	AUSTRALIA	O	M	R	W	Wd	Nb
Imran Khan	10	1	36	3	-	-	McDermott	10	0	44	5	-	-
Saleem Jaffar	6	0	57	0	-	-	Reid	10	2	41	2	-	-
Wasim Akram	10	0	54	0	-	-	Waugh	9	1	51	1	-	-
Abdul Qadir	10	0	39	0	-	-	O'Donnell	10	1	45	0	-	-
Tauseef Ahmed	10	1	39	1	-	-	May	6	0	36	0	-	-
Saleem Malik	4	0	22	1	-	-	Border	4	0	26	1	-	-

INDIA V ENGLAND

RELIANCE WORLD CUP 1987/88 (SEMI-FINAL)

Venue: Wankhede Stadium, Bombay
Date: 5th November 1987
Toss: India
Result: England won by 35 runs
Umpires: AR Crafter, SJ Woodward
Man of the Match: GA Gooch

ENGLAND		R	b	INDIA		R	b
GA Gooch	c Srikkanth b Maninder Singh	115	136	K Srikkanth	b Foster	31	55
RT Robinson	st More b Maninder Singh	13	36	SM Gavaskar	b DeFreitas	4	7
CWJ Athey	c More b Sharma	4	17	NS Sidhu	c Athey b Foster	22	40
*MW Gatting	b Maninder Singh	56	62	M Azharuddin	lbw b Hemmings	64	74
AJ Lamb	not out	32	29	CS Pandit	lbw b Foster	24	30
JE Emburey	lbw b Kapil Dev	6	10	*Kapil Dev	c Gatting b Hemmings	30	22
PAJ DeFreitas	b Kapil Dev	7	8	RJ Shastri	c Downton b Hemmings	21	32
+PR Downton	not out	1	5	+KS More	c and b Emburey	0	5
NA Foster	did not bat			M Prabhakar	c Downton b Small	4	11
GC Small	did not bat			C Sharma	c Lamb b Hemmings	0	1
EE Hemmings	did not bat			Maninder Singh	not out	0	0
Extras	(1 b, 18 lb, 1 w)	20		Extras	(1 b, 9 lb, 3 nb, 6 w)	19	
Total	(6 wickets, 50 overs)	254		Total	(all out, 45.3 overs)	219	

Fall of wickets: 1-40 (Robinson), 2-79 (Athey), 3-196 (Gatting), 4-203 (Gooch), 5-219 (Emburey), 6-231 (DeFreitas)

Fall of wickets: 1-7 (Gavaskar), 2-58 (Srikkanth), 3-73 (Sidhu), 4-121 (Pandit), 5-168 (Kapil Dev), 6-204 (Azharuddin), 7-205 (More), 8-218 (Prabhakar), 9-219 (Sharma), 10-219 (Shastri)

INDIA	O	M	R	W	Wd	Nb	ENGLAND	O	M	R	W	Wd	Nb
Kapil Dev	10	1	38	2	-	-	DeFreitas	7	0	37	1	-	-
Prabhakar	9	1	40	0	-	-	Small	6	0	22	1	-	-
Maninder Singh	10	0	54	3	-	-	Emburey	10	1	35	1	-	-
Sharma	9	0	41	1	-	-	Foster	10	0	47	3	-	-
Shastri	10	0	49	0	-	-	Hemmings	9.3	1	52	4	-	-
Azharuddin	2	0	13	0	-	-	Gooch	3	0	16	0	-	-

AUSTRALIA V ENGLAND

RELIANCE WORLD CUP 1987/88 (FINAL)

Venue: Eden Gardens, Calcutta
Date: 8th November 1987
Toss: Australia
Result: Australia won by 7 runs
Umpires: RB Gupta, Mahboob Shah
Man of the Match: DC Boon

AUSTRALIA		R	b	ENGLAND		R	b
DC Boon	c Downton b Hemmings	75	125	GA Gooch	lbw b O'Donnell	35	57
GR Marsh	b Foster	24	49	RT Robinson	lbw b McDermott	0	1
DM Jones	c Athey b Hemmings	33	57	CWJ Athey	run out (Waugh->Reid)	58	103
CJ McDermott	b Gooch	14	8	*MW Gatting	c Dyer b Border	41	45
*AR Border	run out (Robinson->Downton)	31	31	AJ Lamb	b Waugh	45	55
MRJ Veletta	not out	45	31	+PR Downton	c O'Donnell b Border	9	8
SR Waugh	not out	5	4	JE Emburey	run out (Boon->McDermott)	10	16
SP O'Donnell	did not bat			PAJ DeFreitas	c Reid b Waugh	17	10
+GC Dyer	did not bat			NA Foster	not out	7	6
TBA May	did not bat			GC Small	not out	3	3
BA Reid	did not bat			EE Hemmings	did not bat		
Extras	(1 b, 13 lb, 7 nb, 5 w)	26		Extras	(1 b, 14 lb, 4 nb, 2 w)	21	
Total	(5 wickets, 50 overs)	253		Total	(8 wickets, 50 overs)	246	

Fall of wickets: 1-75 (Marsh), 2-151 (Jones), 3-166 (McDermott), 4-168 (Boon), 5-241 (Border)

Fall of wickets: 1-1 (Robinson), 2-66 (Gooch), 3-135 (Gatting), 4-170 (Athey), 5-188 (Downton), 6-218 (Lamb), 7-220 (Emburey), 8-235 (DeFreitas)

ENGLAND	O	M	R	W	Wd	Nb	AUSTRALIA	O	M	R	W	Wd	Nb
DeFreitas	6	1	34	0	1	1	McDermott	10	1	51	1	-	-
Small	6	0	33	0	-	6	Reid	10	0	43	0	1	2
Foster	10	0	38	1	1	-	Waugh	9	0	37	2	1	1
Hemmings	10	1	48	2	-	-	O'Donnell	10	1	35	1	-	1
Emburey	10	0	44	0	-	-	May	4	0	27	0	-	-
Gooch	8	1	42	1	1	-	Border	7	0	38	2	-	-

MOST RUNS

Player	Mat	Inns	NO	Runs	HS	Ave	BF	SR	100	50	0	4s	6s
GA Gooch (ENG)	8	8	0	471	115	58.87	670	70.29	1	3	0	45	0
DC Boon (AUS)	8	8	0	447	93	55.87	583	76.67	0	5	0	38	3
GR Marsh (AUS)	8	8	1	428	126*	61.14	627	68.26	2	1	0	35	4
IVA Richards (WI)	6	6	0	391	181	65.16	364	107.41	1	3	0	29	13
MW Gatting (ENG)	8	8	1	354	60	50.57	369	95.93	0	3	0	26	2
Rameez Raja (PAK)	7	7	0	349	113	49.85	551	63.33	1	2	0	15	0
Saleem Malik (PAK)	7	7	1	323	100	53.83	354	91.24	1	2	0	30	0
DM Jones (AUS)	8	8	1	314	58*	44.85	404	77.72	0	3	0	9	9
SM Gavaskar (INDIA)	7	7	1	300	103*	50	379	79.15	1	2	0	36	4
AJ Lamb (ENG)	8	7	2	299	76	59.8	315	94.92	0	2	0	20	3
NS Sidhu (INDIA)	7	5	0	276	75	55.2	321	85.98	0	4	0	15	10
Javed Miandad (PAK)	7	7	1	274	103	45.66	374	73.26	1	1	0	18	0
RB Richardson (WI)	6	6	0	271	110	45.16	380	71.31	1	2	1	25	3
A Ranatunga (SL)	5	5	2	252	86*	84	355	70.98	0	3	0	23	2
K Srikkanth (INDIA)	7	7	0	248	75	35.42	299	82.94	0	2	0	29	3
DL Houghton (ZIM)	6	6	0	226	142	37.66	274	82.48	1	1	1	19	6
MD Crowe (NZ)	6	6	0	222	72	37	235	94.46	0	3	0	21	1
DL Haynes (WI)	6	6	0	219	105	36.5	352	62.21	1	0	0	20	1
CWJ Athey (ENG)	6	6	2	211	86	52.75	325	64.92	0	2	0	11	2
KR Rutherford (NZ)	5	5	0	204	75	40.8	276	73.91	0	1	0	15	4
M Azharuddin (INDIA)	7	5	2	190	64	63.33	241	78.83	0	2	0	19	1
AR Border (AUS)	8	8	0	183	67	22.87	225	81.33	0	1	0	16	0
AL Logie (WI)	6	6	2	181	65*	45.25	174	104.02	0	1	0	13	1
JJ Crowe (NZ)	6	6	1	180	88*	36	213	84.5	0	1	0	16	0
AJ Pycroft (ZIM)	6	6	1	174	61	34.8	254	68.5	0	2	0	9	1

HIGH SCORES

Player	Runs	Balls	4s	6s	SR	Team	Opposition	Ground
IVA Richards	181	125	16	7	144.8	West Indies	v Sri Lanka	Karachi
DL Houghton	142	137	13	6	103.64	Zimbabwe	v New Zealand	Hyderabad (Deccan)
GR Marsh	126*	149	12	3	84.56	Australia	v New Zealand	Chandigarh
GA Gooch	115	136	11	0	84.55	England	v India	Mumbai
Rameez Raja	113	148	5	0	76.35	Pakistan	v England	Karachi
GR Marsh	110	141	7	1	78.01	Australia	v India	Chennai
RB Richardson	110	135	8	2	81.48	West Indies	v Pakistan	Karachi
DL Haynes	105	124	10	1	84.67	West Indies	v Sri Lanka	Karachi
SM Gavaskar	103*	88	10	3	117.04	India	v New Zealand	Nagpur
Javed Miandad	103	100	6	0	103	Pakistan	v Sri Lanka	Hyderabad (Sind)

MOST WICKETS

Player	Mat	Inns	Overs	Mdns	Runs	Wkts	BBI	Ave	Econ	SR	4	5
CJ McDermott (AUS)	8	8	73	3	341	18	5/44	18.94	4.67	24.3	1	1
Imran Khan (PAK)	7	6	49.5	6	222	17	4/37	13.05	4.45	17.5	2	0
BP Patterson (WI)	6	6	56	2	253	14	3/31	18.07	4.51	24	0	0
Maninder Singh (IND)	7	7	70	1	280	14	3/21	20	4	30	0	0
EE Hemmings (ENG)	6	6	59.3	4	274	13	4/52	21.07	4.6	27.4	1	0
Abdul Qadir (PAK)	7	7	68	2	242	12	4/31	20.16	3.55	34	1	0
PAJ DeFreitas (ENG)	8	8	69.1	12	283	12	3/28	23.58	4.09	34.5	0	0
SR Waugh (AUS)	8	8	63.3	4	288	11	2/36	26.18	4.53	34.6	0	0
JR Ratnayeke (SL)	6	6	54	2	313	10	3/41	31.3	5.79	32.4	0	0
CA Walsh (WI)	6	6	55.3	6	229	9	4/40	25.44	4.12	37	1	0
M Prabhakar (INDIA)	7	7	59	4	235	9	4/19	26.11	3.98	39.3	1	0
SP O'Donnell (AUS)	7	7	60.4	6	261	9	4/39	29	4.3	40.4	1	0
NA Foster (ENG)	7	7	70	1	313	9	3/47	34.77	4.47	46.6	0	0
CL Hooper (WI)	6	5	41	0	181	7	3/42	25.85	4.41	35.1	0	0
W Watson (NZ)	6	6	53	3	270	7	2/36	38.57	5.09	45.4	0	0
RJ Shastri (INDIA)	7	7	68.2	1	274	7	2/45	39.14	4	58.5	0	0
Wasim Akram (PAK)	7	7	63.2	1	295	7	3/45	42.14	4.65	54.2	0	0
AR Border (AUS)	8	5	32	0	166	6	2/27	27.66	5.18	32	0	0
C Sharma (INDIA)	4	4	36.1	2	170	6	3/51	28.33	4.7	36.1	0	0
AJ Traicos (ZIM)	6	6	58	2	218	6	2/27	36.33	3.75	58	0	0
JE Emburey (ENG)	8	8	79	4	295	6	2/26	49.16	3.73	79	0	0
BA Reid (AUS)	8	8	68	7	303	6	2/38	50.5	4.45	68	0	0
GC Small (ENG)	8	8	68	2	331	6	2/47	55.16	4.86	68	0	0
M Azharuddin (INDIA)	7	7	23.5	0	109	5	3/19	21.8	4.57	28.6	0	0
AH Omarshah (ZIM)	6	5	40	0	179	5	2/34	35.8	4.47	48	0	0

BEST BOWLING

Player	Overs	Mdns	Runs	Wkts	Econ	Team	Opposition	Ground
CJ McDermott	10	0	44	5	4.4	Australia	v Pakistan	Lahore
M Prabhakar	8	1	19	4	2.37	India	v Zimbabwe	Mumbai
Abdul Qadir	10	0	31	4	3.1	Pakistan	v England	Rawalpindi
Imran Khan	8.3	2	37	4	4.35	Pakistan	v West Indies	Lahore
Imran Khan	9	0	37	4	4.11	Pakistan	v England	Karachi
SP O'Donnell	9.4	1	39	4	4.03	Australia	v Zimbabwe	Chennai
CA Walsh	10	1	40	4	4	West Indies	v Pakistan	Lahore
EE Hemmings	9.3	1	52	4	5.47	England	v India	Mumbai
CJ McDermott	10	0	56	4	5.6	Australia	v India	Chennai
M Azharuddin	3.5	0	19	3	4.95	India	v Australia	Delhi

1992

BIGGER, BOLDER, BETTER

BY PHIL WALKER

This one looked, felt and sounded different. The fifth World Cup tumbled forth in a riot of coloured clothing, white balls and post-watershed dramas. It had pinch hitters, spinners opening the bowling, and fielding from another planet. It had leg-spinners altering the course of big matches, and reverse-swing clinching them. It had two white balls, one at each end, for fast bowlers to wreak havoc with. It had South Africa's readmission after 22 years in the sporting wilderness, expanding the show to incorporate a ninth team. And it would all end in Melbourne: in a night-time coalescence between two simmering superpowers, beamed around the world for the very first time.

There wasn't much this one didn't have going for it. Twenty-nine of the 39 matches would be staged in Australia, the spiritual soul of modern ODI cricket since Kerry Packer's late-Seventies revolution, with the rest in New Zealand. After three Lord's finals and a solitary scrap on the subcontinent, cricket was opening itself up. Only the last dying wheeze of a tobacco company sponsoring a world sporting event felt anachronistic. In just about every other conceivable way, this was a portal into cricket's expansionist future.

From the start: a distinct impression of eras shifting, of batons passed. Most glaringly, for the first time in a World Cup, no Vivian Richards; in his stead, a boy named Lara. At least India's colourless campaign, shorn as it was of Gavaskar and Vengsarkar, was somewhat brightened by their own World Cup debutant, Sachin Tendulkar. At certain moments, Zimbabwe and Sri Lanka showed glimpses of what was to come; while the delicate manoeuvres required to pull back the curtain on South Africa would reveal in the form of Jonty Rhodes a new paradigm of fielder, and in Allan Donald the quickest white bowler in the world.

As for the hosts, it was hard to shake the sense that some kind of cricketing teleportation hadn't occurred across the Tasman. For New Zealand's rapt public, cleaving to the story of how Martin Crowe's tactical genius and celestial batting was going to flip the old world order, the show played out like a month-long dream. Contrast that with the living nightmare endured by the reigning champions and pre-tournament favourites, as a dominant build-up fell to nothing on opening night and only got worse from there.

In the case of Pakistan, meanwhile, their treacherous trek along the back-roads to a final reckoning would unmask yet more precocity. Nothing unusual there for those champions of youth, although in the case of those icons-to-be, Mushtaq Ahmed and Inzamam-ul-Haq, it was the stately Imran – for it was *always* Imran – who guided them through.

Last and on this occasion not least, there was England, and its moustachioed company of Gooch, Botham and Lamb marching an otherwise youthful team to the edge of glory. Botham has always asserted that this England team was the best in the tournament. Gooch too. "Oh yeah, we had some top players," he recalls. "I thought we were the best side. Our issue was we peaked too soon, and when it got down to the wire we couldn't produce what we needed to."

And there is much truth in those words. Except that England's final failure is only one version of it. For there was something else going on that night in Melbourne, taking place beyond those mortal scraps between bat and ball. If ever a world tournament, with its galaxies of stars, vaulting ambitions and myriad side-plots, could yield to the dominion of a single individual, then that tournament was this, and that man was Imran Khan.

***

From the outset, a strong political current ran through the tournament. After all, South Africa's cricket team was back.

It all happened with un-cricket-like haste. South Africa had only been readmitted into the cricketing fold in July 1991, following the fall of apartheid and Nelson Mandela's release from incarceration. And for all that a hastily-arranged three-match ODI series against India had been scheduled for November, with those games intended as positive signposts for their sporting future, there was no realistic expectation that the team would feature in the upcoming World Cup – it was all too soon, and politically sensitive; a consensus on the fundamental issue of South Africa's right to be restored to international cricket had not come easily.

And yet there was a core of belief to move nonetheless. What the bid really needed was an unimpeachable voice to carry above people's concerns. It came just a month after South Africa's official readmission, from the purest possible source.

It just so happened that in August of that year, Clive Lloyd, the first World Cup-winning captain, was in Cape Town at the invitation of Dr Ali Bacher, South Africa's cricket supremo. Bacher had hoped that Lloyd's story would inspire young black cricketers in the country. Lloyd was only too happy to make the trip. While he was there, he said to Bacher how he would like to perhaps meet Mandela. Calls were made, and they were granted an audience the next day. A few journalists were there too, and when one of them asked Mandela if he thought South Africa should play in the World Cup, his response was emphatic. "Of course, we *must* play."

Bacher later recalled the seismic effect of those five words. "The message went around the world of cricket and we went to Australia. Till then there was no thought within South African cricket as well as at the ICC about South Africa playing in the World Cup, but Mandela's words changed that immediately. Such was the power of Mandela."

There were, moreover, sound realpolitik reasons for including a ninth team for the first time. The marketing potential around such a huge news story was sufficiently vast to justify the A$600k cost of including an extra team, resulting in eight further fixtures, at a relatively late stage. The simplicity of the format liberated the organisers. With everyone playing each other once, and the top four progressing to the semi-finals, there was no great upheaval involved in bringing another team into it. It was deemed to be a move worth making, with near unanimous backing for South Africa's inclusion, and only the West Indies board arguing against.

***

And so, on the afternoon of 22 February 1992, at an overcast Eden Park with a stiff Auckland wind blowing across the arena, the fifth ICC Cricket World Cup officially began. New Zealand versus Australia. Underdogs versus holders. The match would set the tone for their divergent campaigns.

New Zealand's squad was not heaving with talent. They claimed in wicket-keeper Ian Smith and opener John Wright a pair of skilled streetfighters with bags of experience, and in Chris Cairns and Danny Morrison, a couple of dangerous quicks. But elsewhere, the squad was comprised of mainly workaday cricketers, nagging medium-pacers and middle-order grafters, while the Kenya-born Dipak Patel, a journeyman off-spinner and useful bat who had emigrated to New Zealand from England in the mid-Eighties in search of higher honours, was the only conventional spin option. But they had something else.

Martin Crowe was a free-thinking theorist and a player touched by genius. His former captain Jeremy Coney recalled a strokemaker made of "part dancer, part fencer, part keen-eyed executioner". If New Zealand's limitations were not to be exposed in this tournament, Crowe knew he would need to get funky with his tactics. Somehow he would need to level the field. And bat out of his boots.

The second part of that equation was rarely beyond him. After Crowe had opted to bat first against Australia, he strode out at 13 for 2, the strands of his white bandana dangling from beneath his light-grey helmet. He was soon into his work with a brace of slow-motion off-drives and then the pull shot, executed from an upright stance, the heels closely aligned, hips rotating like an ice skater's revolutions.

He eased to three figures, brought up in the final over and New Zealand had set Australia 249 to win from 50 overs.

Australia's openers David Boon and Geoff Marsh had few concerns against the waspish seam of Chris Cairns, but at the other end, Australia's openers appeared flummoxed by a theory cooked up by Crowe to use the off-spin of Dipak Patel in the early Powerplay overs. Bowling from the end which made it hard for right-handers to hit against the wind into the leg-side, Patel conceded just 19 from seven overs with the new ball, and New Zealand had their first leveller.

It set Australia back. Marsh went for a strained 56-ball 19, precipitating a brief flurry from Dean Jones, then considered the most complete one-day batsman in the game. Jones took on Cairns at deep mid-wicket, whose bullet throw was fired into Smith's gloves hovering by the bails. It was marginal. International cricket may have embraced jazzy kits and white balls, but TV reviews for run-outs and stumpings were still a few months from gestation. Just too late for Dean Jones. His dismissal brought in the captain, Allan Border. Crowe recalled Patel immediately, Border swept and Cairns took an excellent tumbling catch.

Next came the strangle. Australia's powerful middle-order of the Waugh twins and Tom Moody were each extracted by New Zealand's troupe of trundlers, as first Gavin Larsen, then Willie Watson, and finally the portly batsman-cum-golden-arm Rod Latham, suffocated Australia. When Boon went for the second even hundred of the match, Australia were seven down, devoid of batsmen, and sunk.

***

On a blistering opening day, England took on India at Perth. India came into the tournament in miserable form, having lost their last warm-up game to Victoria (for whom Shane Warne, new to Test cricket but not yet considered a one-day option, took 2 for 37), and their luck barely improved as the competition wore on. They had their chances against England. But this tournament was to be Ian Botham's swansong, and while the fitness and agility had begun to wane, the self-belief remained undimmed.

As indeed did his powers of influence. Derek Pringle, who opened the bowling for England in the tournament, wryly recalls the Botham effect in his memoir *Pushing the Boundaries*. Botham had only joined up with the squad in New Zealand – where preparations had been taking place with a string of ODIs against the hosts – after a stint in panto in Bournemouth. "Our one-day plans only really coalesced once Beefy arrived bearing gifts in the shape of a carton of sunglasses from his sponsors, and a Yuletide paunch. Although he huffed and puffed his way through training and the last two one-dayers [against New Zealand], something curious happened between those matches. From batting at five in the first one, a position that saw him make 28 off 43 balls, he somehow persuaded Goochie to let him open the innings in the final one, a role he had not performed in five years." Botham being Botham, he then proceeded to clump a quick 79 to ensure that come the tournament proper, he would be the man to face the new ball with Gooch.

England batted first. Botham laboured to 9 from 21 balls with just the one boundary – albeit a lofted off-drive – before nicking behind to give his great adversary, Kapil Dev, his first wicket. It brought in the back-foot-dominant Robin Smith, who immediately got to work on the WACA's hard, bouncy deck. One pulled six off Subroto Banerjee carried the best part of 100 metres. Smith careered to a 108-ball 91. It would be England's highest individual score of the tournament.

For a time England's 236 didn't seem enough. India started boisterously, with Kris Srikkanth, one of the many helmetless warriors in this World Cup, going up and over the infield. They looked to be favourites at 63 for 0, but their progress was checked when Srikkanth skied an attempted drive, Botham ambling in from extra cover to claim the catch, and when Mohammad Azharuddin edged his first ball from Dermot Reeve to the keeper, it brought in Tendulkar.

A year before, the teenager had constructed a Test innings at Perth against Australia's quicks so pure that Richie Benaud was moved to call it one of the best he'd ever seen. Against England he started in similar vein, cutting the spinners and pulling Phillip DeFreitas hard in front of square. With the game on a knife-edge and Tendulkar on 35, Gooch beckoned Botham into the attack. A little extra effort, a leg-cutter that gripped and held its line, nipping off the pitch to take the edge, and the kid-genius was gone. If the hip-wiggling jig that followed the wicket rather belied the beauty of the delivery itself, it mattered not to Botham. The old stager was into the tournament, and England, with its plethora of seam-bowling all-rounders, had alighted upon a very useful formula. After Sachin, India just fell away. Botham nabbed another, executed a run out to seal it, and moseyed off with the man of the match award.

The other stand-out fixture from the opening round of matches took place at the MCG between the twice-winners West Indies and an injury-hit Pakistan side, shorn of Imran himself, nursing a bad shoulder, and with their main strike bowler Waqar Younis forced to miss the event.

It was a curious game. Pakistan laboured to 220 for 2 from their 50 overs. Notwithstanding the vastness of the playing arena, a final tally of 12 boundaries struck throughout their innings – with the opener Rameez Raja batting through for 102* with just four boundaries – spoke of a lack of thrust and aggression. This was one-day batting from a previous era, shackled to a fading philosophy. Only Javed Miandad showed much imagination, his half-century coming in 56 balls. And here there was added motivation. Miandad, who strained his back in an early practice match, had not been named in Pakistan's original squad; only when their pre-tournament preparations sank from bad to abysmal had he been recalled. Given Miandad's belief that Imran, his old adversary, may have been behind his initial side-lining, those runs at the MCG carried extra resonance.

Still, it was nowhere near enough. Brian Lara and Desmond Haynes withstood the initial barrage, settled in, and constructed an opening partnership that was only ended on 175, seven runs shy of the then-highest opening stand in World Cups, when a Wasim Akram toe-crusher sent Lara hobbling to A&E.

The good folk of New Zealand were enjoying their World Cup. The first weekend of games concluded with a humdinger at the postage-stamp venue of Pukekura Park in New Plymouth. A masterfully judged run-chase by Arjuna Ranatunga ensured that Sri Lanka chased down 312 with four deliveries remaining, but it was a young Zimbabwean keeper-batsman on debut who would claim the man of the match award. Andy Flower's unbeaten 112 would be the first of 16 international centuries.

The tournament was two days old. Eight of the nine teams had played.

***

Like many young South Africans forced by fate to escape their homeland, Kepler Wessels first turned up in Australia in the late Seventies. He was then barely out of his teens, a quiet, intense Afrikaner itinerant whose desire to play cricket had taken him first to England and then, via Sydney club cricket, where he was sledged mercilessly, to Queensland and the personal fiefdom of Allan Border. A kinship ensued. Border's only concern was runs, and Wessels, like Border a left-hander from the getting-it-done school, had the gumption to deliver them by the boatload. It was only a matter of time before Wessels graduated from Queensland's top-order to Australia's, and only a matter of five sessions of cricket before he had an Ashes hundred.

When Mandela walked free and a new nation emerged, the craggy street-scrapper was back in South Africa, ready to take up the fight one more time. He was 34, leading South Africa into its first-ever World Cup. And their first opponents? It had to be Border's Australians.

Wessels was nervous. As much for how his team would be received as for the cricket they hoped to play. Nerves were everywhere. Allan Donald remembers feeling "bloody nervous" before the announcement of the squad itself, and the nervousness barely dissipating until the first ball was bowled in anger. "We were a mature outfit with a lot of experience at domestic level but none in the pressure cauldron of the international arena," Wessels recalls in *Ruling the World*, Jonathan Northall's account of the tournament. "The bus trip was the quietest one I've ever been on. I just looked around, and I saw how everybody was pale and stressed, and I thought, 'Oh, how is this going to work out?'"

In the event, just like this: South Africa would bowl first, Donald would take the new ball, his first delivery would be a pitiless bomb that would take Geoff Marsh's edge, only for the umpire to turn down the appeal, the Sydney Cricket Ground would unite in a chorus of boos, Australia's openers would be pegged back and their middle-order even more so, Border would bag a first-baller, and with the tail exposed Donald would return to crush Tom Moody's front pad and blow away a couple more. Australia would limp to 170-9, and Wessels would knock them off.

For Wessels, South Africa's nine-wicket win was "a golden moment" in his country's cricketing story. For Australia, it was two defeats from two.

***

The tournament was already rousingly unpredictable. Everyone seemed capable of losing to everyone else. Although patterns were hard to detect, the early exchanges threw up two isolated cases of consistency: the potency of England's seam attack, and New Zealand's happy-go-lucky winning streak.

For England, the emergence of the Guyana-born Chris Lewis as a lissom new-ball complement to the old-world skills of Derek Pringle, allied with Phillip DeFreitas' jaffa-potential and backed up by the hirsute schemers Botham and Reeve, provided a sound platform from which to work. Against West Indies at Melbourne in their second match, Lewis tore in against Lara, striking the left-hander in the region around the midriff where many have fallen before. Taking a few minutes to recompose himself, Lara settled in again, the pain still etched into his face, when he sought an ambitious cover drive to an away-swinger that caught the edge. A bruising second-ball duck to go with his retired-hurt 88 against Pakistan. Not long after, Richie Richardson edged Lewis to Botham at slip, followed by an ill-judged pull from the gifted Carl Hooper. When Haynes went to DeFreitas for 38, the Windies were 55 for 4 and in an inextricable mess. Lewis and DeFreitas each finished with three wickets, while the support seamers of Pringle, Reeve and Botham had economy rates of three or under. Fifties for Gooch and Graeme Hick eased England to a second win in a row. Suddenly they were on a roll.

Three days later came a match at Adelaide that would have a profound bearing on the tournament. There was rain around in Australia's driest state capital. The pitch had been covered for 40 hours. The atmosphere was muggy between England and Pakistan.

Their moods coming into the game were contrasting. England were buoyant, having arrived at a formula that was working, whereas Pakistan, having sought to prepare meticulously by arriving three weeks earlier to acclimatise, were finding their best-laid plans unravelling by the day. This was England versus Pakistan (part I). Something had to give. It always did.

The cataclysm would come from above. England were irresistible with the ball while Pakistan edged everything. Rameez Raja was the first to go, picking out the cover fieldsman. Then Inzamam pushed tentatively at DeFreitas, the ball rebounding off Botham's hands at slip into those of Alec Stewart, the scrambling keeper. 5 for 2 soon became 20 for 4, became 35 for 6. When the seventh fell at 42, the books confirmed that Canada's 45 all out in 1979 was under threat, though in the event a few nicks and blows from the tail saw Pakistan clamber up to 74. As it turned out, that scramble proved very valuable indeed.

What happened next brought into sharp relief the inconsistencies of the tournament rain rule. After downpours truncated England's reply at 24 for 1 from eight overs, controversy unfolded when the Most Productive Overs (MPO) method calculated England's revised target as 40 runs from eight more overs. Eventually, with no chance of a resumption, the teams shook hands, and the English shook their heads. A point apiece, then; and how crucial that stolen digit would be for Pakistan come the business end of the tournament.

Over the pond, meanwhile, it was all sunshine and joy for Crowe's Kiwis. Victory over Sri Lanka had been followed with a dominant seven-wicket victory over South Africa to make it three from three. Their win over the Proteas was marked by another of Crowe's tactical masterstrokes, and one that would have far-reaching consequences on ODI batting itself. With the spinner Dipak Patel draining the life from the first 15 overs with the ball, Crowe turned his focus to the batting equation.

Mark Greatbatch was a burly, affable left-hander and an old schoolfriend of Crowe's. They knew each other's games inside out. Crowe knew that Greatbatch was a solid Test match accumulator who stood up to the quicks. He also knew that he would not be overawed by playing a world tournament on home soil. He knew that he packed a punch, and that given the freedom to play his shots, he could make good use of those early fielding restrictions. Crowe also knew that his mate's form coming into the tournament had been borderline abysmal.

Crowe gave him his head. Greatbatch would open with Rod Latham. It was the first time he'd faced the new ball in international cricket, and this particular new ball was in the possession of Allan Donald. No matter. Greatbatch had been instructed to enjoy himself. In Donald's second over he clubbed him through mid-wicket. Three overs later he pumped Brian McMillan over the Eden Park sightscreen. Soon after, Richard Snell was introduced. He was hit for 10 from two balls, with one six going over third man, 180-degrees from where Greatbatch had intended it. Chasing 195 to win, New Zealand were 90-0 after 15 overs, and the southpaw had haymakered a run-a-ball 50. Off the leash, Greatbatch would finish the tournament with 313 runs and a strike rate of 87.92

Cricket wasn't unacquainted with attacking openers. There was Roy Fredericks for the West Indies, with Gordon Greenidge in his slipstream; and in this World Cup, India's Kris Srikkanth had been selected to get on with it, with Botham offering a version himself. But never before, at least in a World Cup, had a player been selected in such defiance of the role's traditional conventions. Crowe had just hatched a plan that would change the face of limited-overs batting. More pressingly, New Zealand had the look of a team that could go all the way.

With their fifth straight win coming up against the Windies at Eden Park – a stroll in the sunshine, with Crowe seeing out the run-chase with an unbeaten 81 and Greatbatch making a punchy 63 – New Zealand became the first team to qualify for the semi-finals.

Less than 24 hours later, England virtually assured their own passage. Their victory against Sri Lanka was a relatively straightforward affair, with runs for Neil Fairbrother, Botham and Hick and a brilliant 36-ball 59 from Stewart setting up a four-wicket blast from Lewis. But a hamstring tweak to Gooch was another injury concern, and with Allan Lamb also sidelined, the latter stages would test their resolve.

***

The tournament's format was proving a huge success. There were no gimmes. Tight games followed surprising upsets. Even though Sri Lanka and Zimbabwe were not yet strong enough to definitively influence proceedings, they still partook in many close games. Every match mattered.

Australia, however, had continued to drift, losing in humiliating fashion to England at Sydney with the best part of 10 overs to spare. This was the last time they would have to deal with Botham, and he honoured it with a rambunctious show, taking four wickets and smashing a quick 50. It was Australia's third defeat in four, with just a one-run squeeze against India to show for their efforts. India themselves were stumbling along, only rousing themselves for the big one against Pakistan. Their 43-run victory at Sydney could have been the catalyst for a charge by Azharuddin's men; instead, in this topsy-turvy tournament, it galvanised their foes.

The WACA in Perth staged Australia v Pakistan, the seventh-placed team playing the eighth. It was already make-or-break.

Until this point, Pakistan had endured a campaign characterised by Osman Samiuddin in his history of Pakistan cricket, *The Unquiet Ones*, as a "great impending disaster, a series of small screw-ups all snowballing into one massive one". Ahead of the showdown, Imran Khan strode into Pakistan's dressing room sporting a tight white T-shirt with an image of a tiger about to pounce. He had been injured and preoccupied with other projects during much of the build-up and the tournament's early stages, and in his absence Pakistan had managed just one win from five games, against Zimbabwe. Now he was back, he had something to say. He told his team to forget everything and play like cornered tigers. Play like this, he said, pointing to his T-shirt, and Pakistan would win the tournament. No ifs, no buts.

Imran kept the T-shirt on for the toss, casually relaying to Border what he'd just told his team. There was no love lost between the sides. Javed Miandad, who was known to Australian fans as the man who raised his bat to a fists-flailing Dennis Lillee, later described it as a "brawl of a match".

It didn't seem much when Pakistan scraped up to 220 for 9, Aamer Sohail hitting 76 and Miandad 46. It was with the ball that their tournament caught fire.

Up until then, Wasim Akram had been searching for control – of the white ball, his front foot stride, his emotions. His new ball partner Aaqib Javed was young, bolshy and quick. They were both, in their own ways, perfect Imran protégés. The captain gave each of them a Test-match field and told them to bowl as fast as they could.

The early stages were electrifying. Aaqib was possessed, Wasim rebooted. Tom Moody nicked off. David Boon was caught at third slip. *Third* slip. Geoff Marsh was shell-shocked into shotlessness. Only Dean Jones offered any kind of riposte and as Marsh ducked and weaved and Jones played expansively off his pads, Australia dragged themselves back into the game. It was tetchy and tense. When the hundred was posted in the 29th over, prompting from Marsh an ugly hoick for four off the inside edge, Jones ostentatiously punched the air as the ball ran away.

The game was never far from boiling point, and when Imran threw the ball to Mushtaq Ahmed, his 22-year-old leg-spinner, Jones sensed blood and charged out of his crease. He got to the pitch but Mushtaq had found some purchase, and a touch of turn took the outer half of Jones' whirring blade. With Imran's words still clattering around in his head ("I could feel that nobody could face me or stop me"), Aaqib Javed positioned himself under the high ball at long off. There was never any doubt. With Jones gone, Australia collapsed, losing their last eight wickets for 53 to leave themselves on the brink of elimination.

***

The biggest story of the group stages, however, was South Africa. What had once seemed impossible, then implausible, had begun to resemble a very real and genuine tilt at the trophy. They had experience and pedigree in Wessels and the well-travelled No.3, Peter Kirsten; they had pace and fire in Donald and McMillan, class in Hansie Cronje, a top-class keeper in Dave Richardson and in Jonty Rhodes, a fielder rewriting the rules. It was estimated that Rhodes was saving between 25-30 runs every innings with his work at backward point, while his run out of Inzamam, diving full length to splatter the stumps ("The fastest way I could cover the last metre and a half was head-first"), would be talked about for years to come. Rarely had fielding seemed so central to a team's identity.

They confronted India at Adelaide knowing that victory would seal a last-four spot. Rain reduced the game to a 30-over thrash, and Donald was pumped, thudding his second delivery into the splice of Srikkanth's bat, the ball looping to Kirsten who clutched it in his fingertips. India regrouped through Azharuddin and Sanjay Manjrekar, but the latter went 53 balls without a boundary before losing his off-stump. Kapil Dev had some fun in the later overs to haul India up to 180 for 6, leaving South Africa with a run-a-ball target.

Kirsten was one of a cohort of brilliant South African cricketers who was reconciled to never playing international cricket. He was 37 when he made his ODI debut in the India series in late 1991. But the years of domestic cricket in South Africa and England had not dulled his eye; at the 1992 World Cup, he was one of the stand-out batsmen. Under the lights at Adelaide, he was inspired, punching a superb 84 from 86 balls, but with the end in sight, he played around a full ball from Kapil, leaving Wessels himself, who had demoted himself for just this scenario, to steer the run-chase and steady the nerves. With four needed off the final over, Cronje bunted the first delivery through mid-wicket.

***

And so to the final round of games. The permutations ran thus: Pakistan were facing an unbeaten New Zealand side knowing they simply had to win. A little later on the same day, the misfiring powerhouses of Windies and Australia would discover what scraps, if any, would be left to fight over. If Pakistan lost, it would be a straight shoot-out. But even though a Pakistan win would knock Australia out, Pakistan would still need West Indies to lose heavily.

But it was starting to happen for Pakistan. Wasim was back on song. Mushtaq was growing into his work. Rameez Raja was in the runs, and Miandad now ensconced in his favoured slot at No.4. With Imran controlling the fates at mid-off, Pakistan dismantled the Kiwi line-up, all out for 166. Despite the loss of Aamer Sohail first ball, Rameez flicked and cuffed his way to an elegant century, his unbeaten 119 the highest score of the tournament (the lowest high of any World Cup) – and after all the discombobulating chaos of previous weeks, this was a breezy stroll to victory. While Crowe's New Zealand were not too downcast – defeat would at least ensure a home semi-final – Pakistan's cricketers scurried back to their hotel to watch the drama unfold elsewhere.

As news filtered across the water to Melbourne, the life drained out of the expectant home crowd. Australia's dominance of the West Indies would count for nothing. David Boon made another even hundred, bookending the tournament with bittersweet centuries, before Lara was run out for 70, removing the last obstacle to Pakistan's implausible progression. That night, as Wasim Akram headed into Auckland to celebrate, he asked his taxi driver for a pen and a scrap of paper. On it, he wrote: "March 19, 1992. Pakistan WILL win the World Cup. Wasim Akram." Then, handing the note to the driver, he disappeared into the night.

It was fitting for a tournament characterised by its rejection of the formbook that there should be one last shock. Zimbabwe had battled hard and well all tournament, but remained winless. England were already through, but creaking a little. This one would forever be known as "Eddo's match". A barrel-chested chicken farmer by trade, Eddo Brandes moonlighted as a decidedly sharp fast bowler, and it was his ferocious opening spell that ensured Zimbabwe claimed another giant upset to go with their stuffing of Australia nine years earlier. Defending just 134, Brandes trapped Gooch first ball and then returned to pluck out their middle order, finishing with four cheap wickets as Zimbabwe stole a famous victory by nine runs.

We had reached the business end of the tournament. The first semi-final would take place at Eden Park between New Zealand and Pakistan. The second would pit England against South Africa under the lights at the SCG.

***

Inzamam-ul-Haq had thus far been an enigmatic presence at the 1992 World Cup. Just 22 yet with the bearing of someone much older, he had hitherto offered little with the bat. If anything, the Jonty Rhodes run out had been his most notable moment so far. Yet stories continued to circle around him. How Imran had seen him bat in the nets and after a few minutes demanded that he be in his squad. How his selection had prompted a Pakistani selector to resign. How he had magic in his hands. How Imran kept saying, meeting after meeting, that the day Inzi performs, he will win the world for Pakistan.

Before the New Zealand match, Inzi would later recall, he was vomiting. "I told Mushtaq Ahmed, as he was senior to me and I felt awkward saying it myself, to tell Imran *bhai* that I was unwell and wouldn't be able to play. So when Mushtaq told me, he laughed and said, 'No matter what, Inzamam, you will play'. While the rest of the team was warming up, I was getting treatment. He still had the confidence that I could perform. Allah made me do something memorable."

Pre-toss, at a windswept Auckland in front of a partisan crowd, Crowe was handed a piece of paper from a local official which read: "Weather forecast 21 March. Heavy thunderstorms by 2.30 pm. Rain all afternoon, worsening". Knowing how the MPO method tended to disadvantage the chasing team, Crowe chose to bat first. It was sound thinking, and with Greatbatch whacking a couple of sixes and the captain holding the middle together, things were going to plan. With a few overs remaining and wickets in hand, Crowe was gearing up for the final assault when he turned for a second run and felt his hamstring tighten. He resolved to carry on, but with his movements restricted, he was duly run out by his designated runner (in a cruel irony, Greatbatch himself) for a supreme 83-ball 91. It meant that New Zealand's final 262 for 7, though hefty, was not insurmountable.

New Zealand's biggest concern – aside from the absence of the predicted rain – was the loss of Crowe, the tournament's top run-scorer, side-lined in the dressing room. It meant that his astonishingly detailed tactical plans – preconceiving 17 bowling changes at specifically designated times – would have to be parked. Not that it seemed to matter as Pakistan spluttered through the first half of their innings.

Inzamam joined the fray at 140 for 4, still 123 shy and the overs ticking by. At least Miandad was still there, lurking. Helmetless yet inscrutable, Inzamam was soon into his stride, square-driving and flicking the seamers to all corners of Eden Park's odd-shaped arena. But it was his extraordinary lofted drive into the wind, dropping almost vertically onto the stone steps beyond the fence, that signalled his intent. With Miandad biding his time at one end, Inzi raced to 60 from just 37 balls, before yet another run out halted the charge. His brilliance – one of the great World Cup cameos – had opened up the match and the tournament. Moin Khan joined Miandad to steer a delirious Pakistan into the final with an over to spare.

***

Without a mid-evening Sydney downpour and the infamous calculations which followed, the semi-final between South Africa and England would have gone very deep indeed. The forgotten stories of the match were many: Donald's ferocity, nicking off Gooch in the early stages; Hick's brilliant 83 with the bat, and Dermot Reeve's unlikely 14-ball 25* at the death; and in South Africa's innings, DeFreitas bowling Kirsten with a jaffa for the ages, and Rhodes scampering a 38-ball 43 as the tension ramped up some more… But sometimes in cricket the sheer drama of a single moment eclipses all which has passed before it; subsuming all the sweat and tears and subplots from a full-blooded game of cricket into one heart-stopping thud.

It came not from events on the pitch, but from numbers on a scoreboard. Numbers which have entered into cricket folklore. It was 9:52pm and South Africa needed 22 from 13 balls when the players scampered off to dodge a passing shower. Eleven minutes later, the players were filing back out again when the scoreboard announced that South Africa had lost one over, and their revised target would now be 22 runs from seven balls. The crowd's disapproval turned to howls when, five minutes later, with McMillan and Richardson out in the middle, the final calculation was beamed onto the board: South Africa had not lost one but *two* overs, and would now, according to the scoreboard, need 22 from just one delivery (later corrected to 21 needed). The fans had been robbed of a grandstand finish, and South Africa of a tilt at greatness. McMillan's disconsolate prod to the last ball offered the perfect, bathetic stop.

Looking back now, Donald is sanguine about how the match ended. "In a way, and I know this sounds crazy, but I think we robbed ourselves. We walked away from that World Cup with the most no balls and wides, probably still, in the history of World Cups. We took a lot of time out of that game with all of our wides and no balls. We were on the brink of doing something amazing and it was a tough pill to swallow. But we knew then, and Kepler said this to us after that game, that we could go toe-to-toe with any team in the world. I think the rest of the world saw us as heroes and we were welcomed back as heroes in South Africa."

***

On 25 March 25 1992, England met Pakistan in a World Cup final for the first time. England had the record; Pakistan the momentum. With a slight chance of rain, Imran won the toss and elected to bat.

Derek Pringle had swung the ball all tournament, but never more than in his opening spell at Melbourne. Hooping the new ball prodigiously, he casually disposed of both openers to set Pakistan back at 24 for 2. The wickets brought Miandad to the crease to join Imran, batting at No.3, and they carefully began a salvage operation. It was painstaking cricket, and at the halfway stage Pakistan had limped to 70 for 2. But a platform had been laid from which the tigers could pounce.

First it was Imran, opening his shoulders to hit a huge six down the ground, signalling to Miandad to keep up. The pair took Pakistan up towards 200, laying the groundwork for Wasim and Inzamam to marmalise England's tiring seamers in a madcap final 10 overs. Inzamam followed his semi-final intervention with a delicate 35-ball 42, while Wasim hit long and merrily, clubbing a crucial 33 from 18 as Pakistan got up to 249 for 6.

As the lights took effect, England's innings got off to the worst possible start when Botham was caught behind off the bowling of Aaqib Javed.

At 59 for 2 Hick and Gooch were building steadily when Mushtaq Ahmed came on for his first bowl. The googly was perfectly pitched, flicking Hick's back pad in front of all three. When Gooch followed, England needed a rebuilding job of their own, and it would come via Fairbrother and Lamb. England were 141 for 4 when Imran beckoned Wasim Akram back into the attack. In two balls, he would change the course of history.

"Those two deliveries were totally planned," Wasim later recalled. "It was always the plan to come round the wicket to Lamb and bowl outswing. He must have thought, 'Left-arm, round the wicket, going away? I don't think so…' It started on middle stump and went away from him against the angle. That ball was absolutely one of the top five balls I ever bowled. Then when Chris Lewis came out to bat, I was about to bowl a yorker. But Imran said he will be expecting a yorker, so just bowl an inswing length ball, and that's exactly what I did. The right pace, the right swing, a little bit of inside edge onto his stumps."

The match and the tournament had bent to Pakistan, and to one man in particular. In the final over, with England nine down and still 22 runs shy, the captain took the ball himself. Two balls in, Richard Illingworth advanced down the pitch and toe-ended a simple catch to Rameez Raja at mid-on.

Imran stood mid-pitch, arms aloft, smiling almost bashfully. The final wicket, the crowning moment, was his.

***

Pakistan's triumph in 1992 was intrinsically, ineluctably Imran's. He was old by cricketing standards, pushing 40, a past master at blunting the slings and arrows of Pakistani cricketing life. He had run the show with as near as anyone got to complete autonomy in Pakistan cricket, and achieved, in the words of his biographer Christopher Sandford, something akin to a sporting miracle, "transforming the perennial cabaret turn of the international circuit into the hyper-aggressive fighting unit that would lift the World Cup".

In the immediate maelstrom which followed, Wasim was named man of the match for his late-innings flourish and his old-ball genius. The magnitude of Pakistan's achievement would take time to fully absorb. "At that moment I didn't realise what we'd done," he would later recall. "It was only after about a week of being back in Pakistan, that we realised we had *really* done something."

1992

RESULTS AND STATISTICS

TABLE

		P	W	L	NR	Pts	Net RR
1	New Zealand	8	7	1	0	14	0.579
2	England	8	5	2	1	11	0.54
3	South Africa	8	5	3	0	10	-0.054
4	Pakistan	8	4	3	1	9	0.282
5	Australia	8	4	4	0	8	0.173
6	West Indies	8	4	4	0	8	0.068
7	India	8	2	5	1	5	0.127
8	Sri Lanka	8	2	5	1	5	-0.686
9	Zimbabwe	8	1	7	0	2	-1.06

NEW ZEALAND V PAKISTAN

BENSON AND HEDGES WORLD CUP 1991/92 (SEMI-FINAL)

Venue: Eden Park, Auckland
Date: 21st March 1992
Toss: New Zealand
Result: Pakistan won by 4 wickets
Umpires: SA Bucknor, DR Shepherd
Referee: PJP Burge
Man of the Match: Inzamam-ul-Haq

NEW ZEALAND		R	b	PAKISTAN		R	b
MJ Greatbatch	b Aaqib Javed	17	22	Aamer Sohail	c Jones b Patel	14	20
JG Wright	c Rameez b Mushtaq Ahmed	13	44	Rameez Raja	c Morrison b Watson	44	55
AH Jones	lbw b Mushtaq Ahmed	21	53	*Imran Khan	c Larsen b Harris	44	93
*MD Crowe	run out	91	83	Javed Miandad	not out	57	69
KR Rutherford	c Moin Khan b Wasim Akram	50	68	Saleem Malik	c sub (RT Latham) b Larsen	1	2
CZ Harris	st Moin b Iqbal Sikander	13	12	Inzamam-ul-Haq	run out	60	37
+IDS Smith	not out	18	10	Wasim Akram	b Watson	9	8
DN Patel	lbw b Wasim Akram	8	6	+Moin Khan	not out	20	11
GR Larsen	not out	8	6	Mushtaq Ahmed	did not bat		
DK Morrison	did not bat			Iqbal Sikander	did not bat		
W Watson	did not bat			Aaqib Javed	did not bat		
Extras	(11 lb, 4 nb, 8 w)	23		Extras	(4 b, 10 lb, 1 w)	15	
Total	(7 wickets, 50 overs)	262		Total	(6 wickets, 49 overs)	264	

Fall of wickets: 1-35 (Greatbatch), 2-39 (Wright), 3-87 (Jones), 4-194 (Rutherford), 5-214 (Harris), 6-221 (Crowe), 7-244 (Patel)

Fall of wickets: 1-30 (Aamer Sohail), 2-84 (Rameez Raja), 3-134 (Imran Khan), 4-140 (Saleem Malik), 5-227 (Inzamam-ul-Haq), 6-238 (Wasim Akram)

PAKISTAN	O	M	R	W	Wd	Nb	NEW ZEALAND	O	M	R	W	Wd	Nb
Wasim Akram	10	1	40	2	2	4	Patel	10	1	50	1	-	-
Aaqib Javed	10	2	45	1	2	-	Morrison	9	0	55	0	1	-
Mushtaq Ahmed	10	0	40	2	-	-	Watson	10	2	39	2	-	1
Imran Khan	10	0	59	0	3	-	Larsen	10	1	34	1	-	-
Iqbal Sikander	9	0	56	1	1	-	Harris	10	0	72	1	-	-
Aamer Sohail	1	0	11	0	-	-							

ENGLAND V SOUTH AFRICA

BENSON AND HEDGES WORLD CUP 1991/92 (SEMI-FINAL)

Venue: Sydney Cricket Ground, Sydney
Date: 22nd March 1992
Toss: South Africa
Result: England won by 19 runs
Umpires: BL Aldridge, SG Randell
Referee: FJ Cameron
Man of the Match: GA Hick

ENGLAND		R	b	SOUTH AFRICA		R	b
*GA Gooch	c Richardson b Donald	2	9	*KC Wessels	c Lewis b Botham	17	21
IT Botham	b Pringle	21	23	AC Hudson	lbw b Illingworth	46	52
+AJ Stewart	c Richardson b McMillan	33	54	PN Kirsten	b DeFreitas	11	26
GA Hick	c Rhodes b Snell	83	90	AP Kuiper	b Illingworth	36	44
NH Fairbrother	b Pringle	28	50	WJ Cronje	c Hick b Small	24	45
AJ Lamb	c Richardson b Donald	19	22	JN Rhodes	c Lewis b Small	43	38
CC Lewis	not out	18	16	BM McMillan	not out	21	21
DA Reeve	not out	25	14	+DJ Richardson	not out	13	10
PAJ DeFreitas	did not bat			RP Snell	did not bat		
GC Small	did not bat			MW Pringle	did not bat		
RK Illingworth	did not bat			AA Donald	did not bat		
Extras	(1 b, 7 lb, 6 nb, 9 w)	23		Extras	(17 lb, 4 w)	21	
Total	(6 wickets, 45 overs)	252		Total	(6 wickets, 43 overs)	232	

Fall of wickets: 1-20 (Gooch), 2-39 (Botham), 3-110 (Stewart), 4-183 (Fairbrother), 5-187 (Hick), 6-221 (Lamb)

Fall of wickets: 1-26 (Wessels), 2-61 (Kirsten), 3-90 (Hudson), 4-131 (Kuiper), 5-176 (Cronje), 6-206 (Rhodes)

SOUTH AFRICA	O	M	R	W	Wd	Nb	ENGLAND	O	M	R	W	Wd	Nb
Donald	10	0	69	2	5	2	Botham	10	0	52	1	3	-
Pringle	9	2	36	2	1	4	Lewis	5	0	38	0	-	-
Snell	8	0	52	1	2	-	DeFreitas	8	1	28	1	1	-
McMillan	9	0	47	1	-	-	Illingworth	10	1	46	2	-	-
Kuiper	5	0	26	0	-	-	Small	10	1	51	2	-	-
Cronje	4	0	14	0	-	-							

ENGLAND V PAKISTAN

BENSON AND HEDGES WORLD CUP 1991/92 (FINAL)

Venue: Melbourne Cricket Ground, Melbourne
Date: 25th March 1992
Toss: Pakistan
Result: Pakistan won by 22 runs
Umpires: BL Aldridge, SA Bucknor
Referee: PJP Burge
Man of the Match: Wasim Akram

PAKISTAN		R	b	ENGLAND		R	b
Aamer Sohail	c Stewart b Pringle	4	19	*GA Gooch	c Aaqib Javed b Mushtaq Ahmed	29	66
Rameez Raja	lbw b Pringle	8	26	IT Botham	c Moin Khan b Wasim Akram	0	6
*Imran Khan	c Illingworth b Botham	72	110	+AJ Stewart	c Moin Khan b Aaqib Javed	7	16
Javed Miandad	c Botham b Illingworth	58	98	GA Hick	lbw b Mushtaq Ahmed	17	36
Inzamam-ul-Haq	b Pringle	42	35	NH Fairbrother	c Moin Khan b Aaqib Javed	62	70
Wasim Akram	run out	33	19	AJ Lamb	b Wasim Akram	31	41
Saleem Malik	not out	0	1	CC Lewis	b Wasim Akram	0	6
Ijaz Ahmed	did not bat			DA Reeve	c Rameez Raja b Mushtaq Ahmed	15	32
+Moin Khan	did not bat			DR Pringle	not out	18	16
Mushtaq Ahmed	did not bat			PAJ DeFreitas	run out	10	8
Aaqib Javed	did not bat			RK Illingworth	c Rameez Raja b Imran Khan	14	11
Extras	(19 lb, 7 nb, 6 w)	32		Extras	(5 lb, 6 nb, 13 w)	24	
Total	(6 wickets, 50 overs)	249		Total	(all out, 49.2 overs)	227	

Fall of wickets: 1-20 (Aamer Sohail), 2-24 (Rameez Raja), 3-163 (Javed Miandad), 4-197 (Imran Khan), 5-249 (Inzamam-ul-Haq), 6-249 (Wasim Akram)

Fall of wickets: 1-6 (Botham), 2-21 (Stewart), 3-59 (Hick), 4-69 (Gooch), 5-141 (Lamb), 6-141 (Lewis), 7-180 (Fairbrother), 8-183 (Reeve), 9-208 (DeFreitas), 10-227 (Illingworth)

ENGLAND	O	M	R	W	Wd	Nb	PAKISTAN	O	M	R	W	Wd	Nb
Pringle	10	2	22	3	3	5	Wasim Akram	10	0	49	3	6	4
Lewis	10	2	52	0	1	2	Aaqib Javed	10	2	27	2	3	1
Botham	7	0	42	1	-	-	Mushtaq Ahmed	10	1	41	3	1	-
DeFreitas	10	1	42	0	1	-	Ijaz Ahmed	3	0	13	0	2	-
Illingworth	10	0	50	1	-	-	Imran Khan	6.2	0	43	1	-	1
Reeve	3	0	22	0	1	-	Aamer Sohail	10	0	49	0	1	-

MOST RUNS

Player	Mat	Inns	NO	Runs	HS	Ave	BF	SR	100	50	0	4s	6s
MD Crowe (NZ)	9	9	5	456	100*	114	502	90.83	1	4	0	45	6
Javed Miandad (PAK)	9	9	2	437	89	62.42	698	62.6	0	5	0	27	0
PN Kirsten (SA)	8	8	2	410	90	68.33	616	66.55	0	4	0	28	2
DC Boon (AUS)	8	8	1	368	100	52.57	534	68.91	2	0	0	34	2
Rameez Raja (PAK)	8	8	2	349	119*	58.16	539	64.74	2	0	0	35	0
BC Lara (WI)	8	8	1	333	88*	47.57	408	81.61	0	4	1		
M Azharuddin (INDIA)	8	7	0	332	93	47.42	425	78.11	0	4	1	29	1
Aamer Sohail (PAK)	10	10	0	326	114	32.6	515	63.3	1	2	1	32	0
AH Jones (NZ)	9	9	2	322	78	46	523	61.56	0	3	0	41	0
MJ Greatbatch (NZ)	7	7	0	313	73	44.71	356	87.92	0	3	0	32	13
KC Wessels (SA)	9	9	2	313	85	44.71	583	53.68	0	3	0	23	0
AC Hudson (SA)	8	8	0	296	79	37	467	63.38	0	3	0	32	0
NH Fairbrother (ENG)	9	7	2	285	75*	57	412	69.17	0	3	0	15	2
SR Tendulkar (INDIA)	8	7	1	283	84	47.16	334	84.73	0	3	0	24	1
DM Jones (AUS)	8	8	1	276	90	39.42	407	67.81	0	2	0	18	3
GA Hick (ENG)	10	9	1	264	83	33	334	79.04	0	3	1	24	2
A Ranatunga (SL)	8	7	2	262	88*	52.4	322	81.36	0	2	0	23	2
AJ Stewart (ENG)	10	8	1	259	77	37	365	70.95	0	2	0	30	1
DL Haynes (WI)	7	7	1	251	93*	41.83	443	56.65	0	1	0	23	2
RS Mahanama (SL)	8	7	0	246	80	35.14	456	53.94	0	3	0	19	0
A Flower (ZIM)	8	8	2	246	115*	41	386	63.73	1	0	0	18	1
KLT Arthurton (WI)	8	7	1	233	58*	38.83	351	66.38	0	2	1	12	4
Inzamam-ul-Haq (PAK)	10	10	0	225	60	22.5	240	93.75	0	1	1	17	1
MAR Samarasekera (SL)	6	6	0	219	75	36.5	273	80.21	0	1	0	24	2
GA Gooch (ENG)	8	8	0	216	65	27	419	51.55	0	3	1	17	0

MOST WICKETS

Player	Mat	Inns	Overs	Mdns	Runs	Wkts	BBI	Ave	Econ	SR	4	5
Wasim Akram (PAK)	10	10	89.4	3	338	18	4/32	18.77	3.76	29.8	1	0
IT Botham (ENG)	10	10	89	7	306	16	4/31	19.12	3.43	33.3	1	0
Mushtaq Ahmed (PAK)	9	8	78	3	311	16	3/41	19.43	3.98	29.2	0	0
CZ Harris (NZ)	9	9	72.1	4	342	16	3/15	21.37	4.73	27	0	0
EA Brandes (ZIM)	8	8	70.1	7	355	14	4/21	25.35	5.05	30	1	0
AA Donald (SA)	9	9	78	5	329	13	3/34	25.3	4.21	36	0	0
M Prabhakar (INDIA)	8	7	57.1	5	245	12	3/41	20.41	4.28	28.5	0	0
AC Cummins (WI)	6	6	59	1	246	12	4/33	20.5	4.16	29.5	1	0
W Watson (NZ)	8	8	79	11	301	12	3/37	25.08	3.81	39.5	0	0
BM McMillan (SA)	9	9	73	7	306	11	3/30	27.81	4.19	39.8	0	0
PAJ DeFreitas (ENG)	10	10	85.3	12	319	11	3/34	29	3.73	46.6	0	0
Aaqib Javed (PAK)	10	10	84.5	11	328	11	3/21	29.81	3.86	46.2	0	0
WKM Benjamin (WI)	8	8	79	8	297	10	3/27	29.7	3.75	47.4	0	0
MR Whitney (AUS)	7	7	66	12	215	9	4/34	23.88	3.25	44	1	0
AP Kuiper (SA)	9	8	41	0	235	9	3/40	26.11	5.73	27.3	0	0
N Kapil Dev (INDIA)	8	7	58	2	251	9	3/41	27.88	4.32	38.6	0	0
GR Larsen (NZ)	9	9	76	7	262	9	3/16	29.11	3.44	50.6	0	0
DA Reeve (ENG)	9	8	34.4	4	126	8	3/38	15.75	3.63	26	0	0
MW Pringle (SA)	7	7	57	6	236	8	4/11	29.5	4.14	42.7	1	0
DN Patel (NZ)	9	8	79	8	245	8	2/26	30.62	3.1	59.2	0	0
CJ McDermott (AUS)	8	8	73	5	246	8	2/29	30.75	3.36	54.7	0	0
J Srinath (INDIA)	8	7	53.1	3	249	8	2/23	31.12	4.68	39.8	0	0
RK Illingworth (ENG)	6	6	58.1	2	250	8	3/33	31.25	4.29	43.6	0	0
SR Waugh (AUS)	8	8	60.4	1	277	8	3/36	34.62	4.56	45.5	0	0
RP Snell (SA)	9	9	72.5	10	310	8	3/42	38.75	4.25	54.6	0	0

HIGH SCORES

Player	Runs	Balls	4s	6s	SR	Team	Opposition	Ground
Rameez Raja	119*	155	16	0	76.77	Pakistan	v New Zealand	Christchurch
A Flower	115*	152	8	1	75.65	Zimbabwe	v Sri Lanka	New Plymouth
Aamer Sohail	114	136	12	0	83.82	Pakistan	v Zimbabwe	Hobart
PV Simmons	110	125	8	2	88	West Indies	v Sri Lanka	Berri
Rameez Raja	102*	158	4	0	64.55	Pakistan	v West Indies	Melbourne
MD Crowe	100*	134	11	0	74.62	New Zealand	v Australia	Auckland
DC Boon	100	133	11	0	75.18	Australia	v New Zealand	Auckland
DC Boon	100	147	8	0	68.02	Australia	v West Indies	Melbourne
DL Haynes	93*	144	7	0	64.58	West Indies	v Pakistan	Melbourne
M Azharuddin	93	102	10	0	91.17	India	v Australia	Brisbane

BEST BOWLING

Player	Overs	Mdns	Runs	Wkts	Econ	Team	Opposition	Ground
MW Pringle	8	4	11	4	1.37	South Africa	v West Indies	Christchurch
EA Brandes	10	4	21	4	2.1	Zimbabwe	v England	Albury
CC Lewis	8	0	30	4	3.75	England	v Sri Lanka	Ballarat
IT Botham	10	1	31	4	3.1	England	v Australia	Sydney
Wasim Akram	9.2	0	32	4	3.42	Pakistan	v New Zealand	Christchurch
AC Cummins	10	0	33	4	3.3	West Indies	v India	Wellington
MR Whitney	10	1	34	4	3.4	Australia	v West Indies	Melbourne
UC Hathurusingha	8	0	57	4	7.12	Sri Lanka	v West Indies	Berri
DR Pringle	8.2	5	8	3	0.96	England	v Pakistan	Adelaide
CZ Harris	4	0	15	3	3.75	New Zealand	v Zimbabwe	Napier

1996

THE SHOCK OF THE NEW

BY ANDREW FIDEL FERNANDO

"It's as if someone had foretold Arjuna Ranatunga that Sri Lanka were going to win," remembers Sidath Wettimuny, former Sri Lanka batsman and team selector for the 1996 World Cup. "He must have been told that by an astrologer, or a soothsayer, or something, you know. He knew it in his bones."

How Ranatunga could have possibly known his team of semi-professionals had what it took to win, hints at both vision and self-delusion, because there was little to suggest they could lift the trophy. Sri Lanka were barely better than minnows in the mid-1990s, having only very recently drummed up a little form in the one-day format. Between 1993 and 1996, they had lost roughly two-thirds of the matches they had played against top-seven opposition. Their batsmen had only chased scores in excess of 250 a handful of times. Their spinners – even the eventually prolific Muttiah Muralitharan – sported decidedly modest averages. That they became the first country to win the World Cup on their home continent is truly remarkable.

Beyond the playing field, the Sri Lanka board was effectively a beggar on the international stage – no more than USD $6,000 in its bank account at the time. Its players all held down jobs at banks or insurance companies to supplement their income from cricket. That Sri Lanka even had an internationally recognised coach for this tournament was thanks to the largesse of the Australia Cricket Board, which had provided Dav Whatmore's salary.

And yet, there Ranatunga was, right through that World Cup campaign, the living, breathing embodiment of zen.

"I used to marvel at some of the things Arjuna used to do in the tournament," Wettimuny says. "He would field in the match, come in, get into his white towel, and when our batsmen were going out to bat, he'd go to sleep. I mean, how cool can you be?

"He would then get up when two wickets fell, and sloooo-wly get ready. Then he's ready to go. I used to get so stressed out. One day I thought I was getting a heart attack and he came and looked at me and laughed. His coolness spread a lot of confidence into that team. It just made everyone think: 'You know, this could happen.'"

***

To tell the story of the 1996 World Cup, and of the rivalry that breathed such dramatic life into the final, it is vital to take stock of the months that preceded the tournament, when Muttiah Muralitharan was called for throwing by umpire Darrell Hair in a Test match in Australia.

Sri Lanka No.3 Asanka Gurusinha says: "Initially we thought he was called for overstepping. When we realised it wasn't for overstepping, something told me this was going to be a big problem. The person that Arjuna was, I knew we were not going to let someone control us and get away with it."

If Hair's decision was the dagger in Sri Lanka's stomach, the affronts the team believed they had endured through the rest of the tour (ball tampering allegations in Perth, the opposition's relentless sledging, and what they perceived to be a partisan Australian media), were the accompanying scrapes and bruises. "That tour we went through a lot of hard times," Gurusinha says. "That's when we really started to get the fire in our bellies."

The Sri Lanka public would soon find a reason to be further aggrieved. Eighteen days before Sri Lanka were to play their World Cup match against Australia in Colombo, a bomb explosion at the city's Central Bank killed 91 and injured as many as 1,400. With the Sri Lankan civil war at a particularly volatile juncture, Australia – along with West Indies – refused to travel to Sri Lanka for their matches.

The withdrawal, though, prompted unity at an international level. "The greatest advantage we had was that we were the little brother in the South Asian triangle," Wettimuny says. Though relations between the two big nations in the region were strained, as ever, Sri Lanka had the affections of both.

Fraternal love was first felt when Pakistan and India sent a combined team to play an exhibition match. "We welcome the golden sons of India and Pakistan," read a banner near the Colombo airport. "As far as the game is concerned, we are all together," said Indian captain Mohammad Azharuddin ahead of the match. For one day, in Khettarama, Sachin Tendulkar and Wasim Akram played in the same side – their own World Cup preparations suspended days out from the start of their campaigns.

***

Thanks in part to the fact that Sri Lanka's first win of the tournament was a walkover victory over the absent Australians, it was not the eventual winners who set the early stages of this12-team (the nine Full Members plus qualifiers UAE, Netherlands and Kenya) tournament alight. New Zealand, led by wicket-keeper Lee Germon (who captained in all but one of his 37 ODIs), were the first real movers and shakers, winning the tournament opener against England by 11 runs, before crushing Netherlands three days later. Before most teams had even played, they had two victories in the bank.

In the following week, a future all-time great of World Cup cricket imposed himself on the tournament. Sachin Tendulkar had had a decent run in the 1992 event, but here he confirmed his status as one of the best batsmen on the planet. He eased himself into the tournament with 127 not out against Kenya, as India comfortably chased down a target of 200, before hitting a match-winning 70 against West Indies three days later.

Two valiant innings in losing causes (something that would soon become a theme of Tendulkar's ODI career) would follow. First he hit 90 off 84 balls against Australia – his team falling 16 runs short of the opposition's 258, with Damian Fleming taking 5 for 36.

The next loss was to Sri Lanka in Delhi. India made a very respectable 271 for 3 with Tendulkar contributing the lion's share – a run-a-ball 137. Where India's 23-year-old opener was producing incandescent lone hands, Sri Lanka were meshing beautifully as a complete batting unit. Sanath Jayasuriya and Romesh Kaluwitharana produced the first of their fast starts, crashing 79 off 76 and 26 off 16 respectively. There was a mild stutter around the mid-way mark, as Jayasuriya and Gurusinha lost their wickets in quick succession, but Ranatunga and Hashan Tillakaratne were on hand to put on 131 and shepherd the team home.

Although Tendulkar would lead the run-scoring charts, eventually finishing with 523 runs at an average of 87.16, another opening batsman was hot on his heels. Like Tendulkar, Mark Waugh also began with a century against Kenya, following that with 126 off 135 balls – the innings that set up that 16-run win over India. And where Tendulkar hit two centuries in the tournament, Waugh mustered three – the first time such a feat had been achieved in a World Cup.

Waugh's best innings came later, against New Zealand, who had hit a commanding 286 for 9. With Australia requiring the second-highest score to win a World Cup match, Waugh stuck an outstanding 110 off 112 balls – an innings so graceful that his rapid rate of scoring almost passed you by. Along the way he put on 86 with older brother Steve, who saw Australia to the target with 59 not out. Where Tendulkar was carrying the India top order (he finished the tournament with 345 runs more than his next-best teammate), Waugh had substantial support – the likes of Ricky Ponting, Stuart Law and Mark Taylor also making important contributions in addition, of course, to Steve.

The one team Australia stumbled against in the group stage, however, was West Indies who themselves had had an odd tournament. They had begun with a crushing win over Zimbabwe – Curtly Ambrose, Courtney Walsh and Ottis Gibson seemingly bowling themselves into form, before suddenly, the team suffered three setbacks in a row. The loss to India was tolerable, perhaps, and the forfeited match against Sri Lanka was expected, but the startling loss to Kenya – by a whopping 73 runs – was the shock of the World Cup. Chasing only 167 for victory in Pune, West Indies collapsed in dramatic fashion –

only Shivnarine Chanderpaul and Roger Harper making it into double figures, as Kenya seam bowler Rajab Ali and off-spinner Maurice Odumbe took three wickets apiece.

Crashing to 93 all out, the loss was humiliating for what appeared to be a disunited West Indies side. Richie Richardson's captaincy had been in jeopardy even before the tournament, while star batsman Brian Lara was reported to be an indifferent presence in the dressing room. The day after the defeat, Richardson presented an apology. "I would say to the West Indian public that we're very, very sorry – we're as disappointed as they are," he said. "I've never felt this bad in all my life. If things are not going well, somebody should be blamed and the people at the top are usually the ones. I'm the captain, but the players are also responsible, the whole set-up is responsible... we're in a very, very deep hole and we're almost at the bottom."

On the verge of being knocked out of the tournament, West Indies required a victory against Australia, who for many were favourites to lift the trophy. Batting first at Jaipur, Australia posted 229 for 6 – Ricky Ponting making his first World Cup hundred, with 102 off 112 balls. Although West Indies had never seemed in such disarray as in the days approaching this game, their batsmen somehow pulled together under the leadership of Richardson, who made 93 off 133 deliveries, forging an 87-run stand with Lara, who made 60 himself. The eventual victory was by four wickets, with seven balls to spare.

The win meant West Indies sneaked into the quarter-finals. Alongside them, the usual suspects: India, Pakistan, England, Australia, New Zealand, South Africa, and of course, Sri Lanka.

***

It's not quite clear when superstition began its descent into the Sri Lankan dressing room, but when it set in, team manager Duleep Mendis ensured it stayed. His order: when our batsmen go out, no one moves from his seat until there is a wicket.

"When Sanath and Kalu were batting, we didn't even want to get up for a cup of tea," says Upul Chandana, the leg-spinner, who was 23 at the time. "All I remember wanting to do was to sit there and watch them bat. I had never seen anything like it."

Pramodya Wickramasinghe remembers a more sinister edge to the routine. "If any of us even shook in our seats, Duleep would start to shout at us. 'If he gets out next ball, you're the idiot I'm blaming,' he used to say. You know, when I think about it, a lot of our actions back then were dictated by the fear of getting an earful from either him or Arjuna."

Having claimed two walkover victories during the group stage, Sri Lanka did not have to work as hard as the other teams to stake a claim to a quarter-final spot. But that does not mean they did not take serious momentum into the knock-out stages. The victory over India was impressive enough, but their campaign was soon to hit overdrive.

Against a Kenyan attack fresh from skittling West Indies for 93, Jayasuriya and Kaluwitharana powered Sri Lanka to 83 off 40 balls, then passed the baton to the seniors. Aravinda de Silva cracked 145 from 115, Gurusinha compiled 84 from 103. And Ranatunga's unbeaten 40-ball 75 propelled Sri Lanka 35 runs further than the previous highest ODI total. It was while amassing 398 for 5 that an unfettered Sri Lanka discovered the full extent of their batting ability.

"The beauty of the tournament for us was that once we qualified for the quarter-final, the pressure was totally off," Wickramasinghe says. "All we needed to prove was that we were in the top eight in the world. Once we did that, the whole team just relaxed. We knew whatever happened, we could face our public."

***

As Sri Lanka were on their flight to Faisalabad for the first quarter-final of the tournament – against England – Jayasuriya was seated next to Wettimuny, both men contemplating the possibilities that hung on Sri Lanka's first entry to the knock-out stages of a World Cup

"Sidath *aiya*," Jayasuriya said. "Whatever happens, all I want to do is earn enough money to finish my house. I just need Rs 175,000 more [around $3,300]. That's enough for me. After that I don't need anything."

Wettimuny smiled. "If you win this match, you will get a lot more than that."

Not long after, Jayasuriya was flicking through the duty-free magazine. "*Sha*! Look at this watch. Beautiful, no? Cartier…"

"I tell you what," Wettimuny said, glancing over. "If you bat 15 overs in the next match, I'll buy you this watch myself.

"Sure?"

"Yes, but 15 overs you have definitely got to bat."

The opener took the challenge to heart while Wettimuny felt that if Jayasuriya got through the fielding restrictions, he would have scored around 50, and given the team a fine start.

Everything appeared to be going according to plan for Jayasuriya when he walked in after Sri Lanka's spinners had trussed England up for 235. He launched Peter Martin through cover point, then savaged Richard Illingworth's left-arm spin for four boundaries on the trot. Phil DeFreitas was slog-swept through cow corner, and Darren Gough picked off over square leg. Jayasuriya reached 50 in 30 balls, then raised the tempo, putting a ball from DeFreitas onto a satellite dish on the roof of the stadium.

In the 13th over, when he was on 82 off 44, Dermot Reeve bowled a leg-side wide. Jayasuriya overbalanced. England wicket-keeper Jack Russell snapped the bails off. "He was thoroughly upset when he came back," Wettimuny remembers. "He had a long face in the dressing room, and then he asked me, 'Sidath *aiya*, I got 80-odd, so isn't that good enough?' I said, 'Sorry, no. The deal was for 15 overs.'" (Wettimuny would later relent. "Even though Sanath didn't technically earn the watch, after teasing him for a day I did eventually buy it for him.")

Such was the haste with which Sri Lanka ran down England's total, perhaps that was the most striking of the quarter-finals, but the other three games had their moments.

With West Indies only having scraped into the knock-out stages, their opponents South Africa were firm favourites heading into their match. And yet, South Africa found a way to lose. It was in Karachi, on 11 March, that they established a reputation for crumbling under pressure that would haunt them for a generation and more. Seemingly headed for a comfortable victory against a misfiring side, South Africa lost their last six wickets for 59 runs, as Roger Harper and Jimmy Adams claimed seven scalps between them.

Lara had hit an outstanding 94-ball 111 to haul West Indies to a competitive total, but for the majority of their innings, South Africa seemed to have the measure of the target of 265. They were 186 for 3 when panic began to take grip. Hansie Cronje was the first to go in the collapse, caught for 40 off the bowling of Adams. Jonty Rhodes, Brian McMillan and Steve Palframan followed soon after, leaving the tail in charge of completing the chase. Predictably, it went poorly – South Africa crashing to 245 all out in the end.

Other World Cup patterns were being established elsewhere in the quarter-finals. Defending champions Pakistan had lost only one match in the group stages, where India had lost two, but despite the hype over this encounter, it was a decidedly dull affair – India cruising to a 39-run victory in Bangalore. For a change, Tendulkar did not top score for India, making only 31 of the team's imposing 287 for 8. Navjot Singh Sidhu had struck 93, and the middle order had chipped in with a string of useful scores, before seamer Venkatesh Prasad and leg-spinner Anil Kumble claimed three Pakistan wickets apiece. Only captain Aamer Sohail crossed 50 for Pakistan – the middle order making a series of insubstantial scores.

Australia's clash with their neighbours New Zealand yielded a similarly straightforward win for the bigger nation. Batting first New Zealand made an excellent 286 for 9, as Chris Harris bashed 130 off 124 balls, forging a 168-run partnership with Germon, who made 89 himself. Then Mark Waugh produced his innings of the tournament, and Australia's middle-order fired, to serve their trans-Tasman rivals a six-wicket defeat.

****

Almost every cricketer in the Sri Lanka team remembers the private conversation with Ranatunga, when a personalised, carefully defined brief was handed down. "Arjuna knew I could hit sixes," Gurusinha says. "But my job was very clear. He asked me to bat through the innings." Jayasuriya had had the team's blessing to attack in the past, but once paired with Romesh Kaluwitharana, attack became his mandate. Roshan

Mahanama was to turn the strike over to the swashbucklers, failing which he and Hashan Tillakaratne had to rebuild. Arjuna saved for himself the role of seeing the thing through.

Sometimes the job description was so bite-sized, it bordered on the mundane. "I was there to make the new ball old," Wickramasinghe says. "It was a bonus if we got wickets, but the main thing was to squeeze. I would have a long spell – maybe eight overs. Vaasy would bowl less, and they would save a few of his overs for the death."

Each spinner was pressed into service at a precise point in the middle overs. Murali was the major menace, and so was first to the bowling crease. The others – more agents of control than fizz and rip – were fed through in sequence. By the knock-outs the bowlers, like the batsmen, had an order. Wickramasinghe, Vaas, Murali, Dharmasena, Jayasuriya, de Silva; like line cooks at a restaurant that serves only one dish.

Quite intentionally, one man was not given a pre-tournament memo. Ranatunga had only one request for Aravinda de Silva the batsman. "You get us a hundred, that's all. You win us the World Cup." In the whole operation, imagined over years, put together over many months, de Silva's was the only free hand. His was the only talent Ranatunga did not limit by the bounds of his own imagination.

De Silva had been the supernova in Sri Lanka's batting galaxy for some time, but about six months before the World Cup, there were whispers he had unlocked something new. He had a summer with Kent in 1995, and somewhere during the run to the one-day final that season, he had found a way around the vagaries of his genius.

"He came back from Kent and suddenly people like Roshan, Hashan and Gura [Gurusinha] were talking about how Ara [de Silva] had become a different batsman almost," says Ravindra Pushpakumara a teammate at domestic level – the two having played together for Nondescripts Cricket Club (NCC). "In '89, '90, '91, he had been the kind of player who would hit a beautiful 25-30 runs and then would play some crazy shot. When we were playing for the club, balls he should maybe have defended, he hooked out of the NCC ground. That changed. He was driven. Serious."

During the World Cup, Wickramasinghe remembers de Silva shadow-batting in hotel rooms for hours. "We had an 11 o'clock curfew, so a bunch of us would always be chatting late into the night, brewing endless pots of tea and coffee. But Aravinda wouldn't just sit and talk. He was always on his feet, with the bat in hand, visualising bowlers he would be facing and practising the shots he would play to them. Just hours and hours of this. Sometimes, someone would ask him, 'Ara, who are you facing now?' and he would say, 'Wasim'. 'What is he bowling, *Ara*?' 'Bouncer.'"

Almost every Sri Lankan over 25 could tell you the context of de Silva's 66 from 47 balls in the semi-final against India, in Calcutta, because their team had never seen a big-match performance quite like it, and arguably, there has not been a better ODI counter-attack ever. Sent in to bat in a tournament where they had preferred chasing, Sri Lanka lost their openers for one run, and a 100,000-strong Eden Gardens was baying. By the eighth over, Sri Lanka's top-order insurance – Gurusinha – had also been dismissed.

If there is an enduring memory from the innings, it is the insane disparity between the speed of de Silva's bat swing and the velocity of the ball after he has hit it. The flick off the toes against Anil Kumble in the second over was almost dopey, but the ball skated across the turf so quick you could barely see it until it stung the boundary board. The square drive off Javagal Srinath in the 13th over was struck with such leisure, the infielders were almost surprised by how quickly it scorched by.

The secret had been a heavy bat he had picked up through the course of the tournament. "Sachin uses a heavy bat, so why shouldn't I try one?" he had asked a team selector. Low intensity, high impact – the heavy bat was a perfect fit for the man. By the time he was dismissed, Sri Lanka were 85 for 4, but having bent the bowlers out of shape and diverted the flow of play, de Silva had set them on course to 251. It would be too many for the opposition. Too much for their fans looking on.

When India collapsed from 98 for 1 to 120 for 8 on a crumbling surface, fires were begun in the stands, projectiles were thrown on to the field, and the match had to be abandoned.

***

If the first semi-final was dramatic, the second was perhaps even more gripping. Having beaten Australia and South Africa in consecutive matches, West Indies suddenly seemed a side reborn – a talented team finally pulling together in the same direction. With Australia having elected to bat in Mohali, the opening exchanges were a dream for West Indies. Ian Bishop was at his devastating finest, bowling Mark Taylor and Steve Waugh in quick succession. Curtly Ambrose was no less intimidating from the other end, trapping Mark Waugh and Ricky Ponting in front of the stumps – the quicks leaving Australia 15 for 4 inside 10 overs.

But Australia just kept dragging themselves back into the match. Stuart Law and Michael Bevan launched a recovery, putting on 138 together for the fifth wicket. That stand, though, was not without good fortune.

"I remember I had Stuart Law caught off a no-ball. I think he flicked one to midwicket," said Bishop. "On reflection, that would have been a significant breakthrough. Even now, it's very disappointing on my part that I couldn't keep my foot behind the line, given the situation Australia were in at the time. Bevan and Law were two quality players, and though Law wasn't very experienced as an international player, we were still not too unhappy with the way things were going despite the no-ball."

Although the middle order bailed Australia out, they could nevertheless cobble together no more than 207 for 8, on a pitch that seemed to hold few terrors for the batsmen. When West Indies settled into their chase – Chanderpaul hitting 80 from the top of the order, while Lara and Richardson contributed 40s – they seemed to be cruising to the target. At 165 for two, it was almost unthinkable that they could fail to advance to the final.

The match then descended into the bizarre. After Chanderpaul was caught at mid-on, West Indies made the strange decision to shuffle the batting order, sending in Roger

Harper and Ottis Gibson over Jimmy Adams and Keith Arthurton. "I think it [the panic] came from my side when the batting order was changed," Bishop said. "I can only speak for myself. I know my ability with the bat. All I had to do was play it a little straighter and work it around. As soon as it got down to a few wickets left, we started realising we were messing this up."

Suddenly, Australia's bowlers – Shane Warne in particular – were irresistible. Warne had Gibson caught behind, and trapped Jimmy Adams and Bishop in front in quick succession. At the other end, Damian Fleming was wreaking havoc. Warne finished with 4 for 36, before Fleming delivered the final blow, bowling Courtney Walsh to leave the opposition five runs short of Australia's score.

"We were so grief-stricken and embarrassed that I don't even remember if the Australians came to see us after the game," said Bishop.

Years later, Mark Waugh was still in disbelief, reflecting in his autobiography: "How the bloody hell did we win that?"

***

On the flight to Lahore, the Sri Lanka players wondered which team the Pakistani fans would favour. Australia were not popular at the time, so there was reason to suggest Sri Lanka would have more support. No one guessed, though, that the fans, the city, the entire nation, would embrace them so willingly. Players who did not turn heads in Colombo couldn't quite understand why these neutrals backed them so energetically.

Even now, it is difficult to pin down exactly why, as some players retell it, Lahoris on bikes, trucks and in hawker stalls, were brandishing Sri Lankan flags on the eve of the final. Pakistan's Lanka love seemed to stem from two major factors: One – Sri Lankans were South Asians. Two – they were not arch-rivals India.

"The day before the match, we wanted to be as relaxed as possible, so we all went shopping," remembers Pushpakumara. "I went into this carpet shop and there was this beautiful carpet there which I really wanted for my parents' place. Problem was, it cost about $500. No way did I have anything near that amount. The shop owner saw me looking and came over. 'You're from the Sri Lanka team?' he said. 'Then today money is no object. You play cricket and we love the way Jayasuriya and Kalu play. Because of the enjoyment your team has given us, you can take this for free.' I was just stunned."

On match day the stands were heaving with Sri Lanka flags, and anti-Australia banners. "Thing is, it wasn't even just like home support," Wickramasinghe says. "It was actually better than home support, because there was no home pressure. When you walk out in a foreign country, and you see support like that for you, you can't help but feel proud. You think, 'We must be playing good cricket. That must be why these people are here.'"

Imran Khan worried that no side had ever won a World Cup final chasing, but by now, Ranatunga's belief was all-pervading. He put Australia in. And the rest of the final was nothing so much as the Aravinda show. Vaas delivered the scalp of the in-form Mark Waugh early, but when Mark Taylor and Ricky Ponting built the second-wicket stand to 101, de Silva shut both men down in quick succession. Taylor was caught top-edging a sweep. Ponting was bowled by one that ripped from well outside off stump.

In the break between spells, de Silva took a running catch from mid-on, then another at backward point, as spin's slow poison worked on the Australian middle order. When he returned to the attack, de Silva dismissed Ian Healy with a delivery that would have done the greatest spinners proud. Tossed up into the rough outside off, the ball dived and jived to whoosh between bat and pad. Australia were kept to 241 for 7. Ranatunga led his team off the field with a strut.

For an innings that lost both openers by the sixth over, the chase was too smooth to believe. The seniors had pow-wowed in the break, and loaded themselves with the job. A gum-chewing Gurusinha broke long, staid spells only to bully bowlers down the ground, reserving for Shane Warne an oozing, intense kind of disdain. De Silva was light-footed and flowing, the ball rarely failing to find the meat of his blade as he clipped to leg and drove on the rise as usual, pacing himself, and by extension, the chase. Over the course of the tournament, the two of them added 566 runs in five third-wicket partnerships, the most added by any pair in a World Cup tournament excluding openers.

The only Sri Lankan who cracked that night was the 12th man. "If I was ever under stress in my life, it was running the drinks in the final," Pushpakumara remembers. "When the water break was coming up, the dressing room was bombarding me with messages to deliver. 'Tell Aravinda this' and 'Make sure Gura doesn't go after the fast bowlers.'

"As I descended the steps, Dav was standing there. He gave me a long, elaborate message as well, but I didn't speak English well at the time. I had no idea what he said. In the end I said, 'Okay Davvy,' and headed out.

"When I got to Aravinda and Gura, I completely choked. There was so much going through my mind, but all I could say was, 'Well played, *aiya*' or something like that. I got back and everyone took turns asking if I had delivered their messages. Of course I told each one that I had. Dav came and asked me too – I didn't understand, but from the way he was speaking, I could tell he was asking about the message. I told him, 'Yes'. The others all believed that I had delivered the messages, but Dav was the only one who looked at me like he wasn't so sure."

***

Perhaps Pushpakumara's meltdown was the last of a litany of improbabilities that prodded Sri Lanka towards triumph, because by the time Gurusinha and de Silva were parted, they had broken the back of the target. Ranatunga arrived with 94 to get, and helped inch Sri Lanka close, before sending Warne down the ground, then over square leg for six – one last thumbing of the nose at the cricketer who six weeks earlier had declared he would not go on holiday to Sri Lanka, let alone on a cricket tour there.

On air, Tony Greig had nailed his colours to the mast early in the tournament when he had declared he loved "the way these little Sri Lankans play" – a phrase that might have been patronising on other lips; only, there was no masking the affection when he said it. As Ranatunga's six cleared the fence, Greig wrote his own legacy into the hearts of a nation: "These Sri Lankans are giving the Aussies a real hiding."

The last act, of course, had to be that glide to third man – the most Ranatunga of all Ranatunga strokes. De Silva had played his piece flawlessly, but the cricket gods knew where this tale began and must end.

Ranatunga had hunted down talented players from around the country, watched his team full of semi-professionals steeled on a spiky tour down under, seen his superstar discover the depths of his talent on a jaunt overseas, and finally, produced the perfectly paced finishing hand. Sri Lanka's captain was ever at the eye of this perfect storm. Maybe that's why, as waves of jubilant teammates rushed the field, and throngs of ecstatic congratulators rushed up to kiss him, Ranatunga was so stoic when the thing was won.

1996

RESULTS AND STATISTICS

GROUP A TABLE

		P	W	L	Pts	Net RR
1	Sri Lanka	5	5	0	10	1.607
2	Australia	5	3	2	6	0.903
3	India	5	3	2	6	0.452
4	West Indies	5	2	3	4	-0.134
5	Zimbabwe	5	1	4	2	-0.939
6	Kenya	5	1	4	2	-1.007

GROUP B TABLE

		P	W	L	Pts	RR
1	South Africa	5	5	0	10	2.043
2	Pakistan	5	4	1	8	0.961
3	New Zealand	5	3	2	6	0.552
4	England	5	2	3	4	0.079
5	United Arab Emirates	5	1	4	2	-1.83
6	Netherlands	5	0	5	0	-1.923

INDIA V SRI LANKA
WILLS WORLD CUP 1995/96 (SEMI-FINAL)

Venue: Eden Gardens, Calcutta
Date: 13th March 1996
Toss: India
Result: Sri Lanka won by a concession
Umpires: RS Dunne, CJ Mitchley
TV Umpire: Mahboob Shah
Referee: CH Lloyd
Man of the Match: PA de Silva

SRI LANKA		R	b	INDIA		R	b
ST Jayasuriya	c Prasad b Srinath	1	3	SR Tendulkar	st Kaluwitharana b Jayasuriya	65	88
+RS Kaluwitharana	c Manjrekar b Srinath	0	1	NS Sidhu	c Jayasuriya b Vaas	3	8
AP Gurusinha	c Kumble b Srinath	1	16	SV Manjrekar	b Jayasuriya	25	48
PA de Silva	b Kumble	66	47	*M Azharuddin	c and b Dharmasena	0	6
RS Mahanama	retired hurt	58	101	VG Kambli	not out	10	29
*A Ranatunga	lbw b Tendulkar	35	42	J Srinath	run out	6	6
HP Tillakaratne	c Tendulkar b Prasad	32	43	AD Jadeja	b Jayasuriya	0	11
HDPK Dharmasena	b Tendulkar	9	20	+NR Mongia	c Jayasuriya b de Silva	1	8
WPUJC Vaas	run out (Azharuddin)	23	16	AR Kapoor	c de Silva b Muralitharan	0	1
GP Wickramasinghe	not out	4	9	A Kumble	not out	0	0
M Muralitharan	not out	5	4	BKV Prasad	did not bat		
Extras	(1 b, 10 lb, 2 nb, 4 w)	17		Extras	(5 lb, 5 w)	10	
Total	(8 wickets, 50 overs)	251		Total	(8 wickets, 34.1 overs)	120	

Fall of wickets: 1-1 (Kaluwitharana), 2-1 (Jayasuriya), 3-35 (Gurusinha), 4-85 (de Silva), 5-168 (Ranatunga), 6-206 (Dharmasena), 7-236 (Tillakaratne), 8-244 (Vaas)

Fall of wickets: 1-8 (Sidhu), 2-98 (Tendulkar), 3-99 (Azharuddin), 4-101 (Manjrekar), 5-110 (Srinath), 6-115 (Jadeja), 7-120 (Mongia), 8-120 (Kapoor)

INDIA	O	M	R	W	Wd	Nb	SRI LANKA	O	M	R	W	Wd	Nb
Srinath	7	1	34	3	-	-	Wickramasinghe	5	0	24	0	2	-
Kumble	10	0	51	1	1	-	Vaas	6	1	23	1	-	-
Prasad	8	0	50	1	2	2	Muralitharan	7.1	0	29	1	1	-
Kapoor	10	0	40	0	-	-	Dharmasena	7	0	24	1	-	-
Jadeja	5	0	31	0	-	-	Jayasuriya	7	1	12	3	1	-
Tendulkar	10	1	34	2	1	-	de Silva	2	0	3	1	1	-

AUSTRALIA V WEST INDIES
WILLS WORLD CUP 1995/96 (SEMI-FINAL)

Venue: Punjab Cricket Association Stadium, Mohali
Date: 14th March 1996
Toss: Australia
Result: Australia won by 5 runs
Umpires: BC Cooray, S Venkataraghavan
TV Umpire: Khizer Hayat
Referee: JR Reid
Man of the Match: SK Warne

AUSTRALIA		R	b	WEST INDIES		R	b
ME Waugh	lbw b Ambrose	0	2	S Chanderpaul	c Fleming b McGrath	80	126
*MA Taylor	b Bishop	1	11	+CO Browne	c and b Warne	10	18
RT Ponting	lbw b Ambrose	0	15	BC Lara	b SR Waugh	45	45
SR Waugh	b Bishop	3	18	*RB Richardson	not out	49	83
SG Law	run out	72	105	RA Harper	lbw b McGrath	2	5
MG Bevan	c Richardson b Harper	69	110	OD Gibson	c Healy b Warne	1	2
+IA Healy	run out	31	28	JC Adams	lbw b Warne	2	11
PR Reiffel	run out	7	11	KLT Arthurton	c Healy b Fleming	0	4
SK Warne	not out	6	6	IR Bishop	lbw b Warne	3	3
DW Fleming	did not bat			CEL Ambrose	run out	2	2
GD McGrath	did not bat			CA Walsh	b Fleming	0	1
Extras	(11 lb, 2 nb, 5 w)	18		Extras	(4 lb, 2 nb, 2 w)	8	
Total	(8 wickets,, 50 overs)	207		Total	(all out, 49.3 overs)	202	

Fall of wickets: 1-0 (ME Waugh), 2-7 (Taylor), 3-8 (Ponting), 4-15 (SR Waugh), 5-153 (Law), 6-171 (Bevan), 7-186 (Reiffel), 8-207 (Healy)

Fall of wickets: 1-25 (Browne), 2-93 (Lara), 3-165 (Chanderpaul), 4-173 (Harper), 5-178 (Gibson), 6-183 (Adams), 7-187 (Arthurton), 8-194 (Bishop), 9-202 (Ambrose), 10-202 (Walsh)

WEST INDIES	O	M	R	W	Wd	Nb	AUSTRALIA	O	M	R	W	Wd	Nb
Ambrose	10	1	26	2	3	-	McGrath	10	2	30	2	-	1
Bishop	10	1	35	2	1	3	Fleming	8.3	0	48	2	1	-
Walsh	10	1	33	0	-	1	Warne	9	0	36	4	1	-
Gibson	2	0	13	0	-	1	ME Waugh	4	0	16	0	-	-
Harper	9	0	47	1	-	-	SR Waugh	7	0	30	1	-	-
Adams	9	0	42	0	1	-	Reiffel	5	0	13	0	-	2
							Bevan	4	1	12	0	-	-
							Law	2	0	13	0	-	-

AUSTRALIA V SRI LANKA

WILLS WORLD CUP 1995/96 (FINAL)

Venue: Gaddafi Stadium, Lahore
Date: 17th March 1996
Toss: Sri Lanka
Result: Sri Lanka won by 7 wickets
Umpires: SA Bucknor, DR Shepherd
TV Umpire: CJ Mitchley
Referee: CH Lloyd
Man of the Match: PA de Silva

AUSTRALIA		R	b	SRI LANKA		R	b
*MA Taylor	c Jayasuriya b de Silva	74	83	ST Jayasuriya	run out	9	7
ME Waugh	c Jayasuriya b Vaas	12	15	+RS Kaluwitharana	c Bevan b Fleming	6	13
RT Ponting	b de Silva	45	73	AP Gurusinha	b Reiffel	65	99
SR Waugh	c de Silva b Dharmasena	13	25	PA de Silva	not out	107	124
SK Warne	st Kaluwitharana b Muralitharan	2	5	*A Ranatunga	not out	47	37
SG Law	c de Silva b Jayasuriya	22	30	HP Tillakaratne	did not bat		
MG Bevan	not out	36	49	RS Mahanama	did not bat		
+IA Healy	b de Silva	2	3	HDPK Dharmasena	did not bat		
PR Reiffel	not out	13	18	WPUJC Vaas	did not bat		
DW Fleming	did not bat			GP Wickramasinghe	did not bat		
GD McGrath	did not bat			M Muralitharan	did not bat		
Extras	(10 lb, 1 nb, 11 w)	22		Extras	(1 b, 4 lb, 1 nb, 5 w)	11	
Total	(7 wickets, innings closed, 50 overs)	241		Total	(3 wickets, 46.2 overs)	245	

Fall of wickets: 1-36 (ME Waugh), 2-137 (Taylor), 3-152 (Ponting), 4-156 (Warne), 5-170 (SR Waugh), 6-202 (Law), 7-205 (Healy)

Fall of wickets: 1-12 (Jayasuriya), 2-23 (Kaluwitharana), 3-148 (Gurusinha)

SRI LANKA	O	M	R	W	Wd	Nb	AUSTRALIA	O	M	R	W	Wd	Nb
Wickramasinghe	7	0	38	0	2	-	McGrath	8.2	1	28	0	-	-
Vaas	6	1	30	1	-	-	Fleming	6	0	43	1	4	-
Muralitharan	10	0	31	1	1	-	Warne	10	0	58	0	1	1
Dharmasena	10	0	47	1	-	1	Reiffel	10	0	49	1	-	-
Jayasuriya	8	0	43	1	5	-	ME Waugh	6	0	35	0	-	-
de Silva	9	0	42	3	3	-	SR Waugh	3	0	15	0	-	1
							Bevan	3	0	12	0	-	-

MOST RUNS

Player	Mat	Inns	NO	Runs	HS	Ave	BF	SR	100	50	0	4s	6s
SR Tendulkar (INDIA)	7	7	1	523	137	87.16	609	85.87	2	3	0	57	7
ME Waugh (AUS)	7	7	1	484	130	80.66	563	85.96	3	1	1	40	6
PA de Silva (SL)	6	6	1	448	145	89.6	416	107.69	2	2	0	57	7
G Kirsten (SA)	6	6	1	391	188*	78.2	434	90.09	1	1	0	33	4
Saeed Anwar (PAK)	6	6	2	329	83*	82.25	343	95.91	0	3	0	29	5
AP Gurusinha (SL)	6	6	0	307	87	51.16	408	75.24	0	3	0	25	11
WJ Cronje (SA)	6	6	1	276	78	55.2	316	87.34	0	2	0	20	6
AC Hudson (SA)	4	4	0	275	161	68.75	271	101.47	1	1	0	32	4
Aamer Sohail (PAK)	6	6	0	272	111	45.33	332	81.92	1	2	0	35	1
BC Lara (WI)	6	6	1	269	111	53.8	256	105.07	1	1	0	33	2
DJ Cullinan (SA)	6	6	2	255	69	63.75	305	83.6	0	2	0	16	3
GP Thorpe (ENG)	6	6	2	254	89	63.5	333	76.27	0	2	0	19	1
A Ranatunga (SL)	6	6	4	241	75*	120.5	210	114.76	0	1	0	29	2
RB Richardson (WI)	6	6	2	236	93*	59	371	63.61	0	1	0	22	1
RT Ponting (AUS)	7	7	0	229	102	32.71	327	70.03	1	0	1	16	1
SR Waugh (AUS)	7	7	2	226	82	45.2	285	79.29	0	3	0	14	2
ST Jayasuriya (SL)	6	6	0	221	82	36.83	168	131.54	0	2	0	29	8
GA Hick (ENG)	5	5	1	212	104*	53	285	74.38	1	1	0	16	2
S Chanderpaul (WI)	6	6	0	211	80	35.16	354	59.6	0	2	0	22	0
SG Law (AUS)	7	6	2	204	72	51	238	85.71	0	1	0	12	2
Ijaz Ahmed (PAK)	6	6	1	197	70	39.4	266	74.06	0	2	1	13	2
SO Tikolo (KENYA)	6	5	0	196	96	39.2	242	80.99	0	2	1	16	6
SP Fleming (NZ)	6	6	0	193	66	32.16	277	69.67	0	1	0	20	0
MA Taylor (AUS)	7	7	0	193	74	27.57	299	64.54	0	2	0	22	2
LK Germon (NZ)	6	6	3	191	89	63.66	225	84.88	0	1	0	13	1

MOST WICKETS

Player	Mat	Inns	Overs	Mdns	Runs	Wkts	BBI	Ave	Econ	SR	4	5
A Kumble (INDIA)	7	7	69.4	3	281	15	3/28	18.73	4.03	27.8	0	0
Waqar Younis (PAK)	6	6	54	5	253	13	4/26	19.46	4.68	24.9	1	0
PA Strang (ZIM)	6	5	42.1	4	192	12	5/21	16	4.55	21	1	1
RA Harper (WI)	6	6	58	6	219	12	4/47	18.25	3.77	29	1	0
DW Fleming (AUS)	6	6	45.2	3	221	12	5/36	18.41	4.87	22.6	0	1
SK Warne (AUS)	7	7	68.3	3	263	12	4/34	21.91	3.83	34.2	2	0
CEL Ambrose (WI)	6	6	56.3	9	170	10	3/28	17	3	33.9	0	0
RW Ali (KENYA)	6	6	41.2	3	190	10	3/17	19	4.59	24.8	0	0
Mushtaq Ahmed (PAK)	6	6	57	2	238	10	3/16	23.8	4.17	34.2	0	0
AA Donald (SA)	4	4	34	0	126	8	3/21	15.75	3.7	25.5	0	0
SLV Raju (INDIA)	4	4	40	4	158	8	3/30	19.75	3.95	30	0	0
DG Cork (ENG)	5	5	48	2	216	8	2/33	27	4.5	36	0	0
J Srinath (INDIA)	7	7	65.4	3	293	8	3/34	36.62	4.46	49.2	0	0
BKV Prasad (INDIA)	7	7	65	1	312	8	3/45	39	4.8	48.7	0	0
Aaqib Javed (PAK)	5	5	39.3	2	189	7	2/18	27	4.78	33.8	0	0
CA Walsh (WI)	6	6	55.3	9	210	7	3/46	30	3.78	47.5	0	0
M Muralitharan (SL)	6	6	57.1	3	216	7	2/37	30.85	3.77	49	0	0
CR Matthews (SA)	6	6	59.3	2	226	7	2/30	32.28	3.79	51	0	0
ST Jayasuriya (SL)	6	6	51	1	231	7	3/12	33	4.52	43.7	0	0
BM McMillan (SA)	6	6	43	5	127	6	3/11	21.16	2.95	43	0	0
PAJ DeFreitas (ENG)	4	4	33.1	6	140	6	3/31	23.33	4.22	33.1	0	0
PL Symcox (SA)	4	4	40	2	149	6	2/22	24.83	3.72	40	0	0
SF Dukanwala (UAE)	5	4	33	1	153	6	5/29	25.5	4.63	33	0	1
DJ Nash (NZ)	4	4	35	4	153	6	3/26	25.5	4.37	35	0	0
Azhar Saeed (UAE)	5	5	31	1	157	6	3/45	26.16	5.06	31	0	0

HIGH SCORES

Player	Runs	Balls	4s	6s	SR	Team	Opposition	Ground
G Kirsten	188*	159	13	4	118.23	South Africa	v U.A.E.	Rawalpindi
AC Hudson	161	132	13	4	121.96	South Africa	v Netherlands	Rawalpindi
PA de Silva	145	115	14	5	126.08	Sri Lanka	v Kenya	Kandy
SR Tendulkar	137	137	8	5	100	India	v Sri Lanka	Delhi
ME Waugh	130	128	14	1	101.56	Australia	v Kenya	Visakhapatnam
CZ Harris	130	124	13	4	104.83	New Zealand	v Australia	Chennai
SR Tendulkar	127*	138	15	1	92.02	India	v Kenya	Cuttack
ME Waugh	126	135	8	3	93.33	Australia	v India	Mumbai
Aamer Sohail	111	139	8	0	79.85	Pakistan	v South Africa	Karachi
BC Lara	111	94	16	0	118.08	West Indies	v South Africa	Karachi

BEST BOWLING

Player	Overs	Mdns	Runs	Wkts	Econ	Team	Opposition	Ground
PA Strang	9.4	1	21	5	2.17	Zimbabwe	v Kenya	Patna
SF Dukanwala	10	0	29	5	2.9	U.A.E.	v Netherlands	Lahore
DW Fleming	9	0	36	5	4	Australia	v India	Mumbai
Waqar Younis	10	0	26	4	2.6	Pakistan	v Netherlands	Lahore
SK Warne	9.3	1	34	4	3.57	Australia	v Zimbabwe	Nagpur
SK Warne	9	0	36	4	4	Australia	v West Indies	Mohali
PA Strang	7.3	1	40	4	5.33	Zimbabwe	v West Indies	Hyderabad (Deccan)
RA Harper	10	0	47	4	4.7	West Indies	v South Africa	Karachi
BM McMillan	8	1	11	3	1.37	South Africa	v U.A.E.	Rawalpindi
ST Jayasuriya	7	1	12	3	1.71	Sri Lanka	v India	Kolkata

1999

THE START OF AN ERA

BY TANYA ALDRED

A wide-eyed, broad-bottomed, luxuriantly hirsute, eye-popping speedster. A chubby-wristed leg-spinner with magic in his hands. A green Thor with bat and ball. A captain with hoarfrost chilling in his veins.

Between them Shoaib Akhtar, Shane Warne, Lance Klusener, and Steve Waugh bestrode the 1999 World Cup – a competition that swung joyfully between farce and pathos, interspersed with moments of cricketing brilliance and breaths of pure high drama. It was a tournament that would mark a sea-change in the way English cricket thought about its fans. It was also the tournament that brought us the very greatest of one-day internationals.

Twenty years on, *that* semi-final is still the greatest. But it came later. Before the sunny uplands, the scrubland.

Critics had aimed fire at the competition's new format and length – 30 first round games, nine Super Sixes, two semi-finals and a final, and its timing – starting in the dubious damp days of mid-May and done and dusted before the summer solstice. In fact neither of those things mattered – the weather was remarkably kind. It was damp for the warm-up games, chilly for the early matches, but only one game was called off through rain and some unfolded in glorious sunshine.

The final bullet the competition had to dodge, was the form of the England team itself.

The summer of 1999 was the first time the World Cup had returned to English (plus Welsh, Scottish, Irish and Dutch) soil since 1983. In that time cricket had slipped down the national agenda, not only because of the slumping fortunes of the national team but also the inexorable rise of the Premier League, the selling off of playing fields and the reduction in the amount of cricket being played in state schools. The world was still four years away from the first T20 competition, so a 50-over World Cup marked the pinnacle of limited overs fun. Unsurprisingly, the ECB viewed the competition as their big chance to reintroduce the nation to cricket. The most obvious way for this to be done was by the national team triumphing, or at least marching masterfully through to the final stages.

Unfortunately, the England team had rather hiccupped through the run-up to the tournament. They'd lost the Ashes 3-1 the previous winter, seven of their 12 one-day internationals on the same tour, and three of four matches in the Coca-Cola Cup between England, Pakistan and India in Sharjah. The one-day captaincy had gone from Adam Hollioake, who had led the team to victory in the 1997 Sharjah Cup, to Alec Stewart, who was desperately out of form. The team had also been embroiled in a row about pay. In the absence of express pace or spin, England had fallen upon "bits and pieces" cricketers, who were experts in early spring conditions.

Mark Ealham was a key member of the side. "I was really happy – we were based in Kent and our hotel was in Ashford where I was born. There was a lot of hype around the competition – and a lot of anticipation for us to do well at home at that time of year. I remember it being really damp for the practice matches and everyone wore long baggy jumpers and looked frozen."

"We had a great start in a what were bowler-friendly conditions. The white ball changed colour to match the pitch so it was difficult for the batsmen to see and there were so many great attacking bowlers in the competition." He also remembers "a meeting about run-rate being really important."

Despite the pre-tournament hitches, England were expected to comfortably make the new Super Six knock-out stage. And, four games in, everything seemed to be going smoothly – eight-wicket, nine-wicket and seven-wicket victories plus a not altogether unexpected, though bad, loss to South Africa, left them on the cusp of qualification. However run-rate was the final determiner in the case of a tie in the qualifying groups. And so when the unthinkable happened in the final round of the group stages and Zimbabwe beat South Africa, it meant that England had to beat India at Edgbaston to qualify. Rain sent the game into the second day and, as panic set in, England were bowled out for 169, losing by 63 runs, and dispatched from the World Cup in the opening rounds for the first time in its history.

Ealham remembers it as the worst moment he ever had in a dressing room: "When we'd walked out at Edgbaston it was like playing an away game. There was a lot of noise, a big atmosphere and we buckled under it. It was very flat afterwards. It is pretty bad when the host nation goes out, we felt like we'd let the country down."

"There are honourable defeats, unfortunate defeats and then ignominious defeats," wrote *The Times* leader writer. "The manner by which England's interest in the cricket World Cup ended yesterday rests, unfortunately, in the final category. "

Captain Alec Stewart was sacked as captain shortly afterwards and the whole thing marked rather a sad end to the tenure of coach David Lloyd, who had pre-announced his parting earlier in the year, presumably with hopes of a happier departure.

And yet... and yet... despite all that, the organisational difficulties, England's early exit, the collective raised eyebrows of a dubious media, the tournament not only survived but bloomed, as 12 teams were slowly, rivetingly, whittled down to one.

The pre-tournament favourites, South Africa, proved to be the very team they were supposed to be until suddenly, in the match that counted more than any other, they faltered. Of the other three semi-finalists, Pakistan were the flair team, the cigar and seat of your pants team, the neutrals' team. New Zealand played their part as plucky outsiders and Australia, with military discipline, turned themselves from a team one defeat away from elimination to an unstoppable, utterly meticulous, banana yellow juggernaut. Of them all, more later.

Kenya and Scotland, two of the three minnows, had their moments, and for the other – Bangladesh – the tournament was life-changing. Their victory over Pakistan would ultimately put them on the road to achieving Test status the following year. For West Indies and the former champions Sri Lanka, as well as for England, it was back to the drawing board. But *in* England, something rather remarkable happened.

Across the country, a spirit was awakening. The deep affection that British Asians had for cricket was no secret in their own communities but it but had not been realised, or tendered to even tacitly, by the cricketing authorities. In the summer of 1999, it broke free.

The affiliations of British immigrants had become a political hot potato in 1990 when the then conservative MP for Chingford, Norman Tebbit, came up with his cricket test. Tebbit questioned whether immigrants and their children could be loyal to Britain if they supported their country of origin rather than England in a cricket match. Here, nine years on, the World Cup played a major part in dismantling such sentiments.

All over the UK, games featuring the four Asian teams brought grounds like Taunton, like Bristol, like Northampton, like Chelmsford, to life with chanting and drumming in a way that was at first alien, then rather wonderful to the traditionally more introverted white British audience. From Sachin Tendulkar's century at Bristol the day after he returned from his father's funeral in Mumbai, via the absolute blast of noise that accompanied the Pakistan v India match at

Headingley, in the words of *Wisden*, a "passionate atmosphere unimaginable in English cricket," to the day of the final itself, it was a joyous thread that looped through the tournament. The other teams too were supported by their diasporas, which lent games an international flavour, almost universally inquisitive and pretty good natured, bar the odd pitch invasion. Even at the India v Pakistan clash, at a time when tensions were high in Kashmir and the two countries were technically at war, there were just three arrests.

The first hint of this fanatical support came at Hove, the day after England easily won the opening game against Sri Lanka on a soggy day at Lord's. The raucous Indian fans who turned up to watch India take on South Africa caused some trepidation amongst the deckchairs, but the late appearance of the sun and a relatively close finish, albeit a win for South Africa, left most people happy.

The Hove game also proved a tasting platter for what was to come – Lance Klusener, XXL shirt billowing in the wind, marching out to bat and hammering his first three balls to the boundary. India's batsmen, always threatening, always classy. Though for the watching media the biggest story was the one-way earpieces that South African captain Hansie Cronje and fast bowler Allan Donald wore when fielding in order to consult with off-field coach Bob Woolmer. Their fun didn't last long though after the earpieces were spotted by an eagle-eyed cameraman and confiscated by the match referee.

India's next game was against Zimbabwe at Leicester, and they were to find themselves in trouble after losing that game too – a humdinger of match that started with an immaculately observed minute's silence for Sachin Tendulkar's father and turned into colourful pandemonium as the two sets of fans partied while a look-a-like Tendulkar, complete with sunglasses and a shellsuit, paraded the boundary. All seemed to be going India's way until the penultimate over when Henry Olonga, the first dreadlocked cricketer to play in a World Cup match, took the final three wickets. The Zimbabwe team bus was peppered with stones as disappointed Indian fans made their way home.

But all was not lost and their batsmen, with four centuries in the next two games, rescued India's World Cup bid. First Tendulkar, on his return, scored 140 dreamlike runs off 101 balls at Bristol, a century he dedicated to his father. Dravid, playing a beautiful second fiddle, made 104 as Kenya were beaten by 94 runs. Then, at Taunton, Sourav Ganguly and Dravid put on 318 in 45 overs as a strangely subdued Sri Lanka were thrashed by 157 runs. It was the end of a disappointing tournament for the reigning champions, who were sent home with only victories over Kenya and Zimbabwe in their back pockets.

While at the bottom of the Group A table Kenya valiantly flayed around but didn't win a game, South Africa were powering ahead at the top. They lost only to Zimbabwe, in the final round, the result that semi-sealed England's fate. Their demolition of Sri Lanka and then England, bowled out for 103, then the lowest total by anyone in an ODI at The Oval, as well as an easy victory over Kenya in

Amstelveen, gave early warning of their steel. Klusener, with mighty club and heavy ball, won the man of the match award in three consecutive games.

Over in Group B, Scotland and Bangladesh were getting their first taste of World Cup cricket. Scotland lost every match but Gavin Hamilton, their young all-rounder, scored more runs than any of England's batsmen – including a 50 against Pakistan. His performances were to catch the roving eyes of the England selectors and he was picked for England the following winter against South Africa. That unfortunately was the highlight. In his only Test at Johannesburg, he scored no runs, took no wickets, and was never picked for England again. He did though pick up with Scotland again four years later.

The Bangladesh victory over Scotland was closer than the 22 runs suggested and no-one foresaw what would happen at the County Ground against Pakistan a week later.

That heady day at Northampton – the ground could have sold out three times over – marked a beacon in Bangladesh's cricketing maturity. It was the first time they had ever beaten a major cricketing power.

Bangladesh worked their way to 223 (28 of them wides) and a jittery Pakistan slipped to 42 for five before the 13th over in reply, and never recovered: Khaled Mahmud took 3 for 31 and there were three run outs. A jubilant pitch invasion by Bangladesh fans couldn't entirely overshadow rumours of match fixing, especially as the match was a dead one, with Pakistan already through to the Super Sixes and Bangladesh already out, but no credible evidence was ever found.

The West Indies side that had spent the early months of the year in a hypnotic and tightly-fought Test and one-day series against Australia, never really got going and nor did their talismanic captain Brian Lara. They lost their opening skirmish against Pakistan at Bristol under heavy skies, a game where Shoaib Akhtar was first revealed to the wider world. Sherwin Campbell was on the receiving end of his first ball of the tournament, accidentally edging it over the slips for six. In his next over Shoaib bowled Campbell, beating him with a ball of blistering speed, and World Cup crowds fell in love. West Indies went on to beat Bangladesh, on a Dublin day so cold that manager Clive Lloyd watched swathed in blankets, New Zealand under leaden skies perfect for seam bowling, and Scotland after George Salmond chose to bat and West Indies reduced them to 29 for 7 – Courtney Walsh with 7-1-7-3 and Curtly Ambrose 10-4-8-2 (the pair were to finish the most economical bowlers of the tournament).

After an acrimonious winter, during which captain Steve Waugh and vice captain Shane Warne fell out, Australia were redefining sluggish. They started with an uninspired win over Scotland, taking nearly 45 overs to overhaul 181, with an unimpressed Steve Waugh describing his side's fielding as "atrocious." A five-wicket loss to New Zealand followed, after Australia were restricted to 213 on a sleepy pitch at Sophia Gardens and then Roger Twose and Chris Cairns made hay with the bat as the sun came out for the New Zealand innings. Pakistan then won a rowdy, thrilling match by 10 runs when Wasim Akram bowled McGrath with two balls to go and Australia's World Cup bid was on the brink of collapse.

But Steve Waugh wasn't going quietly. Australia regrouped, and the strategy of not giving Glenn McGrath the new ball was quietly shelved. Tom Moody was drafted into the team and a quick victory over Bangladesh at Chester-le-Street came thanks largely to his all-round performance – 50 and three wickets. He would remain part of the team for the rest of the competition.

Australia's final group game, at Old Trafford against West Indies, was the bleakest of the whole tournament. Australia needed to win to qualify, but were keen to take West Indies through with them as, in a quirk of the competition, they would then take the points for beating them through to the Super Six stage. Once assured of victory, the funny business started as, in the words of *Wisden*, "run rate became secondary to run-rate manipulation." The final 19 runs took 13 overs and the players walked off to hoots of derision, with many spectators leaving early in disgust.

It was all for nought though when New Zealand, who had done the maths, thrashed Scotland by a large enough margin to skip over the heads of West Indies and join Pakistan and Australia in the Super Sixes.

So the home countries were dispatched back to Lord's and The Grange to lick their wounds and six – Pakistan, Zimbabwe, South Africa, New Zealand, India, Australia – marched on. But if the more parochial fans then turned away, many stayed tuned, especially as the television coverage was shared between terrestrial (the BBC) and satellite (Sky) television.

The Super Six format, in theory, rewarded consistency but it had its flaws. South Africa, easily the best team in Group A, finished top of the group, but went into the Super Six behind Zimbabwe because each team carried forward points and net run rate already gained against fellow Super Six qualifiers. This left India and Australia marooned at the bottom of the table with a mountain to climb – and they were to meet in the first game of the next stage.

More than 18,000 gathered to watch at The Oval in the knowledge that the losing side was going to have very little chance of progressing any further. To the despair of their fans, that side was India. The Indian bowlers had let Australia rack up 282 thanks largely to Mark Waugh's 83 at the top of the order. In reply, Glenn McGrath, now fully into his stride, decimated the top order, including Tendulkar for 0, Dravid for 2 and Azharuddin for 3. Recovery from that was always gong to be tricky and India got nowhere near, despite an undefeated hundred from Ajay Jadeja and 75 from Robin Singh.

The knowledge that every game was a must-win seemed to embolden the Australians, a bot visibly growing in stature as it gorged on its opponents. Emboldened, they marched on to Lord's, where they lost the toss, were put in to bat, and notched up 303 thanks to more runs from Mark Waugh, this time a century – making him the first player to score four World Cup hundreds. Zimbabwe began positively, thanks to Neil Johnson's unbeaten 132, but after a second wicket stand of 114 with Murray Goodwin, wickets tumbled and Zimbabwe were content to gamble on playing the run-rate game.

Then, the big one (part one): South Africa at Headingley. South Africa won the toss and batted. Herschelle Gibbs was at his infuriating best, combining quick singles and risky edges through slips with authoritative slurps to the boundary. His hundred was the innings ballast as Shane Warne rediscovered his form, taking the wickets of Daryll Cullinan and Cronje in the same over, whilst turning the economical screw. It was Klusener, inevitably, who guided the South Africans through the final few overs, ensuring they squeezed the Australians for every run. A target of 272 against Donald, Shaun Pollock and Klusener was never modest, and when Australia wobbled to 48 for 3, it seemed near impossible.

But cometh the hour, cometh the iceman. Steve Waugh, his purpose leaking through every pore, every jagged movement, every adjustment of his equipment, grimly pressed on. Gibbs, with words that must haunt his night hours still, greeted him with: "Let's see how he takes the pressure now." Jacques Kallis was out of the match with an abdominal strain and Ricky Ponting and Waugh took advantage of his dibbly-dobbly replacements, Nicky Boje and Cronje. Then, a moment of high-drama: Cronje summoned back Klusener in the 31st over in an attempt to break the partnership. Waugh, on 56, took an ungainly slap at his sixth ball and sent it to midwicket where Gibbs momentarily clung on before soon – much too soon – throwing the ball up and away in celebration. The ball slipped from his left hand and fell to the grass. Gibbs, sunglasses covering his expression, lips wordlessly apart, looked as if he'd just crashed his father-in-law's antique car. Waugh merely narrowed his eyes, and quipped from the side of his mouth: "Hersch, you've just dropped the World Cup."

Or at least that's how cricket myth has it. Waugh later denied the phrase, claiming to have muttered something much more prosaic, but the damage was done, the aura had been created. Waugh marched onwards to an unbeaten 120 in 110 balls, only his second ODI century. With just three balls to spare he edged Pollock to the boundary, victory by sheer force of personality. Australia's win denied South Africa a top of the table finish and condemned both teams to a re-match in the semi-final.

Pakistan by contrast, did what they had to do, but no more. They eased themselves through to the semi-finals, losing to South Africa and India but thrashing Zimbabwe. The game against South Africa at Trent Bridge was a thriller: a tortoise-like Pakistan batting performance had to be rescued by Moin Khan's 63 – before he was one of three run-outs in the innings. Shoaib Akhtar then turned up the heat with the ball, 95mph thunderbolts dismissing both Gibbs and Cronje in single figures. At 58 for 5 South Africa looked terminal but Pollock and Kallis pushed steadily forward and Klusener struck again. Shoaib had seemed unstoppable when, suddenly, his mastery deserted him in his ninth and last over. Klusener top edged him for four and rocked him over mid-wicket for six before a rattled Shoaib fired one between bat and stumps and across the boundary for four leg byes. With 17 off the over, the impossible was suddenly possible and South Africa won with an over to spare.

India's victory over Pakistan was ultimately irrelevant but it didn't stop their passionate supporters rejoicing long into the night. Dravid, Tendulkar and Azharuddin flared briefly yet the eventual total of 227 hadn't seemed beyond Pakistan's reach. But Srinath and Prasad had other ideas, prising out Saeed Anwar mid-flow and ensuring that no-one scored more than Inzamam-ul-Haq's sloth-like 41. In the end Pakistan fell short by 47 runs – which left them having to beat Zimbabwe to qualify. That they did with ease, three days later, thanks to a century by Saeed Anwar, searing pace from Shoaib and a hat trick (the second in World Cup history) by Saqlain Mushtaq.

New Zealand were the final team to make it through to the semi-finals. Their match with Zimbabwe was washed out after miserable weather in Leeds prevented the minimum number of overs being bowled; they lost to South Africa after having no answer to Gary Kirsten and Gibbs' opening partnership of 176; and then beat India with some flair at Trent Bridge, overhauling their 251 with 10 balls to spare. Geoff Allott's dismissal of Ganguly made him the highest wicket taker at World Cups. New Zealand finished equal fourth with Zimbabwe, but got through thanks to a higher run-rate in the Super Six.

The semi-finals took place on a Wednesday and Thursday in glorious mid-June. In the first, at Old Trafford, in front of adoring, plain-damn-exultant, ear-splittingly noisy Pakistan fans, Wasim Akram's side cruised into the final whilst crushing New Zealand's hopes of reaching it for the first time. The nine-wicket victory was just as much of a trouncing as it sounds. New Zealand batted bravely to notch up 241 in their 50 overs but the adulation went not to Roger Twose or Chris Cairns or Stephen Fleming – all of whom made 40s – but to man of the match Shoaib, who cranked up the swagger and the speed. He knocked out Nathan Astle's leg stump to make the initial breakthrough, uprooted Fleming's off stump with a 92mph toe-snapper to bring an abrupt halt to a promising partnership with Roger Twose, before finally bamboozling Chris Harris and removing his stumps with a slower ball.

Saeed Anwar and Wajahatullah Wasti looked at New Zealand's 241 and laughed, strolling out to the square and promptly putting on 194 for the first wicket, the highest opening stand in World Cup history. Saeed Anwar was unbeaten on a magnificent 113; Ijaz Ahmed joined him for a quick-fire 28 – the end only postponed by a yet another pitch invasion. Fleming suggested in the post-match press conference that, despite the memory of Hillsborough, the English authorities might have to think about fencing grounds: "You are going to have another tragedy, although this time it will happen on the field." That aside, Pakistan would arrive at the final with their mojo roaring.

But all that happened in Manchester turned out to be but a warm-up for Birmingham: Australia v South Africa (part two). Taut because of the situation, taut because of the two protagonists, the game unfolded like a perfectly formed novella

– plot twist following plot twist. And in the end, after all the nerves and the mind-games, 100 overs of high-wire tension, not a slip of lace could divide the two sides. The game finished with scores level – the perfect tie.

"I never said South Africa were chokers," Steve Waugh had said in a pre-match press conference. "I said they couldn't play well under pressure." Thus spake the prescient agitator supreme.

With six overs of the match left South Africa needed 53, with five wickets remaining. Warne's next over went for 15 but included the wicket of Kallis, caught by Steve Waugh for 53. That brought in Klusener, who duly carved Fleming's first ball through mid-wicket for four but lost his partner Pollock in the same over. Just five came from McGrath's next over, then seven from Fleming's. With two overs left, 18 runs were needed, three wickets in hand. McGrath knocked out Boucher's middle stump and Elworthy followed after a sharp-elbowed throw from Paul Reiffel ran him out. Klusener, now going for broke, charged at a McGrath full toss. The ball flew high and far, but at long on Reiffel – hero to zero – parried the ball over the boundary for six. The final six balls: nine wickets required, one wicket left.

Waugh threw the ball to Fleming, veteran of the last over of the 1996 World Cup semi-final. His first ball was a pitch-perfect yorker – Klusener crashed it through the covers for four. Another attempted yorker followed. Thud! This time the ball parted mid-off and extra cover. Just one run needed. Klusener tapped the next ball to mid-on, into the grasping hands of Darren Lehmann. Donald, who couldn't hear in the din, started backing up too far and had to scramble back. Had Lehmann hit, he'd have been out.

Breathe.

Fleming again, another yorker. Klusener swung and ran. Donald didn't. He turned round and watched the ball, ran his bat in, then realised Klusener was up his end. As Mark Waugh flicked the ball towards the non-striker's end – had it hit, it would have run out both men – Donald dropped his bat in slow-motion panic. He hesitated, again, and then started, fruitlessly, to run. Fleming picked up the ball and rolled it down to the waiting Adam Gilchrist who removed the bails. Eleven exultant Australians. One South African already nearly off the field – Klusener, the running man. One standing, distraught, without his bat, while celebration happened all around him. The teams had to be separated, and were, by run-rate. Australia went through to the final.

That the Australians had earlier totted up 213 was thanks largely to Michael Bevan and Steve Waugh; that they didn't score any more was down to razor-sharp bowling from Shaun Pollock (5 for 36) and Donald, whose four wickets came in two bursts in two overs. South Africa's reply was stymied by Warne, suddenly on top of his form. He took three of the first four wickets to reduce South Africa from 48 for 0 to 61 for 4: a repeat of his ball of the century to Gibbs, a furiously spinning leg-break that caught off-stump; before bowling a slog-sweeping Gary Kirsten and having Cronje out caught off his boot. Jonty Rhodes and Jacques Kallis then steadied the ship until Klusener so nearly got them over the line.

For South Africa, out in the semi-final for the second time in the three tournaments since they were readmitted to international cricket, it was heart-breaking. Allan Donald, who would later tell the *Guardian*: "I don't think that disappointment comes in bigger packages than that", was to be given a break from cricket mid-season by Warwickshire. Cronje couldn't sleep for two weeks. The South Africans played and replayed the game in their heads. But history repeated itself as they also went on to lose semi-finals in 2007 and 2015.

And so to the final, three days later. But it turned out the final had already been played. Australia v Pakistan at Lord's was the popped balloon after the wedding; the hangover after the party. Pakistan were utterly overawed – though their loyal fans did their best, filling the roads around St John's Wood with chants of *Zindabad Pakistan* and the poop poop of car horns. Only about 3,000 Pakistan fans made it into the ground, but there was a gigantic roar when Saeed Anwar cut Glenn McGrath for four with regal ease from the third ball of the game. That, however, was as good as it got.

Both openers were out by time Pakistan had made 22 – and when Steve Waugh threw the ball to Warne, Pakistan's batsmen were shortly to be toast. A dreamy leg-break landed on Ijaz Ahmed's leg-stump and spun back, and back again, to knock out the off stump. Moin Khan and Shahid Afridi followed. And when Wasim Akram got down on one-knee for an ill-advised swipe after Inzamam-ul-Haq was given out to a ball from Paul Reiffel that he didn't hit, television sets switched off all over Lahore. Extras top scored with 25 out of the eventual total of 132 (indeed, in the tournament as a whole, extras accounted for 1,982 runs, a record 11.7 per cent of the total).

Australia overtook that in 20.1 overs, Adam Gilchrist guiding Australia to victory; Pakistan's fabled bowlers with nothing to play with.

As champagne sprayed over the Lord's balcony, and Steve Waugh lifted the trophy high over his head, Warne praised "an inner strength and belief in your ability, and a belief in your teammates." And, of course, producing the goods when it mattered. Warne took four wickets in both the semi-final and final but had not taken four wickets in an ODI in his previous 60 matches, over two and a half years and, after the 1999 final, only achieved the feat once more in the last 67 ODIs of his career.

A still-stunned Lance Klusener was awarded a car as man of the tournament. He had scored 281 runs off 230 balls in eight innings, in which he was out only twice (average 140.5), and took 17 wickets, at 20.5. Only one other player has achieved a World Cup tournament double of 15 wickets and 250 runs – Yuvraj Singh for India in 2011 (362 runs, average 90.5; 15 wickets average 25.1).

The Pakistan side were praised by Wasim Akram but booed by their supporters. Inzamam-ul-Haq would later bemoan Pakistan for misreading the wicket at Lord's, but said: "I still believe this was the strongest Pakistan side to date to have featured in an ICC Cricket World Cup, at least, in the five ICC showcase events in which I had been involved."

A third of Australia's population was said to have watched the final, which confirmed that the world's No.1 Test team were also the world's No.1 one-day team. They would go on to win three of the next four tournaments. It was something the rest of the world were going to have to get used to.

1999

RESULTS AND STATISTICS

GROUP A TABLE

		P	W	L	NR	Pts	Net RR	Bow SR
1	South Africa	5	4	1	0	8	0.859	32.317
2	India	5	3	2	0	6	1.285	33.595
3	Zimbabwe	5	3	2	0	6	0.017	37.806
4	England	5	3	2	0	6	-0.331	34.651
5	Sri Lanka	5	2	3	0	4	-0.809	46.281
6	Kenya	5	0	5	0	0	-1.198	69.789

GROUP B TABLE

		P	W	L	NR	Pts	Net RR	Bow SR
1	Pakistan	5	4	1	0	8	0.526	30.319
2	Australia	5	3	2	0	6	0.731	39.243
3	New Zealand	5	3	2	0	6	0.575	34.487
4	West Indies	5	3	2	0	6	0.497	31.381
5	Bangladesh	5	2	3	0	4	-0.543	38.033
6	Scotland	5	0	5	0	0	-1.928	41.48

SUPER SIX TABLE

		P	W	L	NR	Pts	Net RR	Bow SR
1	Pakistan	5	3	2	0	6	0.654	35.024
2	Australia	5	3	2	0	6	0.358	40.611
3	South Africa	5	3	2	0	6	0.174	48.323
4	New Zealand	5	2	2	1	5	-0.520	40.459
5	Zimbabwe	5	2	2	1	5	-0.786	34.556
6	India	5	1	4	0	2	-0.153	40.194

NEW ZEALAND V PAKISTAN

ICC WORLD CUP 1999 (SEMI-FINAL)

Venue: Old Trafford, Manchester
Date: 16th June 1999
Toss: New Zealand
Result: Pakistan won by 9 wickets
Umpires: DB Hair, P Willey
TV Umpire: DL Orchard
Referee: CW Smith
Man of the Match: Shoaib Akhtar

NEW ZEALAND		R	b	PAKISTAN		R	b
MJ Horne	b Abdur Razzaq	35	48	Saeed Anwar	not out	113	148
NJ Astle	b Shoaib Akhtar	3	18	Wajahatullah Wasti	c Fleming b Cairns	84	123
CD McMillan	c Moin Khan b Wasim Akram	3	19	Ijaz Ahmed	not out	28	21
*SP Fleming	b Shoaib Akhtar	41	57	Inzamam-ul-Haq	did not bat		
RG Twose	c Ijaz Ahmed b Abdur Razzaq	46	83	Abdur Razzaq	did not bat		
CL Cairns	not out	44	48	Shahid Afridi	did not bat		
CZ Harris	b Shoaib Akhtar	16	21	+Moin Khan	did not bat		
+AC Parore	b Wasim Akram	0	4	*Wasim Akram	did not bat		
DJ Nash	not out	6	10	Azhar Mahmood	did not bat		
GR Larsen	did not bat			Saqlain Mushtaq	did not bat		
GI Allott	did not bat			Shoaib Akhtar	did not bat		
Extras	(4 b, 14 lb, 12 nb, 17 w)	47		Extras	(3 lb, 7 nb, 7 w)	17	
Total	(7 wickets,, 50 overs)	241		Total	(1 wicket, 47.3 overs)	242	

Fall of wickets: 1-20 (Astle, 5.3 ov), 2-38 (McMillan, 10.3 ov), 3-58 (Horne, 15.1 ov), 4-152 (Fleming, 33.5 ov), 5-176 (Twose, 39.3 ov), 6-209 (Harris, 45.4 ov), 7-211 (Parore, 46.4 ov)

Fall of wickets: 1-194 (Wajahatullah Wasti, 40.3 ov)

PAKISTAN	O	M	R	W	Wd	Nb	NEW ZEALAND	O	M	R	W	Wd	Nb
Wasim Akram	10	0	45	2	7	4	Allott	9	0	41	0	1	1
Shoaib Akhtar	10	0	55	3	1	2	Nash	5	0	34	0	2	2
Abdur Razzaq	8	0	28	2	1	-	Larsen	10	0	40	0	-	1
Saqlain Mushtaq	8	0	36	0	1	-	Cairns	8	0	33	1	-	3
Azhar Mahmood	9	0	32	0	3	-	Harris	6	0	31	0	-	-
Shahid Afridi	5	0	27	0	2	2	Astle	7.3	0	41	0	1	-
							McMillan	2	0	19	0	1	-

AUSTRALIA V SOUTH AFRICA

ICC WORLD CUP 1999 (SEMI-FINAL)

Venue: Edgbaston, Birmingham
Date: 17th June 1999
Toss: South Africa
Result: Match tied
Umpires: DR Shepherd, S Venkataraghavan
TV Umpire: SA Bucknor
Referee: R Subba Row
Man of the Match: SK Warne

AUSTRALIA		R	b	SOUTH AFRICA		R	b
+AC Gilchrist	c Donald b Kallis	20	39	G Kirsten	b Warne	18	42
ME Waugh	c Boucher b Pollock	0	4	HH Gibbs	b Warne	30	36
RT Ponting	c Kirsten b Donald	37	48	DJ Cullinan	run out (Bevan)	6	30
DS Lehmann	c Boucher b Donald	1	4	*WJ Cronje	c ME Waugh b Warne	0	2
*SR Waugh	c Boucher b Pollock	56	76	JH Kallis	c SR Waugh b Warne	53	92
MG Bevan	c Boucher b Pollock	65	101	JN Rhodes	c Bevan b Reiffel	43	55
TM Moody	lbw b Pollock	0	3	SM Pollock	b Fleming	20	14
SK Warne	c Cronje b Pollock	18	24	L Klusener	not out	31	16
PR Reiffel	b Donald	0	1	+MV Boucher	b McGrath	5	10
DW Fleming	b Donald	0	2	S Elworthy	run out (Reiffel->McGrath)	1	1
GD McGrath	not out	0	1	AA Donald	run out (ME Waugh->Fleming->Gilchrist)	0	0
Extras	(1 b, 6 lb, 6 nb, 3 w)	16		Extras	(1 lb, 5 w)	6	
Total	(all out, 49.2 overs)	213		Total	(all out, 49.4 overs)	213	

Fall of wickets: 1-3 (ME Waugh, 0.5 ov), 2-54 (Ponting, 13.1 ov), 3-58 (Lehmann, 13.6 ov), 4-68 (Gilchrist, 16.6 ov), 5-158 (SR Waugh, 39.3 ov), 6-158 (Moody, 39.6 ov), 7-207 (Warne, 47.6 ov), 8-207 (Reiffel, 48.1 ov), 9-207 (Fleming, 48.3 ov), 10-213 (Bevan, 49.2 ov)

Fall of wickets: 1-48 (Gibbs, 12.2 ov), 2-53 (Kirsten, 14.1 ov), 3-53 (Cronje, 14.3 ov), 4-61 (Cullinan, 21.2 ov), 5-145 (Rhodes, 40.3 ov), 6-175 (Kallis, 44.5 ov), 7-183 (Pollock, 45.5 ov), 8-196 (Boucher, 48.2 ov), 9-198 (Elworthy, 48.4 ov), 10-213 (Donald, 49.4 ov)

SOUTH AFRICA	O	M	R	W	Wd	Nb	AUSTRALIA	O	M	R	W	Wd	Nb
Pollock	9.2	1	36	5	-	-	McGrath	10	0	51	1	1	-
Elworthy	10	0	59	0	1	2	Fleming	8.4	1	40	1	3	-
Kallis	10	2	27	1	1	1	Reiffel	8	0	28	1	-	-
Donald	10	1	32	4	1	-	Warne	10	4	29	4	1	-
Klusener	9	1	50	0	-	3	ME Waugh	8	0	37	0	-	-
Cronje	1	0	2	0	-	-	Moody	5	0	27	0	-	-

AUSTRALIA V PAKISTAN

ICC WORLD CUP 1999 (FINAL)

Venue: Lord's Cricket Ground, St John's Wood
Date: 20th June 1999
Toss: Pakistan
Result: Australia won by 8 wickets
Umpires: SA Bucknor, DR Shepherd
TV Umpire: S Venkataraghavan
Referee: RS Madugalle
Reserve Umpire: CW Smith (West Indies)
Man of the Match: SK Warne

PAKISTAN		R	b	AUSTRALIA		R	b
Saeed Anwar	b Fleming	15	17	ME Waugh	not out	37	52
Wajahatullah Wasti	c ME Waugh b McGrath	1	14	+AC Gilchrist	c Inzamam-ul-Haq b Saqlain Mushtaq	54	36
Abdur Razzaq	c SR Waugh b Moody	17	51	RT Ponting	c Moin Khan b Wasim Akram	24	27
Ijaz Ahmed	b Warne	22	46	DS Lehmann	not out	13	9
Inzamam-ul-Haq	c Gilchrist b Reiffel	15	33	*SR Waugh	did not bat		
+Moin Khan	c Gilchrist b Warne	6	12	MG Bevan	did not bat		
Shahid Afridi	lbw b Warne	13	16	TM Moody	did not bat		
Azhar Mahmood	c and b Moody	8	17	SK Warne	did not bat		
*Wasim Akram	c SR Waugh b Warne	8	20	PR Reiffel	did not bat		
Saqlain Mushtaq	c Ponting b McGrath	0	4	DW Fleming	did not bat		
Shoaib Akhtar	not out	2	6	GD McGrath	did not bat .		
Extras	(10 lb, 2 nb, 13 w)	25		Extras	(1 lb, 3 nb, 1 w)	5	
Total	(all out, 39 overs)	132		Total	(2 wickets, 20.1 overs)	133	

Fall of wickets: 1-21 (Wajahatullah Wasti, 4.4 ov), 2-21 (Saeed Anwar, 5.1 ov), 3-68 (Abdur Razzaq, 19.4 ov), 4-77 (Ijaz Ahmed, 23.4 ov), 5-91 (Moin Khan, 27.1 ov), 6-104 (Inzamam-ul-Haq, 30.1 ov), 7-113 (Shahid Afridi, 31.6 ov), 8-129 (Azhar Mahmood, 36.6 ov), 9-129 (Wasim Akram, 37.2 ov), 10-132 (Saqlain Mushtaq, 39 ov)

Fall of wickets: 1-75 (Gilchrist, 10.1 ov), 2-112 (Ponting, 17.4 ov)

AUSTRALIA	O	M	R	W	Wd	Nb	PAKISTAN	O	M	R	W	Wd	Nb
McGrath	9	3	13	2	-	-	Wasim Akram	8	1	41	1	1	2
Fleming	6	0	30	1	4	2	Shoaib Akhtar	4	0	37	0	-	1
Reiffel	10	1	29	1	2	-	Abdur Razzaq	2	0	13	0	-	-
Moody	5	0	17	2	1	-	Azhar Mahmood	2	0	20	0	-	-
Warne	9	1	33	4	2	-	Saqlain Mushtaq	4.1	0	21	1	-	-

MOST RUNS

Player	Mat	Inns	NO	Runs	HS	Ave	BF	SR	100	50	0	4s	6s
R Dravid (INDIA)	8	8	1	461	145	65.85	539	85.52	2	3	0	49	1
SR Waugh (AUS)	10	8	3	398	120*	79.6	512	77.73	1	2	0	35	6
SC Ganguly (INDIA)	7	7	0	379	183	54.14	467	81.15	1	1	0	39	8
ME Waugh (AUS)	10	10	1	375	104	41.66	492	76.21	1	2	1	39	1
Saeed Anwar (PAK)	10	10	1	368	113*	40.88	511	72.01	2	0	0	42	0
NC Johnson (ZIM)	8	8	1	367	132*	52.42	496	73.99	1	3	0	43	4
RT Ponting (AUS)	10	10	1	354	69	39.33	532	66.54	0	1	0	32	5
HH Gibbs (SA)	9	9	0	341	101	37.88	467	73.01	1	2	1	34	4
RG Twose (NZ)	9	9	5	318	80*	79.5	426	74.64	0	3	1	29	4
JH Kallis (SA)	8	8	2	312	96	52	470	66.38	0	4	2	18	4
A Jadeja (INDIA)	8	7	1	285	100*	47.5	379	75.19	1	1	0	23	4
L Klusener (SA)	9	8	6	281	52*	140.5	230	122.17	0	2	0	26	10
MG Bevan (AUS)	10	8	3	264	65	52.8	391	67.51	0	2	0	18	2
Inzamam-ul-Haq (PAK)	10	9	1	254	81	31.75	409	62.1	0	2	1	15	1
SR Tendulkar (INDIA)	7	7	1	253	140*	42.16	281	90.03	1	0	1	30	3
Moin Khan (PAK)	10	9	2	242	63	34.57	219	110.5	0	1	0	20	6
G Kirsten (SA)	9	9	0	229	82	25.44	417	54.91	0	1	1	22	1
AC Gilchrist (AUS)	10	10	0	224	63	22.4	284	78.87	0	2	1	27	2
GM Hamilton (SCOT)	5	5	1	217	76	54.25	316	68.67	0	2	0	15	4
DJ Cullinan (SA)	9	9	1	216	50	27	391	55.24	0	1	1	21	3
SP Fleming (NZ)	9	9	1	208	69	26	338	61.53	0	1	1	23	0
RD Jacobs (WI)	5	4	2	205	80*	102.5	408	50.24	0	2	0	18	3
MW Goodwin (ZIM)	8	8	0	201	57	25.12	315	63.8	0	1	0	25	0
MJ Horne (NZ)	8	8	0	199	74	24.87	354	56.21	0	1	0	29	0
N Hussain (ENG)	5	5	2	194	88*	64.66	330	58.78	0	2	0	22	1

MOST WICKETS

Player	Mat	Inns	Overs	Mdns	Runs	Wkts	BBI	Ave	Econ	SR	4	5
GI Allott (NZ)	9	9	87.4	7	325	20	4/37	16.25	3.7	26.3	2	0
SK Warne (AUS)	10	10	94.2	13	361	20	4/29	18.05	3.82	28.3	2	0
GD McGrath (AUS)	10	10	95.4	9	367	18	5/14	20.38	3.83	31.8	0	1
L Klusener (SA)	9	9	75.5	5	350	17	5/21	20.58	4.61	26.7	0	1
Saqlain Mushtaq (PAK)	10	10	83.4	4	379	17	5/35	22.29	4.52	29.5	0	1
AA Donald (SA)	9	9	82	7	325	16	4/17	20.31	3.96	30.7	2	0
Shoaib Akhtar (PAK)	10	10	80.5	6	391	16	3/11	24.43	4.83	30.3	0	0
Wasim Akram (PAK)	10	10	90.4	6	342	15	4/40	22.8	3.77	36.2	1	0
DW Fleming (AUS)	10	10	88	9	362	14	3/57	25.85	4.11	37.7	0	0
Abdul Razzaq (PAK)	9	9	77	5	302	13	3/25	23.23	3.92	35.5	0	0
Azhar Mahmood (PAK)	10	10	84	4	349	13	3/24	26.84	4.15	38.7	0	0
NC Johnson (ZIM)	8	7	50	4	233	12	4/42	19.41	4.66	25	1	0
J Srinath (INDIA)	8	8	73.2	11	313	12	3/37	26.08	4.26	36.6	0	0
CL Cairns (NZ)	9	9	69.5	4	333	12	3/19	27.75	4.76	34.9	0	0
CA Walsh (WI)	5	5	47	8	108	11	4/25	9.81	2.29	25.6	1	0
D Gough (ENG)	5	5	48.4	4	192	11	4/34	17.45	3.94	26.5	1	0
HH Streak (ZIM)	8	8	68	3	326	11	3/35	29.63	4.79	37	0	0
AD Mullally (ENG)	5	5	50	6	176	10	4/37	17.6	3.52	30	1	0
MA Ealham (ENG)	5	5	50	5	191	10	2/28	19.1	3.82	30	0	0
JAR Blain (SCOT)	5	5	37.1	1	210	10	4/37	21	5.65	22.3	1	0
DS Mohanty (INDIA)	6	6	52	2	260	10	4/56	26	5	31.2	1	0
S Elworthy (SA)	8	8	72	9	262	10	2/20	26.2	3.63	43.2	0	0
GP Wickramasinghe (SL)	5	5	49	3	208	9	3/30	23.11	4.24	32.6	0	0
CZ Harris (NZ)	9	9	54.1	2	255	9	4/7	28.33	4.7	36.1	1	0
BKV Prasad (INDIA)	7	7	64.5	4	266	9	5/27	29.55	4.1	43.2	0	1

HIGH SCORES

Player	Runs	Balls	4s	6s	SR	Team	Opposition	Ground
SC Ganguly	183	158	17	7	115.82	India	v Sri Lanka	Taunton
R Dravid	145	129	17	1	112.4	India	v Sri Lanka	Taunton
SR Tendulkar	140*	101	16	3	138.61	India	v Kenya	Bristol
NC Johnson	132*	144	14	2	91.66	Zimbabwe	v Australia	Lord's
SR Waugh	120*	110	10	2	109.09	Australia	v South Africa	Leeds
Saeed Anwar	113*	148	9	0	76.35	Pakistan	v New Zealand	Manchester
R Dravid	104*	109	10	0	95.41	India	v Kenya	Bristol
ME Waugh	104	120	13	0	86.66	Australia	v Zimbabwe	Lord's
Saeed Anwar	103	144	11	0	71.52	Pakistan	v Zimbabwe	The Oval
HH Gibbs	101	134	10	1	75.37	South Africa	v Australia	Leeds

BEST BOWLING

Player	Overs	Mdns	Runs	Wkts	Econ	Team	Opposition	Ground
GD McGrath	8.4	3	14	5	1.61	Australia	v West Indies	Manchester
L Klusener	8.3	3	21	5	2.47	South Africa	v Kenya	Amstelveen
BKV Prasad	9.3	2	27	5	2.84	India	v Pakistan	Manchester
RR Singh	9.3	0	31	5	3.26	India	v Sri Lanka	Taunton
Saqlain Mushtaq	10	1	35	5	3.5	Pakistan	v Bangladesh	Northampton
SM Pollock	9.2	1	36	5	3.85	South Africa	v Australia	Birmingham
CZ Harris	3.1	0	7	4	2.21	New Zealand	v Scotland	Edinburgh
AA Donald	8	1	17	4	2.12	South Africa	v England	The Oval
CA Walsh	10	0	25	4	2.5	West Indies	v Bangladesh	Dublin
SK Warne	10	4	29	4	2.9	Australia	v South Africa	Birmingham

2003

CROSSING CONTINENTS

BY TELFORD VICE

Rugby had got there first and made a roaring success of it. Then came football. Ditto. Now it was cricket's turn: the "New South Africa" – and it really was new, from its flag to the first half of its anthem to most of its electorate and the reinvention of what it meant to consider yourself fully part of the country that clung to the sharp tip of Africa – was to host the 2003 ICC Cricket World Cup.

Nelson Mandela was always going to be an impossible act to follow. The story that culminated in the tall, beaming icon of the best humanity could be, happily at home in a Springbok jersey buttoned all the way up, handing Francois Pienaar the Webb Ellis Cup after South Africa had beaten New Zealand, the only rugby opponents who matter to them, in the 1995 World Cup final at Johannesburg's Ellis Park would have been laughed out of Hollywood as outrageously implausible had it arrived as a film script. Instead it landed in reality with the thump of unshakeable truth, which John Carlin chronicled in *Playing the Enemy: Nelson Mandela and the Game That Made a Nation* and hit the silver screen as *Invictus*, starring Morgan Freeman and Matt Damon – who were both nominated for Oscars – and directed by Clint Eastwood.

No book was written nor movie made about football's 1996 Africa Cup of Nations, which was also staged in South Africa. But the impact of Bafana Bafana's triumph – Mark Williams struck twice in as many minutes in the second half of the final against Tunisia at Soccer City in Soweto – resounded much more deeply with the nation than what the Springboks had achieved. South Africa's football team are nowhere near as competitive on the world stage as their cricket and rugby counterparts, not least because there are far more champions-in-waiting in football than there are in cricket and rugby combined. But a disproportionate chunk of the nation's heart belongs to Bafana regardless.

Rugby had Mandela. Football had victory. What did South African cricket have in its bid to make a fist of things? PT Barnum in pads. At least, he used to wear pads.

He also used to captain what was called South Africa's team, even though it looked nothing like most South Africans. His name is Ali Bacher.

Few figures in the game's history have been as complex. Bacher emerged from the privileged classes as a medical doctor but also as part of the Jewish minority in an age and in a society in which kneejerk racism was the default. He became a standard-bearer for that society, captaining first Transvaal then South Africa before being consigned to a generation of players who will forever be left asking what might have been had the policies and behaviour of the apartheid state not led to the isolation of the country's teams from international sport.

In his next incarnation, as the South African Cricket Union's managing director, he welcomed teams to South Africa during their isolation and it was this role in the ongoing saga of South Africa that led Bacher to the light, as Mike Gatting's rebel tour turned sour.

"That tour nearly finished me off emotionally," Bacher would say years later. "We lived in a cocoon here, you must remember; including myself. I must confess that if I had known the anger and the hurt that those tours would cause I would have thought twice about them. It was very hurtful for me. I had been a liberal all my life."

Somewhere in all that Bacher had seen the error of his ways, and became cricket's equivalent of the reformed smoker in the cigarette factory. Instead of plotting more rebel tours he forged towards racial unity in a still racially segregated state. It bears pointing out that when cricket in South Africa first spoke with a voice of all colours and creeds, on June 29 1991, the country was almost three years away from its inaugural democratic election. The game hurtled into its future: in November 1991 South Africa undertook their first tour to India – indeed, their first engagement against any team who weren't entirely white – and in February 1992 they made their World Cup debut. A return to Test cricket followed in Barbados in April 1992, and that November a new generation of South Africans was introduced to the format in their own backyards when India arrived.

Bacher was the indefatigable energy at the heart of the miracle, a zealot who never tired of preaching his gospel, who would call back two minutes after talking to a reporter and tweak the punctuation of what he had said in order to turn a long sentence into two pithier pronouncements. He was a consummate communicator and a superb salesperson. Central to his message was the importance of opening elite cricket's doors to all who played the game, whatever their background, community and culture.

So it was no surprise that Bacher had secured the hosting of the 2003 ICC Cricket World Cup, a truth that felt like destiny for so many South Africans. Neither was it unusual that Bacher's vision for the tournament burst the country's banks: matches would also be played in Zimbabwe and Kenya. Political and security issues complicated that grand plan, and affected games scheduled for both the latter countries – most famously when Zimbabwe's Andy Flower and Henry Olonga wore black armbands to, as they said in a statement, "mourn the death of democracy in our beloved Zimbabwe" during a match against Namibia in Harare. But it is to cricket's and the ICC's credit that they were given the space and the opportunity to express their views in dignified fashion to a vast, worldwide audience despite Zimbabwe's tense political and social situation.

The other major news story from the tournament was the sending home in disgrace, and before the first round, of cricket's biggest box office star of the age and a fine player besides. That's how big Shane Warne was when he tested positive for a banned diuretic. Perhaps Warne felt he was too big for his own good: the bad medicine was contained in a slimming agent he had consumed, he said, on the advice of his mother.

The events of 3 March at Kingsmead didn't constitute a controversy. But, for South Africans who had lived through the shambles of the tied semi-final against Australia at Edgbaston that saw their team jettisoned from the 1999 tournament, what happened on that drizzly Durban night was too much to bear. Despite batting with a Duckworth/Lewis sheet in his pocket and consulting it, Mark Boucher blocked a delivery from Muttiah Muralitharan because he believed South Africa would win if the rain ended the match at that point. It duly did, but the figure Boucher read was, of course, what was required to tie. And that wasn't enough to stop the South Africans from being kicked out of their own tournament after the first round.

Would they take with them the rising tide of public interest in the event? No, because the still novel truth of being welcomed back into the world was more important. Besides, and maybe because they had been declared undesirable for 22 long years, South Africans typically wouldn't dream of not buying the best crockery there is to buy if they know they will be receiving illustrious visitors. It meant so much that the finest cricketers of the time had come to town, perhaps even more than finding out how their own players would fare against many of them.

Couple those factors with the lubricating lack of formality in how things get done in South Africa and it shouldn't be difficult to accept that, except for the issues mentioned above, more or less everything else went off without a significant hitch. The memories are mostly of an impressive seamlessness that proved Africa doesn't only make things tough. It also makes them terrific.

Much is made of the devotion to cricket of people in Asia, England and Australia, and so it should be. The passion for the game in those places is a key reason for its continued growth in everything from financial to cultural terms. Consequently, the BBC not offering ball-by-ball coverage of the first semi-final in 2003 earned Radio 4 more than 300 angry telephone calls, a number that would likely have been exponentially dwarfed had social media been as prominent a noticeboard for unhappiness then as it is now. That the match was played on a Tuesday, started at 9am (UK time) and involved not England but Australia and Sri Lanka was of little import in the complaints its absence from the BBC engendered.

Even so, South Africa's contribution to the cause of unconditional love for cricket is not inconsiderable. They don't have the sheer numbers to rival India's influence nor an economy big enough to dictate terms in the global arena. But that shouldn't lead anyone to doubt their quietly burning passion. "Cricket is not a game," JM Coetzee famously wrote. "It is the truth of life." For a writer known for crafting sparse, taut, clear prose, that's as close to gushing as it gets. Just as famously, Coetzee was born South African. That he became in 2006, and apparently of his own free will, Australian is something his erstwhile compatriots would rather not discuss. But, in Cape Town, they're still talking about the time he turned up at what Archie Henderson, a former sports editor of the *Cape Argus*, called "one of those Sunday social games, which was played with the intensity of a league match". The venue was Pinelands Cricket Club, on the fringes of Newlands forest, deep in leafy suburbia.

"There was this bloke with a beard that I bowled to," Henderson remembered. "Vaguely familiar. He was called John by his teammates, who mostly treated him with great deference: 'John, would you mind fielding at slip? No? OK, then where…?'

"I figured he must have been that bloke who wrote something about the Barbarians, whether it was the Goths or the rugby team didn't matter as long as he included Phil Bennett's try against the All Blacks.

"Anyway when they came into bat, he was soon at the crease and I bowled to him. The best I could say was that I made him play every ball. And the bloke could play!

"There were beers afterwards, but by that time John had disappeared. Not much of a socialiser, their captain said. Was he the writer? 'I think so,' said the captain."

Henderson should not feel aggrieved. John Maxwell Coetzee has been reclusive enough to not collect his Booker price, even when he became the first writer to win it twice. He did, however, deem bagging the Nobel prize – in 2003, no less – worthy of putting in an appearance.

***

That no previous ICC World Cup had involved as many as 14 teams – four of them ICC Associate Members – mattered little, as did the fact that of all the 15 grounds used for the tournament only the Wanderers could hold 30,000 people or more. The tournament had Bacher, who had perfected the art of proclaiming accomplishments even as the paint on them was still drying. It had millions of other South Africans – among them a small army of World Cup volunteers – who saw a patriotic duty in making sure the country presented itself properly to the world. And it shimmered with some of the most celebrated players ever to step over a boundary rope: Sachin Tendulkar, Ricky Pointing and Herschelle Gibbs; Glenn McGrath, Zaheer Khan and Muttiah Muralitharan.

Twenty-one centuries – two of more than 150 and 10 unbeaten – were struck on invariably willing pitches, which nevertheless yielded a dozen five-wicket hauls, all of them at comfortably less than a run a ball, and two each of six and seven wickets.

There were nine totals of more than 300, one of which climbed above 350, and three double century stands among the 25 of 100 or more.

Eight times victory was achieved by more than 100 runs, once by more than 250, and thrice by 10 wickets. There were also wins by two wickets, and three and six runs.

It was a good tournament for tail-enders. Heath Streak made an unbeaten 72 for Zimbabwe batting at No.8 against New Zealand, Australia got 64 out of their No.9, Andy Bichel, against New Zealand and Shoaib Akhtar threw his bat at England's bowlers to score 43 at No.11. They remain the record scores in an ICC World Cup for players batting in those positions.

Even so, bowlers had something to shout about in the shape of the facts that the collective tournament batting average, 25.7, was the third lowest in ICC World Cup history. That, and more ducks – 96 out of 902 innings – than ever before or since. But the batsmen claimed the second-highest conversation rate of 50s to 100s, a sturdy 19 per cent.

One team shone out, earning more mentions in dispatches than any other as the tournament wore on. They put up four of the biggest 10 totals, supplied half of the leading 10 run-scorers, and three of the leading 10 wicket-takers. They were Australia, and no eyebrows were raised when they cruised into the final unbeaten despite being deprived of Warne's services for the duration and without ace fast bowler Jason Gillespie, who took seven wickets in the first four matches before limping home with a heel injury.

That Australia were able to deal so easily in the final with India, beating clearly the event's second-best team by 125 runs at the Wanderers to become the first side in World Cup history to win a third trophy and all of the matches they played at a single tournament, surprised some. But there was no quibble that ODI cricket's most deserving team had duly won its biggest prize.

And that Tendulkar was the finest batsman in the game. Going into the 2019 ICC Cricket World Cup, the Indian master's 2003 aggregate of 673 remains the highest number of runs any player has piled up at a single edition of the event. He forged past 80 three times in making seven half-centuries (the only time a player has reached 50 more than five times in a World Cup) and scored a towering 152 studded with 18 fours against Namibia in Pietermaritzburg. But, more than those cold facts, Tendulkar's legion of devotees will remember the tournament for his performance in that blue riband of modern cricket clashes: India versus Pakistan. Always a match exponentially bigger than the sum of its constituent parts, the occasion, in Centurion, was lent an extra gilt edge by its global context. Tendulkar said later people had wanted to talk to him about the showdown since the fixtures were announced a year before the tournament, and admitted that he hadn't slept well for a dozen nights before it finally loomed.

Pakistan, powered by Saeed Anwar's 101, came to the party by posting a challenging 273 for 7. Would India be up for the fight against an attack that bristled with Wasim

Akram, Waqar Younis and Shoaib? Tendulkar answered the question in the second over of his team's reply. It was bowled by the fire-breathing Shoaib, who tore into his run like a man possessed. Which he was: by the desire to give of his best against his team's most valued opponents on the biggest stage of all. Three runs in wides, a single and two dot balls accrued before Tendulkar lashed at a short, wide delivery and sent it steepling emphatically over third man for six. It was a stroke of astounding audacity, a thing of wonder especially as it was the creation of a player who had built his career on nerveless, measured excellence. Tendulkar followed that with consecutive boundaries – through square leg and down the ground – to set India inexorably on the path to victory, which they clinched by six wickets with 26 balls to spare. To Shoaib went the glory of dismissing Tendulkar just two runs shy of a century. But there was no denying Tendulkar had won their duel.

That Australia were the team to beat and Tendulkar was a giant of the game were hardly in question when cricket's worldwide audience trained its attention on South Africa in 2003.

Not that the World Cup plodded along predictably in lockstep with the form book and received wisdom. The hosts' shock removal from the equation in the first round was one entry on a list of jarring eventualities that also saw England, Pakistan and West Indies go home early. On top of that, the latter teams' forfeiture of matches in Harare and Nairobi over security fears put Zimbabwe in the Super Sixes and made Kenya the only team from a non-Test playing country in the semi-finals.

The tournament grabbed eyeballs from its opening game, between the hosts and West Indies at Newlands. Shaun Pollock had had Wavell Hinds caught behind and bowled Chris Gayle when Brian Lara walked out to play his first match in earnest in five months due to illness. Not quite seven overs had been bowled and there were seven runs on the board. The eighth came from the first ball Lara faced – but from the edge of his bat and with the help of a dropped catch by Jacques Kallis diving at second slip after Makhaya Ntini had earned the chance. Lara grafted hard for his first 50, which took him 78 deliveries, and partied hard for the second, which flew off 43. Ntini did get his man, but in the 46th over after Lara had scored a shimmering 116 that, with worthy support from Shivnarine Chanderpaul and Carl Hooper and an unbroken stand of 63 between Ricardo Powell and Ramnaresh Sarwan, propelled the Windies to 278 for 5.

The South Africans, perhaps blinded by the glitz of the opening ceremony – or was it Lara's batting – barely looked in the game in their reply, and when Gary Kirsten's guardianship of the innings ended, caught and bowled by Merv Dillon for 69, they were 155 for five. Or 124 runs away from the target with fewer than 18 overs still at their disposal. Enter Lance Klusener to reprise his master-blasting role of four years previously with a blistering 57, 36 of them hammered in sixes. He was still there when Vasbert Drakes glided in to bowl the last over with nine required. But Drakes had the heaving Klusener caught on the boundary with his third delivery and Ntini taken at deep cover with his fifth, and it didn't matter that Nicky Boje hit the last for four: West Indies won by three runs.

In the second match of the tournament in Harare, Zimbabwe held it together well enough, despite the distraction of Flower's and Olonga's protest, to put up 340 for 2 after Namibia put them in to bat. Craig Wishart was in rasping form, reaching 30 before his opening partner, Mark Vermeulen, had scored a run. Wishart stood tall all the way to the end of the innings for his undefeated 172. With him in a partnership of 166 was Grant Flower, whose 78 was the product of 55 balls faced. Namibia had subsided to 104 for five when rain ended the match after 25.1 overs of their reply. Had the umpires waved on the groundstaff two balls earlier, the match would have ended inconclusively. Instead, Zimbabwe won by 86 runs on the Duckworth/Lewis method.

The third match day, in Bloemfontein, saw Sanath Jayasuriya score the first of his career total of three ICC World Cup centuries in his 17th innings in the tournament, his 120 and Hashan Tillakaratne's 81 – and their stand of 170 – the only efforts of more than 20 in Sri Lanka's 272 for seven. Jayasuriya might have been given out caught behind to Daryl Tuffey for 18 had umpire Neil Mallender spotted the edge, while Tillakaratne was overcome by cramp and called for a runner. Jacob Oram went wicketless in New Zealand's seven-man attack, but his economy rate of 3.70 was a valuable contribution. Despite a plasticine pitch that should have made the New Zealanders feel at home they more than matched their opponents for feckless batting. Scott Styris, last out for a stirring 141, and Chris Cairns, who made 32, were their only decent answers to the questions asked by the canny Sri Lankans, whose spinners bowled all but 15 of the 45.3 overs they needed to dismiss the Kiwis and win by 47 runs.

The Australian juggernaut shuddered into gear with 310 for 8 against Pakistan at the Wanderers, a total built on Andrew Symonds' 143 not out – a 125-ball assault that bristled with 18 fours and two sixes. And that from a player who had cracked the selectorial nod only because Ricky Ponting had a hunch he could do something special, and who had almost chucked in cricket for a career in rugby league, and on the same day that Warne announced his imminent return home in less than ideal circumstances. Less heralded was Brad Hogg and Ian Harvey sharing 70 and 54 in their stands with Symonds. Then Hogg and Harvey shared seven wickets as Pakistan were sent packing for 228.

Canada, eight of their XI born in different countries and playing in their first senior international since 1979, snatched a stunning upset win, by 60 runs, over Bangladesh at Kingsmead. The key performance was Austin Codrington, a Jamaica-born apprentice plumber and fast bowler, taking 5 for 27.

South Africa got their campaign back on the tracks with a 10-wicket thumping of Kenya in Potchefstroom, where Klusener took 4 for 16, and India overcame collapsing for 204 to Tim de Leede – who took 4 for 35 – and the lesser lights of the Netherlands attack to win by 68 runs in Paarl, where Javagal Srinath and Anil Kumble claimed four wickets each.

The hosts were soon on the skids again, losing to New Zealand by nine wickets in a rain-affected match at the Wanderers despite Herschelle Gibbs' 143 studding their 306 for six. Stephen Fleming's unbeaten 134 proving the decisive performance.

James Anderson's sniping bowling earned him 4 for 29 in a Pakistan total of 134 at Newlands that would have been far smaller without Shoaib's outrageous 43, which he smote off 16 balls and with just five of his runs not reaped in fours and sixes. England won by 112 runs.

Kenya, ably steered to 210 for nine by opener Kennedy Otieno's 60, delivered the first real shock of the tournament by dismissing Sri Lanka for 157 in Nairobi. Leg-spinner Collins Obuya took 5 for 24 but the real star was the home side's wonderful display in the field.

The Kenyans then travelled south to Johannesburg, where they beat Bangladesh by 32 runs to seal a place in the second round and become the only non-Test playing side to defeat more than one of the game's elite club. Maurice Odumbe owned the headlines, scoring 52 not out and taking 4 for 38 to send Bangladesh crashing to their 30th consecutive defeat in completed ODIs.

India brought Kenya back to earth in the second Super Sixes game at Newlands, beating them by six wickets with Sourav Ganguly making 107 not out. But the upstarts regrouped to down their only remaining fellow Africans, Zimbabwe, by seven wickets in Bloemfontein.

Then the bubble burst: Kenya were no match for India in their semi-final at Kingsmead, where Sourav Ganguly made an undefeated 111 and Zaheer Khan took 3 for 13 in the Indians' 91-run success.

In their semi at St George's Park, Australia put up a barely middling 212 for 7 with Andrew Symonds' 91 not out the key innings and Adam Gilchrist's decision to walk – caught behind, he said – despite being given not out by the umpire on the field sparking incredulity. But Sri Lanka failed to seize their chance to repeat their triumph over the same opponents in the 1996 ICC Cricket World Cup final and dwindled to 123 for 7 in pursuit of their revised target of 172.

And so to the Wanderers on 23 March for the final. A thunderstorm of Macbethian proportions the night before might have muddled Ganguly into choosing to bowl first, which was soon revealed to be a serious error. Gilchrist and Matthew Hayden racked up 105 for the first wicket before Ponting strode to the middle to play the most commanding innings yet seen in a match of this magnitude. The Australian captain was in complete control for all of the 121 balls he faced to score an undefeated 140. He and Damien Martyn shared 234 for the unbroken third wicket – the highest partnership in a World Cup knock-out match – and built Australia's total to 359 for 2, the first time in World Cup history any side had reached 350 with only two wickets down. That proved an ominous number for India. The 234, that is, which is what they were dismissed for as Australia sealed their triumph with ease. This time there was no brilliance from Tendulkar, who blooped a simple return catch to McGrath in the first over of India's reply.

"It's been an outstanding effort from the whole team," Ponting offered in the giddy afterglow of his team's win. "It says a lot about the team that we've known for a long time. But when a World Cup comes around you've got to play at your best when it counts, and we've managed to do that."

Years later reflection had burnished his memory: "It had taken me about 70 balls to get to 50 [74, in fact]. And because the game was so under control and we were scoring quickly, I wanted to make sure I was there at the end. The 12th man came out and I said, 'Tell the boys to strap the seatbelts on, I'm going to go flat-out from now and see what happens'. I got most of them in the middle from there on in." He did, scoring 86 runs off the 41 balls he faced in the last 10 overs of the innings and becoming the first player to hit eight sixes in a World Cup innings in a display of controlled aggression that has yet to be surpassed.

Time has also allowed Tendulkar's views on what happened that day to mature in the mind: "We were all charged up when we went out to field, and right from over one, it was that big moment and we were unbelievably charged up. [If the] same players were given the same opportunity, we would approach [that game] differently."

Tendulkar had a thoroughly modern argument behind his reasoning: "We would play differently only because of the introduction of T20. In those days [chasing] 359 looked a herculean task. It would be today as well but it will be closer than it was in 2003. We have also on a number of occasions got 325, 340 runs and that is because the format has changed and the rules have changed a little bit. The conditions have also changed [from] what we got there. I just feel the mindset has changed because of the introduction of T20 and the calculations are different."

Those who had worked long and hard on the 2003 ICC Cricket World Cup – from the administrators to the groundstaff to the press – weren't thinking thoughts like those as the sun went down on the Wanderers after the final, and not only because cricket was still a few years away from discovering the heady rush that would be given to the game by the shortest format.

But, on that late summer Sunday, it was scarcely believable that, after more than six weeks and 54 games, it was finally over and the circus would soon leave town. South Africa had not, as it had done when rugby and football had pitched their tents, risen to the challenge on the field. But there was no questioning that the country had won the even bigger battle. The world had come to South Africa, and South Africa had done its best to make the world at home. Now it was time to say goodbye to all that. There was also a big goodbye to be said to Bacher, whose career in cricket was done after more than 40 years of high-level involvement as a player and an administrator.

At the presentation ceremony on the field after the final the then ICC president, Malcolm Gray, took the podium amid the pandemonium to say: "Forty-three days ago we placed the spirit of cricket in the hands of southern Africa. I thank you, the people of this outstanding country and enchanting continent for upholding and enhancing that spirit. You have helped write a glorious chapter, not only in the history of our sport but also in the history of southern Africa.

"Special thanks go to the many thousands of volunteers who have enlightened the tournament with their vivid purple uniforms and their even brighter smiles. But cricket is all about the players, and today we saw the very best players in the world compete honourably for the ultimate prize in our noble sport. Many congratulations to Ricky Ponting and his team. Well done to Sourav Ganguly and his team. Thank you for entertaining us all so splendidly today and throughout the tournament. This ICC Cricket World Cup may end this evening but the spirit and enthusiasm of everyone involved will ensure that a positive legacy will be taken to the West Indies in 2007. The world has been watching, and southern Africa, you have delivered."

JM Coetzee could no doubt have written Gray's speech more eloquently and Nelson Mandela would have delivered it with more gravitas. But it was no less true all the same.

2003

RESULTS AND STATISTICS

POOL A TABLE

		P	W	T	L	NR	Adj	Pts	Net RR	Bow SR
1	Australia	6	6	0	0	0	0	24	2.045	24.263
2	India	6	5	0	1	0	0	20	1.108	31.646
3	Zimbabwe	6	3	0	2	1	0	14	0.504	41.481
4	England	6	3	0	3	0	0	12	0.821	30.756
5	Pakistan	6	2	0	3	1	0	10	0.227	30.425
6	Netherlands	6	1	0	5	0	0	4	-1.454	35.581
7	Namibia	6	0	0	6	0	0	0	-2.955	54.545

POOL B TABLE

		P	W	T	L	NR	Adj	Pts	Net RR	Bow SR
1	Sri Lanka	6	4	1	1	0	0	18	1.204	26.704
2	New Zealand	6	4	0	2	0	0	16	0.99	37
3	Kenya	6	4	0	2	0	0	16	-0.691	34.486
4	West Indies	6	3	0	2	1	0	14	1.103	32.159
5	South Africa	6	3	1	2	0	0	14	1.73	39
6	Canada	6	1	0	5	0	0	4	-1.989	31.758
7	Bangladesh	6	0	0	5	1	0	2	-2.046	44.655

SUPER SIX TABLE

		P	W	T	L	NR	Adj	Pts	Net RR	Bow SR
1	Australia	5	5	0	0	0	4	24	1.854	28.630
2	India	5	4	0	1	0	4	20	0.886	30.027
3	Kenya	5	3	0	2	0	2	14	0.354	34.828
4	Sri Lanka	5	2	0	3	0	3.5	11.5	-0.844	35.600
5	New Zealand	5	1	0	4	0	4	8	-0.896	44.000
6	Zimbabwe	5	0	0	5	0	3.5	3.5	-1.254	60.227

AUSTRALIA V SRI LANKA

ICC WORLD CUP 2002/03 (SEMI-FINAL)

Venue: St George's Park, Port Elizabeth
Date: 18th March 2003
Toss: Australia
Result: Australia won by 48 runs
Umpires: RE Koertzen, DR Shepherd
TV Umpire: BF Bowden
Referee: CH Lloyd
Man of the Match: A Symonds

AUSTRALIA		R	b	SRI LANKA		R	b
+AC Gilchrist	c Sangakkara b de Silva	22	20	MS Atapattu	b Lee	14	17
ML Hayden	c Tillakaratne b Vaas	20	38	*ST Jayasuriya	c Symonds b McGrath	17	24
*RT Ponting	c Jayasuriya b Vaas	2	8	HP Tillakaratne	c Gilchrist b Lee	3	15
DS Lehmann	b Jayasuriya	36	66	DA Gunawardene	c Ponting b Lee	1	4
A Symonds	not out	91	118	PA de Silva	run out (Bichel)	11	16
MG Bevan	c Sangakkara b Jayasuriya	0	1	+KC Sangakkara	not out	39	70
GB Hogg	st Sangakkara b de Silva	8	19	DPMD Jayawardene	c Gilchrist b Hogg	5	8
IJ Harvey	c Sangakkara b Vaas	7	10	RP Arnold	c Lee b Hogg	3	27
AJ Bichel	not out	19	21	WPUJC Vaas	not out	21	50
B Lee	did not bat			M Muralitharan	did not bat		
GD McGrath	did not bat			PW Gunaratne	did not bat		
Extras	(3 lb, 1 nb, 3 w)	7		Extras	(4 b, 1 lb, 2 nb, 2 w)	9	
Total	(7 wickets, 50 overs)	212		Total	(7 wickets, 38.1 overs)	123	

Fall of wickets: 1-34 (Gilchrist, 5.2 ov), 2-37 (Ponting, 6.5 ov), 3-51 (Hayden, 12.2 ov), 4-144 (Lehmann, 34.6 ov), 5-144 (Bevan, 36.1 ov), 6-158 (Hogg, 40.3 ov), 7-175 (Harvey, 43.5 ov)

Fall of wickets: 1-21 (Atapattu, 3.6 ov), 2-37 (Jayasuriya, 8.5 ov), 3-37 (Tillakaratne, 9.3 ov), 4-43 (Gunawardene, 11.2 ov), 5-51 (de Silva, 13.1 ov), 6-60 (Jayawardene, 16.1 ov), 7-76 (Arnold, 24.2 ov)

SRI LANKA	O	M	R	W	Wd	Nb	AUSTRALIA	O	M	R	W	Wd	Nb
Vaas	10	1	34	3	1	1	McGrath	7	1	20	1	-	-
Gunaratne	8	0	60	0	1	-	Lee	8	0	35	3	2	2
de Silva	10	0	36	2	1	-	Bichel	10	4	18	0	-	-
Muralitharan	10	0	29	0	-	-	Hogg	10	1	30	2	-	-
Jayasuriya	10	0	42	2	-	-	Harvey	2.1	0	11	0	-	-
Arnold	2	0	8	0	-	-	Lehmann	1	0	4	0	-	-

INDIA V KENYA

ICC WORLD CUP 2002/03 (SEMI-FINAL)

Venue: Kingsmead, Durban
Date: 20th March 2003
Toss: India
Result: India won by 91 runs
Umpires: SA Bucknor, DJ Harper
TV Umpire: SJA Taufel
Referee: MJ Procter
Man of the Match: SC Ganguly

INDIA		R	b	KENYA		R	b
V Sehwag	c Odumbe b Ongondo	33	56	+KO Otieno	c Dravid b Srinath	15	43
SR Tendulkar	c DO Obuya b Tikolo	83	101	RD Shah	lbw b Khan	1	17
*SC Ganguly	not out	111	114	PJ Ongondo	c Khan b Nehra	0	5
M Kaif	run out (CO Obuya)	15	20	TM Odoyo	c Sehwag b Nehra	7	15
Yuvraj Singh	c DO Obuya b Odoyo	16	10	*SO Tikolo	b Tendulkar	56	83
+RS Dravid	not out	1	1	MO Odumbe	c Khan b Yuvraj Singh	19	16
D Mongia	did not bat			HS Modi	c Dravid b Khan	9	25
J Srinath	did not bat			DO Obuya	run out (Kaif->Harbhajan)	3	23
A Nehra	did not bat			CO Obuya	lbw b Tendulkar	29	42
Z Khan	did not bat			MA Suji	b Khan	1	8
Harbhajan Singh	did not bat			AY Karim	not out	0	1
Extras	(2 nb, 9 w)	11		Extras	(16 b, 8 lb, 15 w)	39	
Total	(4 wickets, 50 overs)	270		Total	(all out, 46.2 overs)	179	

Fall of wickets: 1-74 (Sehwag, 18.3 ov), 2-177 (Tendulkar, 37.5 ov), 3-233 (Kaif, 45.5 ov), 4-267 (Yuvraj Singh, 49.3 ov)

Fall of wickets: 1-20 (Shah, 8.2 ov), 2-21 (Ongondo, 10.1 ov), 3-30 (Otieno, 13.1 ov), 4-36 (Odoyo, 14.3 ov), 5-63 (Odumbe, 18.4 ov), 6-92 (Modi, 26.4 ov), 7-104 (DO Obuya, 33.1 ov), 8-161 (Tikolo, 43.4 ov), 9-179 (CO Obuya, 45.4 ov), 10-179 (Suji, 46.2 ov)

KENYA	O	M	R	W	Wd	Nb	INDIA	O	M	R	W	Wd	Nb
Suji	10	1	62	0	-	-	Khan	9.2	2	14	3	3	-
Odoyo	10	1	45	1	1	2	Srinath	7	1	11	1	1	-
Ongondo	10	1	38	1	-	-	Nehra	5	1	11	2	2	-
Karim	4	0	25	0	1	-	Harbhajan Singh	10	1	32	0	-	-
Tikolo	10	0	60	1	2	-	Yuvraj Singh	6	0	43	1	-	-
CO Obuya	6	0	40	0	1	-	Sehwag	3	1	16	0	1	-
							Tendulkar	6	0	28	2	3	-

Top left: Viv Richards batting against Pakistan in Karachi.

Top right: Graham Gooch sweeps to victory in the semi-final against India, when he made a brilliant 115 as England triumphed by 35 runs at the Wankhede in Bombay.

Bottom: Eden Gardens Calcutta hosts the final between England and Australia.

Top: Mike Gatting, purring along on 41, opts to reverse sweep Allan Border's first delivery in the final and is caught behind.

Bottom: Border, with Dean Jones and Geoff Marsh alongside, and man of the match David Boon behind, celebrate Australia's win.

Top: The eight captains pose in front of the Sydney Opera House, wearing coloured clothing in the World Cup for the first time.

Bottom: A wry grin from Ian Botham as Brian McMillan was left with the impossible task of scoring 22 from one ball in the semi-final.

Top: The return of South Africa to the fold saw the brilliance of Jonty Rhodes' fielding revealed to the world.

Middle: The scoreboard at the SCG after the controversial rain calculations had taken place and consigned South Africa to defeat.

Bottom: Imran, with Inzamam by his side, celebrates Pakistan's victory.

Top: Sachin Tendulkar, not for the first time, topped the scoring, with 523. Here he hits Shane Warne over the top during an 84-ball 90.

Bottom: Warne has Ian Bishop lbw with the West Indies needing five to win with four balls remaining in the semi-final.

Top: Sachin Tendulkar awaits the umpire's decision in the semi-final against Sri Lanka in Calcutta. Once he was given out stumped, India capitulated before crowd trouble meant they conceded the match.

Middle: Aravinda de Silva completes a brilliant, match-winning hundred in the final.
Bottom: Arjuna Ranatunga lifts the trophy in Lahore as Sri Lanka become the fifth different winner of the World Cup.

Top: A chastened captain and coach, Alec Stewart and David Lloyd, face the press afer England's early exit.

Bottom: Pakistan's Shoaib Akhtar was a constant menace during the tournament with his raw pace.

Top: All 11 Australian players celebrate as Adam Gilchrist runs out South Africa's Allan Donald to complete what is commonly considered to be the best ever World Cup game.

Bottom: Man of the match Shane Warne and sipper Steve Waugh, who had done so much to keep Australia in the competiton, with the trophy in the Lord's pavilion.

AUSTRALIA V INDIA
ICC WORLD CUP 2002/03 (FINAL)

Venue: New Wanderers Stadium, Johannesburg
Date: 23rd March 2003
Toss: India
Result: Australia won by 125 runs
Umpires: SA Bucknor, DR Shepherd
TV Umpire: RE Koertzen
Referee: RS Madugalle
Man of the Match: RT Ponting

AUSTRALIA		R	b	INDIA		R	b
+AC Gilchrist	c Sehwag b Harbhajan Singh	57	48	SR Tendulkar	c and b McGrath	4	5
ML Hayden	c Dravid b Harbhajan Singh	37	54	V Sehwag	run out (Lehmann)	82	81
*RT Ponting	not out	140	121	*SC Ganguly	c Lehmann b Lee	24	25
DR Martyn	not out	88	84	M Kaif	c Gilchrist b McGrath	0	3
DS Lehmann	did not bat			+RS Dravid	b Bichel	47	57
MG Bevan	did not bat			Yuvraj Singh	c Lee b Hogg	24	34
A Symonds	did not bat			D Mongia	c Martyn b Symonds	12	11
GB Hogg	did not bat			Harbhajan Singh	c McGrath b Symonds	7	8
AJ Bichel	did not bat			Z Khan	c Lehmann b McGrath	4	8
B Lee	did not bat			J Srinath	b Lee	1	4
GD McGrath	did not bat			A Nehra	not out	8	4
Extras	(2 b, 12 lb, 7 nb, 16 w)	37		Extras	(4 b, 4 lb, 4 nb, 9 w)	21	
Total	(2 wickets, 50 overs)	359		Total	(all out, 39.2 overs)	234	

Fall of wickets: 1-105 (Gilchrist, 13.6 ov), 2-125 (Hayden, 19.5 ov)

Fall of wickets: 1-4 (Tendulkar, 0.5 ov), 2-58 (Ganguly, 9.5 ov), 3-59 (Kaif, 10.3 ov), 4-147 (Sehwag, 23.5 ov), 5-187 (Dravid, 31.5 ov), 6-208 (Yuvraj Singh, 34.5 ov), 7-209 (Mongia, 35.2 ov), 8-223 (Harbhajan Singh, 37.1 ov), 9-226 (Srinath, 38.2 ov), 10-234 (Khan, 39.2 ov)

INDIA	O	M	R	W	Wd	Nb	AUSTRALIA	O	M	R	W	Wd	Nb
Khan	7	0	67	0	6	2	McGrath	8.2	0	52	3	-	-
Srinath	10	0	87	0	2	3	Lee	7	1	31	2	2	4
Nehra	10	0	57	0	3	-	Hogg	10	0	61	1	2	-
Harbhajan Singh	8	0	49	2	-	-	Lehmann	2	0	18	0	-	-
Sehwag	3	0	14	0	-	-	Bichel	10	0	57	1	4	-
Tendulkar	3	0	20	0	1	-	Symonds	2	0	7	2	1	-
Mongia	7	0	39	0	-	2							
Yuvraj Singh	2	0	12	0	-	-							

MOST RUNS

Player	Mat	Inns	NO	Runs	HS	Ave	BF	SR	100	50	0	4s	6s
SR Tendulkar (INDIA)	11	11	0	673	152	61.18	754	89.25	1	6	0	75	4
SC Ganguly (INDIA)	11	11	3	465	112*	58.12	565	82.3	3	0	1	30	15
RT Ponting (AUS)	11	10	2	415	140*	51.87	472	87.92	2	1	0	29	13
AC Gilchrist (AUS)	10	10	0	408	99	40.8	387	105.42	0	4	0	56	7
HH Gibbs (SA)	6	6	2	384	143	96	381	100.78	1	2	0	52	10
MS Atapattu (SL)	10	10	3	382	124	54.57	452	84.51	2	1	1	50	0
A Flower (ZIM)	8	7	0	332	71	47.42	459	72.33	0	3	0	30	1
ML Hayden (AUS)	11	11	1	328	88	32.8	410	80	0	1	0	37	5
A Symonds (AUS)	9	5	3	326	143*	163	360	90.55	1	2	1	32	6
DR Martyn (AUS)	10	8	3	323	88*	64.6	395	81.77	0	4	2	21	1
SP Fleming (NZ)	8	8	1	321	134*	45.85	374	85.82	1	0	0	51	2
ST Jayasuriya (SL)	10	10	2	321	120	40.12	420	76.42	1	2	0	30	2
R Dravid (INDIA)	11	10	5	318	62	63.6	496	64.11	0	2	0	21	1
V Sehwag (INDIA)	11	11	0	299	82	27.18	345	86.66	0	2	0	37	7
CB Wishart (ZIM)	8	7	1	293	172*	48.83	343	85.42	1	0	0	33	3
SB Styris (NZ)	8	7	2	268	141	53.6	263	101.9	1	1	0	12	9
PA de Silva (SL)	10	8	0	267	92	33.37	299	89.29	0	2	1	27	7
RD Shah (KENYA)	9	9	0	265	61	29.44	438	60.5	0	2	1	34	0
BC Lara (WI)	6	6	0	248	116	41.33	306	81.04	1	1	0	25	7
Yuvraj Singh (INDIA)	11	10	3	240	58*	34.28	281	85.4	0	2	1	23	2
JM Davison (CAN)	6	6	0	226	111	37.66	190	118.94	1	1	1	21	12
DS Lehmann (AUS)	10	8	3	224	56*	44.8	272	82.35	0	2	0	20	3
CL Cairns (NZ)	8	7	1	223	54	37.16	273	81.68	0	1	0	15	6
Saeed Anwar (PAK)	5	5	1	218	101	54.5	303	71.94	1	0	0	19	1
NJ Astle (NZ)	7	7	2	213	102*	42.6	266	80.07	1	1	3	23	0

MOST WICKETS

Player	Mat	Inns	Overs	Mdns	Runs	Wkts	BBI	Ave	Econ	SR	4	5
WPUJC Vaas (SL)	10	10	88	14	331	23	6/25	14.39	3.76	22.9	1	1
B Lee (AUS)	10	10	83.1	9	394	22	5/42	17.9	4.73	22.6	0	1
GD McGrath (AUS)	11	11	87	18	310	21	7/15	14.76	3.56	24.8	0	1
Z Khan (INDIA)	11	11	88.2	5	374	18	4/42	20.77	4.23	29.4	1	0
SE Bond (NZ)	8	8	78	12	305	17	6/23	17.94	3.91	27.5	0	1
M Muralitharan (SL)	10	10	87.4	7	319	17	4/28	18.76	3.63	30.9	1	0
AJ Bichel (AUS)	8	8	57	7	197	16	7/20	12.31	3.45	21.3	0	1
VC Drakes (WI)	6	6	51.5	7	208	16	5/33	13	4.01	19.4	0	2
J Srinath (INDIA)	11	11	91.1	4	369	16	4/30	23.06	4.04	34.1	2	0
A Nehra (INDIA)	9	9	69.1	9	289	15	6/23	19.26	4.17	27.6	1	1
JDP Oram (NZ)	8	8	70	8	295	14	4/52	21.07	4.21	30	1	0
GB Hogg (AUS)	10	9	75.4	4	322	13	3/46	24.76	4.25	34.9	0	0
CO Obuya (KENYA)	9	9	77.5	4	374	13	5/24	28.76	4.8	35.9	0	1
Wasim Akram (PAK)	6	5	47.3	4	201	12	5/28	16.75	4.23	23.7	0	1
Shoaib Akhtar (PAK)	6	5	44	2	252	11	4/46	22.9	5.72	24	1	0
TBM de Leede (NL)	6	6	45.5	0	253	11	4/35	23	5.52	25	1	0
Harbhajan Singh (IND)	10	9	85.2	5	335	11	2/28	30.45	3.92	46.5	0	0
M Ntini (SA)	6	6	52.1	6	176	10	4/24	17.6	3.37	31.3	1	0
JM Davison (CAN)	6	6	42	5	187	10	3/15	18.7	4.45	25.2	0	0
JM Anderson (ENG)	5	5	47	3	225	10	4/25	22.5	4.78	28.2	2	0
ST Jayasuriya (SL)	10	8	64	1	315	10	3/30	31.5	4.92	38.4	0	0
AR Adams (NZ)	7	7	57.4	3	347	10	4/44	34.7	6.01	34.6	1	0
SO Tikolo (KENYA)	9	6	36.3	1	153	9	3/14	17	4.19	24.3	0	0
C White (ENG)	5	5	45	5	179	9	3/33	19.88	3.97	30	0	0
TM Odoyo (KENYA)	7	7	54	3	219	9	4/28	24.33	4.05	36	1	0

HIGH SCORES

Player	Runs	Balls	4s	6s	SR	Team	Opposition	Ground
CB Wishart	172*	151	18	3	113.9	Zimbabwe	v Namibia	Harare
SR Tendulkar	152	151	18	0	100.66	India	v Namibia	Pietermaritzburg
A Symonds	143*	125	18	2	114.4	Australia	v Pakistan	Johannesburg
HH Gibbs	143	141	19	3	101.41	South Africa	v New Zealand	Johannesburg
SB Styris	141	125	3	6	112.8	New Zealand	v Sri Lanka	Bloemfontein
RT Ponting	140*	121	4	8	115.7	Australia	v India	Johannesburg
SP Fleming	134*	132	21	0	101.51	New Zealand	v South Africa	Johannesburg
KJJ van Noortwijk	134*	129	11	3	103.87	Netherlands	v Namibia	Bloemfontein
MS Atapattu	124	129	18	0	96.12	Sri Lanka	v South Africa	Durban
JF Kloppenburg	121	142	6	4	85.21	Netherlands	v Namibia	Bloemfontein

BEST BOWLING

Player	Overs	Mdns	Runs	Wkts	Econ	Team	Opposition	Ground
GD McGrath	7	4	15	7	2.14	Australia	v Namibia	Potchefstroom
AJ Bichel	10	0	20	7	2	Australia	v England	Port Elizabeth
A Nehra	10	2	23	6	2.3	India	v England	Durban
SE Bond	10	2	23	6	2.3	New Zealand	v Australia	Port Elizabeth
WPUJC Vaas	9.1	2	25	6	2.72	Sri Lanka	v Bangladesh	Pietermaritzburg
CO Obuya	10	0	24	5	2.4	Kenya	v Sri Lanka	Nairobi (Gym)
A Codrington	9	3	27	5	3	Canada	v Bangladesh	Durban
Wasim Akram	9	1	28	5	3.11	Pakistan	v Namibia	Kimberley
VC Drakes	10	2	33	5	3.3	West Indies	v Kenya	Kimberley
B Lee	9.1	2	42	5	4.58	Australia	v New Zealand	Port Elizabeth

2007

WORLD DOMINATION

BY BENJ MOOREHEAD

It was February 2007, and the mighty Australians had just exacted revenge upon the Poms with a clean sweep in the Ashes and were happily bulldozing their way through the one-day tri-series which followed. Nothing seemed more certain than a third consecutive triumph at the ICC Cricket World Cup due to begin in the Caribbean a month later. Then, without warning, they did something utterly un-Australian: they started losing cricket matches – four times in 10 days against England (including the two tri-series finals) and three times in less than a week against New Zealand in the Chappell-Hadlee Trophy. It was their worst losing streak in a decade and it knocked them off top spot in the ODI rankings for the first time since they were introduced in 2002. "I feel pretty demoralised really," said Australia's Mike Hussey.

Glenn McGrath had even become the subject of ridicule when England beat Australia in the first tri-series final at the MCG. The match fell on his 37th birthday and he suddenly looked creaky after spilling a crucial catch, fumbling a simple run-out chance and being carted around the enormous ground by Paul Collingwood.

As if sensing its moment, ill-fortune rained down on the Australians. Brett Lee, the fastest bowler in the world, was ruled out the World Cup after tearing ankle ligaments in practice. Matthew Hayden and Andrew Symonds, the two beasts of the Aussie line-up, were sweating over injuries. Adam Gilchrist was expected to miss some of the tournament to attend the birth of his child.

"The luck has deserted Australia along with the confidence and sureness of touch. It always does when a side starts to lose," wrote Simon Barnes in *The Times*. After well over a decade of virtually unchallenged dominance, were the Aussies finally flaking? Had they become too old, too arrogant and – dare we say it – soft?

No chance. Not yet anyway. Australia's victory in the 2007 World Cup was the most crushing of them all. Played 11, won 11. And all of them won handsomely. South Africa briefly went toe to toe with the Aussies in the group stage, and Sri Lanka had a faint sniff when chasing in the final, but that was it. No one else came anywhere close. Australia thus extended their unbeaten record in the World Cup to 29 matches.

On practically every statistical measure, Australia came out on top. Six batsmen averaged 60 or more and four scored more than 400 runs. Their run-rate of 6.54 was vastly superior to anyone else's – South Africa were next with 5.58. The four main bowlers took 86 wickets between them, each at less than 21. The emergence of Shaun Tait more than made up for the loss of Lee. Nathan Bracken, the one-day specialist, was at his miserly best and nobody could pick Brad Hogg's left-arm wrong 'uns. McGrath? Twenty-six wickets at 13.73. Player of the tournament. Leading wicket-taker in World Cups.

"You can say that this was a team of legends," says Russel Arnold, a member of the Sri Lankan side who took on Australia in the final. "Even with the bowling, there was plenty of variety, there was speed, there was experience. There was no weak link, no one who you could really decide to target. The squad was so strong that there was great competition among themselves. Anyone could just walk in to the side, be cool, and show courage. And they were terriers in the field, all of them."

It didn't pay for opponents to look at the batting line-up. If you got past Hayden and Gilchrist, there was Ponting, Clarke, Symonds. And then Hussey, the No.1-ranked ODI batsman, who as it turned out was barely called upon because his mates up the order were just too darn good.

Ricky Ponting was at his brilliant hip-swivelling best and his 25-year-old understudy, Michael Clarke, came of age. But nothing came to symbolise Australia's irresistible force more than the hulking, gum-chewing figure of Matthew Hayden.

Hayden was merciless on a succession of flat Caribbean pitches, often advancing at fast bowlers and baseballing them through midwicket or straight down the ground. Clump. It all looked so simple. "Bowlers might target a particular area, a yorker on his foot or whatever it may be, but against Hayden it was no good because he just walks at you," says Arnold. "And, of course, he was a very fierce competitor. He had great balance too: that allowed him to express himself." Hayden made 659 runs in all, 384 of them crashed to the boundary.

He could do no wrong – even when he wasn't playing. On the day England were dumped out of the tournament, he went fishing off the coast of Grenada with Ponting and Gilchrist, presumably to celebrate another Pom bashing, and emerged triumphant after a 25-minute battle with an enormous fish. "We had about 80 people there to greet us when we got to the shore," Hayden said after posing for photos, a 300lb marlin in one hand and a bottle of Moët in the other. "It was magnificent. My arms are sore. I might get a massage this afternoon."

***

This was the first World Cup held in the West Indies. Much had changed in the Caribbean since Clive Lloyd's team had breathed life into the tournament in the 1970s, not least the fortunes of West Indian cricket. The infrastructure had undergone a $300m makeover which included four new stadiums in St Kitts, Guyana, St Lucia and Antigua. Sabina Park (Jamaica), Kensington Oval (Barbados) and Queen's Park Oval (Trinidad) had all been substantially renovated. And the pitches were a world away from the hard tracks on which the West Indies quicks had terrorised batsmen in the 1980s.

The format was slightly tweaked to accommodate a 16-team tournament, the most in a World Cup. The first two from each of the four groups qualified for the Super Eight, a round-robin stage from which the top four went through to the semi-finals. In all there were 51 matches spread across a shade over six weeks, making it the longest-ever World Cup.

There was much debate about the inclusion of six Associate nations – Bermuda, Canada, Ireland, Kenya, Netherlands and Scotland. Some saw it as a boost to the aspiring minnow nations, others thought it would compromise the standard of the competition. A glance at Bermuda's results does not make for pretty reading: defeats by 243 runs, 257 runs and seven wickets. But, improbably, it was a Bermudan who provided a moment that has gone down in World Cup folklore.

Dwayne Leverock. Twenty stone. His favourite dish was "spaghetti with hamburger mixed in". They called him Sluggo because of the way he biffed the bowling on the streets of his local neighbourhood. He was a 35-year-old policeman known to celebrate his wickets with a little jig. For obvious reasons, he fielded at slip.

India had been asked to bat first in Trinidad and were 3 without loss after the first over. Seventeen-year-old Malachi Jones came running in to deliver his first ball in a World Cup. You know what comes next. "The fridge has opened, he has flown like a gazelle!" chortled David Lloyd on commentary. And then, watching the full scale of Leverock's dive for glory in slow-motion: "The earth shook! Oh what a catch!" Maniacal Bermudan fielders were haring from all corners of the ground. Some of them pursued Leverock; in vain. Jones burst into tears, overcome with his achievement.

This was Bermuda's World Cup debut (they have not appeared since). With a population of 66,000, they are the smallest nation to have played in the tournament. For players like Jones, it was an extraordinary experience just to rub shoulders with the best players in the world. The match against India was almost too much for all-rounder Lionel Cann. "He loves India," said captain Irvine Romaine when asked about Cann ahead of the match. "He has named his child India. His favourite player is actually Tendulkar. Right now I'm hoping Tendulkar does not hit a catch to him because he will probably drop it to watch him bat."

***

Ahead of the tournament, Jonathan Agnew was asked for his predictions: "The team I think should do well is India. They've got great attacking batsmen at the top of the order, controlling batsmen in the middle and then lunatics at the very end. It's a batting line-up to die for. And with the ball they've got every option covered… With everyone expecting the pitches to be slow, they should be a real factor."

Shahid Afridi was less equivocal about Pakistan's chances. "Our team will definitely win the World Cup," he said.

Yet five days into the tournament and Pakistan were out, while India's chances hung by a thread following a shock defeat to Bangladesh in their first group match.

This was a landmark tournament for Bangladesh. They had beaten Pakistan in the 1999 ICC Cricket World Cup and received ICC full-member status a year later but their first steps as a Test nation had been a baptism of fire. Now, under the sharp eye of Australian coach Dav Whatmore, who had coached Sri Lanka to World Cup success in 1996, and led by the veteran Habibul Bashar, there emerged a crop of fearless teenagers who would form the backbone of the side that would become genuine contenders over the next decade. Tamim Iqbal was a 17-year-old batting prodigy, while future captains Shakib al Hasan and Mushfiqur Rahim were both 19. Then there was the enigmatic Mohammad Ashraful, 22, who probably had the most beautiful cover-drive in the world but never scored the runs his talent demanded.

But it was Bangladesh's clutch of left-arm spinners – along with the hostile Mashrafe Mortaza – who were the architects of India's demise at Queen's Park Oval. Virender Sehwag, Sachin Tendulkar – who made just 64 runs in the tournament – Rahul Dravid and MS Dhoni mustered 23 between them, and it took a three-hour 66 from Sourav Ganguly to steer India towards a barely competitive total, all out for 191 in the final over of the innings. Tamim then launched the sort of outrageous assault that became his trademark, charging the Indian seamers and trusting his eye for a brisk 51, before Mushfiqur and Shakib put on a nerveless 84 to set up a famous victory with nine balls to spare. Back home in Bangladesh an interim military government had placed a ban on public gatherings but thousands of locals chose to ignore it and filled the streets of Dhaka. Victory against South Africa later in the tournament was confirmation that Bangladesh had finally arrived in international cricket.

For India, everything came down to the final group game against the Sri Lankans but the much-vaunted batting failed again, with their old nemesis Muttiah Muralitharan taking 3 for 41 in a 69-run win. In less than a year India would win the first-ever World T20, a prelude to their 2011 World Cup triumph on home soil. But first they would have to pick themselves up off the floor.

Pakistan's exit arrived in even more dramatic circumstances. They had lost the curtain-raiser to hosts West Indies, who went on to top the group. But victory against Ireland and Zimbabwe would ensure qualification for the Super Eight stage.

This was Ireland's first World Cup but they were not a team to be underestimated, containing a number of players who would become seasoned county pros, such as Will Porterfield, Boyd Rankin and the feisty O'Brien brothers, Kevin and Niall. Also among them was an unorthodox left-hander on Middlesex's books: Eoin Morgan, then only 20.

Their leader was the experienced Trent Johnston, a Sydney-born all-rounder whose first-class career had stalled at New South Wales after he slipped off the team bus and broke his arm. Johnston found a new lease of life in Dublin, where he played as an overseas pro and eventually became a citizen by dint of marriage. Described by his wife as "a big foot-stamper with no co-ordination and all elbows", Johnston's chicken-dance celebrations became one of the images of the World Cup.

A pulsating tie against Zimbabwe in their first match might have been regarded as a missed opportunity, but then came the miracle in Jamaica. Pakistan were inserted on a pitch "as green as Larry's leprechaun suit", according to one correspondent, and subsided to Ireland's battery of medium-pacers, all out for 132. The Irish made heavy weather of the chase, and things were looking shaky at 113 for 7, with Niall O'Brien back in the hutch after a brilliant 72. But the eighth-wicket pair eked out the remaining 20 runs to the delight of some 2,500 Irish fans calling themselves the Blarney Army. To cap it all, it was St Patrick's Day.

Johnston had sealed the victory with a six. "Apart from my two kids being born, [it was] the greatest day of my life," he reflected some years later. "To change the fortune of a sport in a country where it's very much a minority sport and put it on the front pages and on every radio station and media outlet around the world that Ireland had beaten Pakistan... It was a very special moment."

Teammate John Mooney, who played in three World Cups, has described the match as "the biggest game of cricket Ireland has ever played... Even though we've beaten England since then, it would never have happened without beating Pakistan."

It should have been a time to revel in the glory of the underdog. Yet within hours of Ireland's victory Bob Woolmer, the 58-year-old coach of Pakistan, was found dead in his hotel room. Initial reports indicated that Woolmer had suffered a heart attack but within days the Jamaican police opened a murder investigation. The Pakistan players were interviewed by the police, and for many days a feverish mood of suspicion and conspiracy hung over the World Cup. It wasn't until three months later that the enquiry concluded that Woolmer had died from natural causes (though a subsequent coroner's inquest declared an "open verdict").

Pakistan's final group match, against Zimbabwe at Kingston, was played out to a ghostly air. Imran Nazir hit 160 – then the eighth-highest score in a World Cup but also one of the least significant innings in the competition's history. Inzamam-ul-Haq wept as he walked through a guard of honour after making 37 in his final innings for Pakistan.

***

Events in the other two groups went to script, producing the four expected qualifiers: New Zealand, England, Australia and South Africa. These last two had been pooled in the same group, and there was much anticipation about their meeting in St Kitts. Both sides were already assured of their places in the Super Eight stage, but there were plenty of psychological points at stake.

Their rivalry had grown fierce in recent years. South Africa had just usurped Australia as the No.1-ranked ODI team and only they, it seemed, had the ability to go toe to toe with the Aussies. The uncompromising captain Graeme Smith headed a nucleus of steely seniors which included Jacques Kallis, Ashwell Prince, Mark Boucher and Shaun Pollock. Smith's opening partner was one of the game's hottest talents, AB de Villiers, then only 23, and lurking in the middle-order was the alpha male Herschelle Gibbs, who had become only the third batsman in the game's history to hit six sixes in an over when he carted Netherlands leg-spinner Daan van Bunge to all corners in South Africa's first group game at St Kitts.

Almost exactly a year earlier Gibbs had shaken off a hangover to smash the Australians for a match-winning 175 off 111 balls in the famous "438 game" at Johannesburg, when the record for the highest ODI total was twice broken. Here was evidence that South Africa could beat Australia at their own game. It was aggressive, full-throttle cricket, each seeking to outdo the other, no quarter given, pride verging on vanity.

For a time at St Kitts it seemed we were on for a repeat. Australia batted first and there were a brace of sparkling 90s from Ponting and Clarke but Hayden was the driving force behind a formidable total of 377 for 6 in more than ways than one. His 66-ball hundred was then the fastest-ever in a World Cup. Shaun Pollock, one of the most respected seamers of his generation, was treated like a punch bag, returning the worst figures of his ODI career: 10-0-83-0.

Naturally South Africa came out swinging. Smith, belligerent as ever, and de Villiers, altogether more stylish, cruised to 160 in the 21st over with such ease that it seemed only divine intervention could prevent them from charging to victory… The last ball of the 20th over was flicked to the left of long leg, from where Shane Watson sent in a bullet throw which crashed into the stumps before de Villiers could complete a second run. The match was turned, Australia going on to win by 83 runs. It was an emphatic statement to any pretenders to their World Cup crown: if our bowlers don't get you, our fielders will.

***

But Australia and South Africa were not the only riders in town as the tournament moved into the Super Eight stage.

New Zealand, led by the unflappable Stephen Fleming, were determined to make their traditional strength in one-day cricket count on the big stage. Their lumping all-rounder Jacob Oram had raised the stakes ahead of the tournament when asked about his recovery from a broken finger: "If it means cutting the finger off, if that's the worst-case scenario, if that's the last resort, I'll do that. There's no way I'm missing this." The squad was blessed with talented all-rounders and contained some outstanding individuals right through the side, from the elegant Fleming at the top of the order down to Daniel Vettori, the canniest spinner around, and the world's most in-form pace bowler, Shane Bond. Filling in between were a pair of ferocious young hitters: Brendon McCullum and Ross Taylor.

New Zealand's breezy win against England in their group match was the first of six straight victories – none of them by fewer than six wickets or 114 runs – completed when Ireland were dispatched in Guyana three weeks later. Another comfortable win against South Africa in Grenada assured them of a place in the last four. Scott Styris was in the form of his life and would go on to score 499 runs in the tournament, then a New Zealand record, as well as contributing nine wickets at less than 27. No one could lay a bat on Bond. By the end of the Super Eight stage he had tournament figures of 59.4-8-154-12.

Like everyone else, they were pummelled by Australia and by Matthew Hayden, who clobbered his third hundred of the tournament to help inflict a 215-defeat on New Zealand, still their biggest loss in a one-day international. Bond and Oram had both been missing and there was nothing riding on the match, but it knocked the stuffing out of the Kiwis on the eve of their semi-final against Sri Lanka, the only other team to have beaten them.

The tournament fell at just the right time for the Sri Lankans. Sanath Jayasuriya, Chaminda Vaas and Muttiah Muralitharan were still going strong, while the classical masters Mahela Jayawardene and Kumar Sangakkara were just coming into their prime. "It was an exciting group to be part of," says Russel Arnold. "We had been together for a while so the understanding was there, along with the trust that each player would perform his role. Some of our batsmen were probably not the most technically correct, but we had guys like Tillakaratne Dilshan who could tear a game apart. We relied on our flair and would do something outside the box to surprise the opposition and take them out of their comfort zone. We felt we could upset anyone."

No one produced unorthodox cricketers like Sri Lanka, from the whirlwind batting of Jayasuriya to the trickery of Murali. In 2007 they unleashed 23-year-old Lasith Malinga. He wore a blonde-streaked afro on his head and a ring on his eyebrow, and his bowling arm came slamming round from nowhere, like a slingshot. For batsmen, it wasn't so much about picking length as picking up the ball at all.

Malinga had made his international debut two years earlier. "When he started playing first-class cricket he just had the one length: short," says Arnold. "Soon after he had two lengths: the yorker and the bouncer. But it was around 2007 that he suddenly became the complete bowler. He was exceptional because he kept improving day by day, he would surprise everyone. He came to understand what a force he could be, and the importance of bringing variation and control to his bowling. People don't give him enough credit for the head on his shoulders."

The game was never over if Malinga had the ball in his hand, as South Africa discovered in their opening Super Eight match at Guyana when they needed four to win with five wickets in hand and plenty of time. Shaun Pollock and Andrew Hall were duped by successive slower balls at the end of Malinga's seventh over before Jacques Kallis chased a full one and was caught behind to complete the hat trick off the first ball of his eighth. The second produced a trademark dismissal, a vicious in-swinging toe-crusher which knocked back Makhaya Ntini's middle stump to send Malinga aeroplaning into the covers. No bowler had ever taken four wickets in four balls in one-day cricket. South Africa's last pair wriggled to victory, but the Slinga had arrived.

Sri Lanka bounced back quickly from that narrow defeat, easing past West Indies in Guyana, and qualified for the semi-finals with two games to spare, thanks in large part to the runs of Jayasuriya and Jayawardene. Murali was warming to the task.

It was no surprise that England and hosts West Indies did not make the knockout stage. Lara's team had won all three of their group matches but they could not swim with the big boys, their only victory in the Super Eight phase coming against Bangladesh. The bowling was a shadow of what it once was and, despite the impudence of a young Chris Gayle and the old pro Shivnarine Chanderpaul, the batsmen could not make up the deficit. Lara was struggling for form and often cut a distracted figure. He appeared to forget to use a Powerplay against South Africa, leaving West Indies at the mercy of Gibbs and Boucher at the end of the innings. In truth the match had already been wrestled from them by de Villiers' 146 from 130 balls, the first of 25 ODI hundreds he would score over the next decade.

England had been buoyed by their shock victory in the tri-series Down Under, but this was a team still reeling from the winter's Ashes whitewash. The Vaughan–Fletcher axis was on its last legs and an early exit seemed inevitable once the Fredalo affair – you remember the one, Flintoff and the pedalo – provided the English press with front-page headlines early in the tournament. Yet England came within a whisker of beating Sri Lanka in Antigua, Ravi Bopara bowled off the final ball for a heroic but futile 51 as England went down by two runs, and hard-earned victories against Bangladesh and Ireland took them into their penultimate match against South Africa in Barbados with all to play for. Their hopes were dashed by medium-pacer Andrew Hall, whose five-wicket haul triggered a collapse of 7 for 43 as England were rolled out for 154 in 48 excruciating overs. South Africa needed less than 20 to knock off the runs.

England and West Indies met in the last game of the Super Eight stage, a match which carried no significance save for one matter: this was to be Brian Lara's last appearance in a maroon shirt. With ticket prices lowered and locals flooding in, the

Kensington Oval took on the carnival atmosphere that had been missing for much of the tournament. The match was a humdinger, lit up by the explosive batting of Chris Gayle and Kevin Pietersen and going right down to the wire, England's last-wicket pair sealing victory off the penultimate ball. The great disappointment for West Indians was not so much the result as the low-key exit of Lara, run out by his partner for 18.

***

After 48 matches in 40 days, we had arrived at the semi-finals with four teams who were clearly a cut above the rest: Sri Lanka, New Zealand, Australia, South Africa.

A hundred of classical beauty by Mahela Jayawardene set his side on course for an 81-run victory over the Kiwis in the first semi-final in Jamaica, where a slow track played into the hands of the Sri Lankans. Bond had a rare off day, conceding 59 runs from his 10 overs and dropping Jayawardene on the square-leg boundary when he was just starting to purr. New Zealand's hopes of chasing 290 were alive while Styris was in flow, but his dismissal for 37 exposed the middle-order to the wiles of Murali (4 for 31).

Attention turned to the showdown between Australia and South Africa at St Lucia, which promised to be another slugfest with plenty of edge. Ponting raised the ante in the build-up by questioning the ability of Jacques Kallis to keep up with the tempo of his teammates: "We all know that if we bowl a certain way and put him under pressure, we can keep him reasonably quiet." Kallis had been criticised for his 63-ball 48 during South Africa's defeat by the Australians earlier in the tournament.

Whether the goading of Kallis had any effect is open to question. But the reckless manner in which South African batsmen threw away their wickets spoke of a team which had revved up its engine to the point of meltdown. The match was effectively over inside the first 10 overs, by which stage Australia had their opponents 27 for 5. Smith was bowled advancing down the track, Kallis lost his off stump trying to make room to hit through the covers, de Villiers was caught behind driving wildly at a full ball, and Prince was caught slashing at a wide one. Only Boucher, prodding at a beauty from McGrath for a first-ball duck, was blameless. Justin Kemp dragged South Africa to a painstaking 149 all out before Australia, in no hurry, cruised to the target in the 32nd over.

South Africa had come up short again when it mattered, prompting their cricket board to launch an official review into the mental strength of its cricketers. De Villiers admitted in his autobiography that the occasion got the better of them: "We wanted so badly to overcome South Africa's historic World Cup jinx that we departed from our carefully developed plans and went for the Australians too hard and too soon. We needed to stay calm and play our normal game."

So it would be a repeat of the 1996 final: Australia against Sri Lanka, the unbreakable Antipodeans against the mystical South Asians. "It was always going to be a very difficult task to take on Australia," says Arnold. "But we were quietly confident. Beating them in a five-match series would have probably been a step too far, but to win one game that mattered, to catch them on the wrong foot, to pull off something special, to surprise them – we thought we had that in us."

There was little to glean from their earlier clash, when Sri Lanka had already qualified and chose to rest Murali, Vaas and Malinga. Arnold played as the main spinner in that game and hasn't forgotten that he dismissed both openers before the Australians cantered to victory: "I still joke with Murali that if he'd listened to me about how to bowl to Hayden and Gilchrist then we would have won the World Cup."

***

The blistering form of his opening partner had masked what, until now, had been a modest World Cup for Adam Gilchrist, then in the twilight of a glorious career. His two fifties had come against lesser opposition and he had been dismissed for one in his previous two innings. "For the majority of that World Cup I was pining to be at home with my family," wrote Gilchrist in his autobiography. "My new-born Archie – I'd barely seen him. On so many lonely nights in the West Indies I'd been thinking, 'Gee, I don't need this any more.'" But here he was on a true pitch in Barbados for the World Cup final; he might as well have a go.

"Ahead of that match, we felt all we needed was a 'normal' game," says Arnold. "But the rain came in so we started a bit late. And Gilchrist had decided he was going to slog everything in the final.

"We got caught in something extra special, an innings that you would rarely see. The ball was flying to all parts of the ground. Gilchrist was in a different frame of mind. He felt he had nothing to lose in that innings. The pressure of the World Cup final, getting out – all that was gone. When that sort of thing happens and it comes off, I don't think you can do that much. It's just meant to be."

Hayden was reduced to a mere sidekick, contributing 38 to an opening partnership of 172 in 23 overs. Gilchrist brought up his 72-ball hundred, the fastest in a World Cup final, with another belting drive over long on. Almost half of his runs that day were scored "in the V", including five of his eight sixes. This was unusual for a batsman famed for his rasping shots square on the off-side. The answer lay in the palm of his hand – to be precise, the bottom hand, which he held up to the dressing room for all to see after reaching his century. There was a mysterious bulge in the middle of the glove. Only later did we get the full story.

Of late Gilchrist had become worried about the dominance of his bottom hand, which made it difficult to drive straight when the ball was pitched up (only a fool would bowl short to him). To correct the fault, his batting coach Bob Meuleman suggested he wedge a squash ball into his bottom glove. Meuleman later recalled: "He had a few hits before he went off to the World Cup. He didn't have the squash ball in and he hit them like he couldn't even play fourth grade. He put it in and he then hit the ball so good." But Gilchrist grew frustrated at the lack of big scores in the Caribbean and even ditched the squash ball for the semi-final against South Africa. It was recalled for the final – with devastating results. Some questioned its legality, but it was hard not to admire the sort of ingenious innovation which would have made Bob Woolmer smile.

Australia's formidable total of 281 for 4 – in a match reduced by weather to 38 overs a side – was built almost entirely on Gilchrist's 104-ball 149, the highest score ever made in a World Cup final. Sri Lanka's famed trio of Vaas, Malinga and Murali were vaporised, their 23 overs haemorrhaging 147 runs. Surely there was no way back for Sri Lanka.

Yet the chase was still just about on nearly 20 overs into the reply, with Jayasuriya and Sangakkara adding 116 for the second wicket. For a fleeting moment, the Australians appeared vulnerable. But the dark clouds that were circling over the Kensington Oval were a bad omen for the Sri Lankans. Sangakkara pulled Hogg to midwicket before Jayasuriya, perhaps mindful of the Duckworth-Lewis equation, took a swipe at Michael Clarke and was bowled by a low-bouncing turner.

A break for rain revised the target to 269 off 36 overs but Sri Lanka's momentum was lost. Australia chipped away at the middle order and the task became impossible. At the end of the 33th over, with Sri Lanka needing 63 from 18 balls, the batsmen effectively raised the white flag by accepting an offer for bad light. But to everyone's surprise – not least the players' – umpires Aleem Dar and Rudi Koertzen insisted that the remaining three overs could be bowled on tomorrow's reserve day (a misjudgement since both innings had passed the minimum 20 overs to constitute a match). Seeing sense, the two captains agreed to complete the formalities in virtual darkness. When at last the deed was done, it was barely possible to glimpse the ecstatic Australians dancing in the middle.

***

The 2007 World Cup was the last major success of the great Australian era. Shane Warne and Justin Langer had retired after the 2006–07 Ashes and McGrath followed suit after the World Cup. Within two years Gilchrist and Hayden were gone too. Australia's aura went with them. Henceforth they would have to settle with jostling for position at the top of the international game.

Australia were not the only team in transition after the World Cup. In fact there was change wherever you looked; nearly every team who took part in the tournament had a new captain and coach within a year of its completion. There was also a sense of a changing of the guard – McGrath, Lara, Inzamam, Kumble, Ganguly, Fleming and Vaas all on their way out – and a glimpse of those who would shape the game's future, the likes of de Villiers, Pietersen, Gayle, Dilshan, Malinga, Morgan and McCullum. Virat Kohli made his India debut the following year.

Cricket itself was changing. In September 2007 the inaugural World Twenty20 took place in South Africa and the two-week tournament, won by India, was an instant hit. Then in 2008 the Indian Premier League was born.

RESULTS AND STATISTICS

POOL A TABLE

		P	W	T	L	NR	A	Pts	Net RR
1	Australia	3	3	0	0	0	0	6	3.433
2	South Africa	3	2	0	1	0	0	4	2.403
3	Netherlands	3	1	0	2	0	0	2	-2.527
4	Scotland	3	0	0	3	0	0	0	-3.793

POOL B TABLE

		P	W	T	L	NR	A	Pts	Net RR
1	Sri Lanka	3	3	0	0	0	0	6	3.493
2	Bangladesh	3	2	0	1	0	0	4	-1.523
3	India	3	1	0	2	0	0	2	1.206
4	Bermuda	3	0	0	3	0	0	0	-4.345

POOL C TABLE

		P	W	T	L	NR	A	Pts	Net RR
1	New Zealand	3	3	0	0	0	0	6	2.138
2	England	3	2	0	1	0	0	4	0.418
3	Kenya	3	1	0	2	0	0	2	-1.194
4	Canada	3	0	0	3	0	0	0	-1.389

POOL D TABLE

		P	W	T	L	NR	A	Pts	Net RR
1	West Indies	3	3	0	0	0	0	6	0.764
2	Ireland	3	1	1	1	0	0	3	-0.092
3	Pakistan	3	1	0	2	0	0	2	0.089
4	Zimbabwe	3	0	1	2	0	0	1	-0.886

SUPER EIGHT TABLE

		P	W	T	L	NR	A	Pts	Net RR
1	Australia	7	7	0	0	0	0	14	2.400
2	Sri Lanka	7	5	0	2	0	0	10	1.483
3	New Zealand	7	5	0	2	0	0	10	0.253
4	South Africa	7	4	0	3	0	0	8	0.313
5	England	7	3	0	4	0	0	6	-0.394
6	West Indies	7	2	0	5	0	0	4	-0.566
7	Bangladesh	7	1	0	6	0	0	2	-1.514
8	Ireland	7	1	0	6	0	0	2	-1.730

NEW ZEALAND V SRI LANKA

ICC WORLD CUP 2006/07 (SEMI-FINAL)

Venue: Sabina Park, Kingston
Date: 24th April 2007
Toss: Sri Lanka
Result: Sri Lanka won by 81 runs
Umpires: RE Koertzen, SJA Taufel
TV Umpire: DJ Harper (Australia)
Referee: MJ Procter (South Africa)
Reserve Umpire: Asad Rauf (Pakistan)
Man of the Match: DPMD Jayawardene

SRI LANKA		R	b	NEW ZEALAND		R	b
WU Tharanga	b Vettori	73	74	PG Fulton	c Silva b Jayasuriya	46	77
ST Jayasuriya	b Franklin	1	6	*SP Fleming	lbw b Malinga	1	4
+KC Sangakkara	c Fleming b Franklin	18	42	LRPL Taylor	lbw b Vaas	9	25
*DPMD Jayawardene	not out	115	109	SB Styris	c Jayawardene b Dilshan	37	38
LPC Silva	lbw b Bond	21	33	JDP Oram	c and b Muralitharan	3	7
TM Dilshan	lbw b Oram	30	27	+BB McCullum	c Silva b Muralitharan	0	1
RP Arnold	not out	14	14	CD McMillan	b Jayasuriya	25	20
WPUJC Vaas	did not bat			DL Vettori	lbw b Muralitharan	0	4
SL Malinga	did not bat			JEC Franklin	not out	30	38
M Muralitharan	did not bat			SE Bond	b Muralitharan	2	4
CRD Fernando	did not bat			JS Patel	c Fernando b Dilshan	34	38
Extras	(3 lb, 5 nb, 9 w)	17		Extras	(5 b, 2 lb, 6 nb, 8 w)	21	
Total	(5 wickets, 50 overs)	289		Total	(all out, 41.4 overs)	208	

Fall of wickets: 1-13 (Jayasuriya, 2.3 ov), 2-67 (Sangakkara, 13.1 ov), 3-111 (Tharanga, 25.1 ov), 4-152 (Silva, 34.3 ov), 5-233 (Dilshan, 45.1 ov)

Fall of wickets: 1-2 (Fleming, 1.3 ov), 2-32 (Taylor, 10.3 ov), 3-105 (Styris, 21.5 ov), 4-114 (Oram, 23.5 ov), 5-114 (McCullum, 23.6 ov), 6-115 (Fulton, 24.3 ov), 7-116 (Vettori, 25.4 ov), 8-144 (McMillan, 30.2 ov), 9-149 (Bond, 31.4 ov), 10-208 (Patel, 41.4 ov)

NEW ZEALAND	O	M	R	W	Wd	Nb	SRI LANKA	O	M	R	W	Wd	Nb
Franklin	9	1	46	2	2	2	Vaas	8	1	25	1	1	-
Bond	10	1	59	1	3	1	Malinga	7	2	21	1	-	1
Oram	10	0	60	1	1	2	Fernando	5	0	45	0	1	5
Vettori	10	0	51	1	1	-	Muralitharan	8	0	31	4	1	-
Patel	10	0	62	0	-	-	Jayasuriya	9	0	57	2	3	-
Styris	1	0	8	0	1	-	Dilshan	4.4	0	22	2	1	-

AUSTRALIA V SOUTH AFRICA

ICC WORLD CUP 2006/07 (SEMI-FINAL)

Venue: Beausejour Stadium, Gros Islet
Date: 25th April 2007
Toss: South Africa
Result: Australia won by 7 wickets
Umpires: Aleem Dar, SA Bucknor
TV Umpire: BF Bowden (New Zealand)
Referee: JJ Crowe (New Zealand)
Reserve Umpire: MR Benson (England)
Man of the Match: GD McGrath

SOUTH AFRICA		R	b	AUSTRALIA		R	b
*GC Smith	b Bracken	2	5	+AC Gilchrist	b Langeveldt	1	5
AB de Villiers	c Gilchrist b Tait	15	34	ML Hayden	c Smith b Pollock	41	60
JH Kallis	b McGrath	5	9	*RT Ponting	b Nel	22	25
HH Gibbs	c Gilchrist b Tait	39	49	MJ Clarke	not out	60	86
AG Prince	c Gilchrist b McGrath	0	2	A Symonds	not out	18	16
+MV Boucher	c Hayden b McGrath	0	1	MEK Hussey	did not bat		
JM Kemp	not out	49	91	SR Watson	did not bat		
AJ Hall	c Gilchrist b Tait	3	8	GB Hogg	did not bat		
SM Pollock	c and b Hogg	5	13	NW Bracken	did not bat		
A Nel	c Clarke b Tait	8	41	SW Tait	did not bat		
CK Langeveldt	b Watson	6	10	GD McGrath	did not bat		
Extras	(4 lb, 13 w)	17		Extras	(5 lb, 3 nb, 3 w)	11	
Total	(all out, 43.5 overs)	149		Total	(3 wickets, 31.3 overs)	153	

Fall of wickets: 1-7 (Smith, 2.3 ov), 2-12 (Kallis, 5.3 ov), 3-26 (de Villiers, 8.5 ov), 4-27 (Prince, 9.4 ov), 5-27 (Boucher, 9.5 ov), 6-87 (Gibbs, 22.5 ov), 7-93 (Hall, 26.1 ov), 8-103 (Pollock, 29.4 ov), 9-130 (Nel, 40.1 ov), 10-149 (Langeveldt, 43.5 ov)

Fall of wickets: 1-1 (Gilchrist, 1.1 ov), 2-44 (Ponting, 8.6 ov), 3-110 (Hayden, 24.4 ov)

AUSTRALIA	O	M	R	W	Wd	Nb	SOUTH AFRICA	O	M	R	W	Wd	Nb
Bracken	7	2	15	1	-	-	Pollock	5	1	16	1	-	-
McGrath	8	1	18	3	1	-	Langeveldt	6	0	34	1	1	1
Tait	10	0	39	4	5	-	Kallis	5	1	20	0	1	1
Watson	8.5	0	49	1	-	-	Nel	7	1	31	1	1	-
Hogg	10	2	24	1	3	-	Hall	6.3	0	43	0	-	1
							Kemp	2	0	4	0	-	-

AUSTRALIA V SRI LANKA

ICC WORLD CUP 2006/07 (FINAL)

Venue: Kensington Oval, Bridgetown
Date: 28th April 2007
Toss: Australia
Result: Australia won by 53 runs
Umpires: Aleem Dar, SA Bucknor
TV Umpire: RE Koertzen (South Africa)
Referee: JJ Crowe (New Zealand)
Reserve Umpire: BF Bowden (New Zealand)
Man of the Match: AC Gilchrist

AUSTRALIA		R	b	SRI LANKA		R	b
+AC Gilchrist	c Silva b Fernando	149	104	WU Tharanga	c Gilchrist b Bracken	6	8
ML Hayden	c Jayawardene b Malinga	38	55	ST Jayasuriya	b Clarke	63	67
*RT Ponting	run out (Jayawardene)	37	42	+KC Sangakkara	c Ponting b Hogg	54	52
A Symonds	not out	23	21	*DPMD Jayawardene	lbw b Watson	19	19
SR Watson	b Malinga	3	3	LPC Silva	b Clarke	21	22
MJ Clarke	not out	8	6	TM Dilshan	run out (Clarke->McGrath)	14	13
MEK Hussey	did not bat			RP Arnold	c Gilchrist b McGrath	1	2
GB Hogg	did not bat			WPUJC Vaas	not out	11	21
NW Bracken	did not bat			SL Malinga	st Gilchrist b Symonds	10	6
SW Tait	did not bat			CRD Fernando	not out	1	6
GD McGrath	did not bat			M Muralitharan	did not bat		
Extras	(4 lb, 3 nb, 16 w)	23		Extras	(1 lb, 14 w)	15	
Total	(4 wickets, 38 overs)	281		Total	(8 wickets, 36 overs)	215	

Fall of wickets: 1-172 (Hayden, 22.5 ov), 2-224 (Gilchrist, 30.3 ov), 3-261 (Ponting, 35.4 ov), 4-266 (Watson, 36.2 ov)

Fall of wickets: 1-7 (Tharanga, 2.1 ov), 2-123 (Sangakkara, 19.5 ov), 3-145 (Jayasuriya, 22.6 ov), 4-156 (Jayawardene, 25.5 ov), 5-188 (Dilshan, 29.6 ov), 6-190 (Silva, 30.1 ov), 7-194 (Arnold, 31.5 ov), 8-211 (Malinga, 33.6 ov)

SRI LANKA	O	M	R	W	Wd	Nb	AUSTRALIA	O	M	R	W	Wd	Nb
Vaas	8	0	54	0	1	2	Bracken	6	1	34	1	1	-
Malinga	8	1	49	2	-	-	Tait	6	0	42	0	2	-
Fernando	8	0	74	1	4	1	McGrath	7	0	31	1	1	-
Muralitharan	7	0	44	0	2	-	Watson	7	0	49	1	3	-
Dilshan	2	0	23	0	1	-	Hogg	3	0	19	1	-	-
Jayasuriya	5	0	33	0	-	-	Clarke	5	0	33	2	2	-
							Symonds	2	0	6	1	-	-

MOST RUNS

Player	Mat	Inns	NO	Runs	HS	Ave	BF	SR	100	50	0	4s	6s
ML Hayden (AUS)	11	10	1	659	158	73.22	652	101.07	3	1	0	69	18
DPMD Jayawardene (SL)	11	11	2	548	115*	60.88	644	85.09	1	4	0	40	10
RT Ponting (AUS)	11	9	1	539	113	67.37	565	95.39	1	4	0	53	11
SB Styris (NZ)	10	9	3	499	111*	83.16	598	83.44	1	4	0	45	6
JH Kallis (SA)	10	9	3	485	128*	80.83	578	83.91	1	3	0	43	7
ST Jayasuriya (SL)	11	11	1	467	115	46.7	475	98.31	2	2	0	47	14
AC Gilchrist (AUS)	11	11	1	453	149	45.3	436	103.89	1	2	0	58	10
KP Pietersen (ENG)	9	9	1	444	104	55.5	548	81.02	2	3	0	36	5
GC Smith (SA)	10	10	1	443	91	49.22	424	104.48	0	5	0	55	6
MJ Clarke (AUS)	11	9	4	436	93*	87.2	459	94.98	0	4	0	40	7
RR Sarwan (WI)	9	9	1	375	92	46.87	481	77.96	0	2	0	32	5
AB de Villiers (SA)	10	10	0	372	146	37.2	369	100.81	1	2	4	47	9
SP Fleming (NZ)	10	10	1	353	102*	39.22	409	86.3	1	3	1	40	9
LPC Silva (SL)	11	10	2	350	64	43.75	452	77.43	0	4	0	28	4
KC Sangakkara (SL)	11	11	1	350	76	35	465	75.26	0	4	1	30	2
HH Gibbs (SA)	10	8	2	342	72	57	373	91.68	0	4	0	20	14
S Chanderpaul (WI)	9	9	1	315	102*	39.37	517	60.92	1	2	0	23	9
WU Tharanga (SL)	11	11	0	298	73	27.09	446	66.81	0	3	1	27	2
PG Fulton (NZ)	8	8	0	297	83	37.12	424	70.04	0	2	1	29	2
PD Collingwood (ENG)	9	9	3	276	90	46	368	75	0	2	0	24	4
BC Lara (WI)	9	8	1	269	77	38.42	330	81.51	0	1	0	19	5
CH Gayle (WI)	9	9	0	228	79	25.33	272	83.82	0	1	0	28	6
CD McMillan (NZ)	10	9	2	228	71	32.57	261	87.35	0	1	0	14	9
TM Dilshan (SL)	11	9	2	217	58	31	236	91.94	0	1	0	15	2
MN Samuels (WI)	8	8	1	216	63	30.85	285	75.78	0	2	0	22	6

MOST WICKETS

Player	Mat	Inns	Overs	Mdns	Runs	Wkts	BBI	Ave	Econ	SR	4	5
GD McGrath (AUS)	11	11	80.5	5	357	26	3/14	13.73	4.41	18.6	0	0
M Muralitharan (SL)	10	10	84.4	1	351	23	4/19	15.26	4.14	22	2	0
SW Tait (AUS)	11	11	84.3	1	467	23	4/39	20.3	5.52	22	1	0
GB Hogg (AUS)	11	11	82.5	6	332	21	4/27	15.8	4	23.6	2	0
SL Malinga (SL)	8	8	58.2	6	284	18	4/54	15.77	4.86	19.4	1	0
NW Bracken (AUS)	10	10	71.4	10	258	16	4/19	16.12	3.6	26.8	1	0
DL Vettori (NZ)	10	10	97.4	2	447	16	4/23	27.93	4.57	36.6	1	0
A Flintoff (ENG)	8	8	69	3	298	14	4/43	21.28	4.31	29.5	1	0
AJ Hall (SA)	9	9	76	5	335	14	5/18	23.92	4.4	32.5	0	1
CK Langeveldt (SA)	8	8	66	3	361	14	5/39	25.78	5.46	28.2	0	1
DBL Powell (WI)	9	9	85	9	385	14	3/38	27.5	4.52	36.4	0	0
SE Bond (NZ)	8	8	69.4	9	213	13	3/31	16.38	3.05	32.1	0	0
WPUJC Vaas (SL)	10	10	77.4	15	286	13	3/33	22	3.68	35.8	0	0
Abdur Razzak (BDESH)	9	9	73.4	4	344	13	3/20	26.46	4.66	34	0	0
DJ Bravo (WI)	9	8	64.5	4	361	13	3/42	27.76	5.56	29.9	0	0
A Nel (SA)	6	6	52.2	6	217	12	5/45	18.08	4.14	26.1	0	1
WB Rankin (IRE)	9	9	59.2	4	324	12	3/32	27	5.46	29.6	0	0
JEC Franklin (NZ)	9	9	65.2	7	331	11	3/74	30.09	5.06	35.6	0	0
WK McCallan (IRE)	9	8	58.4	3	233	10	2/12	23.3	3.97	35.2	0	0
JDP Oram (NZ)	9	9	62.3	7	252	10	3/23	25.2	4.03	37.5	0	0
MF Maharoof (SL)	6	6	44	5	198	9	4/23	22	4.5	29.3	2	0
SB Styris (NZ)	10	9	57	3	242	9	4/43	26.88	4.24	38	1	0
Mashrafe Mortaza (BDESH)	9	9	71.2	8	323	9	4/38	35.88	4.52	47.5	1	0
Syed Rasel (BDESH)	7	7	62	7	239	8	2/25	29.87	3.85	46.5	0	0
DT Johnston (IRE)	8	7	50.2	3	258	8	2/40	32.25	5.12	37.7	0	0

HIGH SCORES

Player	Runs	Balls	4s	6s	SR	Team	Opposition	Ground
Imran Nazir	160	121	14	8	132.23	Pakistan	v Zimbabwe	Kingston
ML Hayden	158	143	14	4	110.48	Australia	v West Indies	North Sound
AC Gilchrist	149	104	13	8	143.26	Australia	v Sri Lanka	Bridgetown
AB de Villiers	146	130	12	5	112.3	South Africa	v West Indies	St George's
JH Kallis	128*	109	11	5	117.43	South Africa	v Netherlands	Basseterre
BJ Hodge	123	89	8	7	138.2	Australia	v Netherlands	Basseterre
JP Bray	115*	137	10	2	83.94	Ireland	v Zimbabwe	Kingston
DPMD Jayawardene	115*	109	10	3	105.5	Sri Lanka	v New Zealand	Kingston
ST Jayasuriya	115	101	10	4	113.86	Sri Lanka	v West Indies	Providence
V Sehwag	114	87	17	3	131.03	India	v Bermuda	Port of Spain

BEST BOWLING

Player	Overs	Mdns	Runs	Wkts	Econ	Team	Opposition	Ground
AJ Hall	10	2	18	5	1.8	South Africa	v England	Bridgetown
CK Langeveldt	10	1	39	5	3.9	South Africa	v Sri Lanka	Providence
A Nel	10	1	45	5	4.5	South Africa	v Bangladesh	Providence
NW Bracken	9.4	3	19	4	1.96	Australia	v Sri Lanka	St George's
M Muralitharan	5	0	19	4	3.8	Sri Lanka	v Ireland	St George's
MF Maharoof	7	1	23	4	3.28	Sri Lanka	v Bermuda	Port of Spain
DL Vettori	8.4	1	23	4	2.65	New Zealand	v Ireland	Providence
MF Maharoof	10	3	25	4	2.5	Sri Lanka	v Ireland	St George's
GB Hogg	4.5	0	27	4	5.58	Australia	v Netherlands	Basseterre
GB Hogg	6.5	1	29	4	4.24	Australia	v New Zealand	St George's

2011

THE BIG ONE

BY JO HARMAN

"This will be the mother and father of all World Cups that have been played up to now," said former Indian all-rounder Ravi Shastri in the lead-up to the 2011 tournament in India, Sri Lanka and Bangladesh. "Rest assured it will be exactly that, because there will be more people watching it, there'll be more sponsorship at this event, there'll be more eyeballs around the world than at any World Cup before. The enthusiasm and the atmosphere, it'll be fever pitch."

The spectacle that followed delivered and then some on Shastri's promise, with a combined TV audience of 2.2 billion worldwide tuning in to watch a tournament which featured nail-biting finishes, one of the most memorable shocks in World Cup history, grand farewells to some of the game's all-time greats and, ultimately, the dreams of a cricket-obsessed nation realised.

Never before had a team won the World Cup on home soil, and never before had a host nation been under so much pressure to do so. India, captained by the dashing MS Dhoni, were considered marginal favourites in a tight field but scars from the 2007 tournament in the Caribbean, when Rahul Dravid's side calamitously crashed out in the group stage after losing to Bangladesh and Sri Lanka, were still fresh.

The pressure was ramped up further still by the realisation that this would be Sachin Tendulkar's final World Cup, and perhaps his farewell to ODI cricket. The 37-year-old entered the tournament with 97 international centuries, on the verge of becoming the first batsman to achieve the historic landmark of 100 hundreds.

Muttiah Muralitharan, the Sri Lankan spin wizard who two years previously had surpassed Wasim Akram to become the all-time leading wicket-taker in ODIs, was also in the twilight of his career, and announced before the tournament that he would be retiring from international cricket at its conclusion.

After six weeks of enthralling action, featuring 49 matches played across 12 venues, Sachin and Murali would meet at the Wankhede Stadium in Mumbai for a fantasy match-up – two bona fide legends of the game going toe-to-toe to decide the outcome of the biggest match in cricket.

***

The tournament began on 19 February with two of the host nations, India and Bangladesh, facing off in Group B – which also featured South Africa, England, West Indies, Ireland and the Netherlands – at the Shere Bangla National Stadium in Dhaka. India were strong favourites but the underdogs could draw on the memory of their famous World Cup win four years previously in Trinidad and were boosted by fervent local support – Tendulkar estimated that 30,000 fans turned up just to watch the teams practise, many of them camping outside the stadium the night before the match.

Speaking before the game, Virender Sehwag, India's freewheeling opening batsman, insisted the team had to ignore the outside pressure and focus on the task in hand, and he showed no sign of nerves as he crunched the first ball of the tournament to the cover boundary. It set the tone for the innings as Sehwag brought up his hundred in 94 balls before finally being dismissed for 175 – the fifth-highest score in World Cup history at the time. India's total of 370 for 4 was also the fifth-highest in the competition's 36-year history.

Tendulkar missed out on a chance to add to his tally of centuries when he was run out for 28, but his 22-year-old protégé announced himself on the World Cup stage with a hundred of his own.

Virat Kohli – who hit 100 not out, his fourth ODI hundred – had been inspired to become an international cricketer after watching Tendulkar on TV. "As a kid the innings that really pushed me to work towards my dream of playing for India were Sachin's back-to-back hundreds against Australia in Sharjah – the 'Desert Storm' knocks," he told *Wisden Cricket Monthly* in 2018.

"When India were playing I would go to the shops and get my pack of chips and chocolate to prepare myself to watch him bat. I did exactly the same with both those games as well, and he batted for so long that I had to refill my snacks! It was worth it, watching him play in a manner that at that stage no one else was doing. It was literally a change happening in front of my eyes. I was like, 'Wow, this sport can be played in *this* manner'. It was just so exciting. I asked my father to get me enrolled in a cricket academy and two or three months later I joined. And from there the whole journey started."

After a pulsating start to their reply, Bangladesh's innings petered out, right-arm seamer Munaf Patel taking 4 for 48 in an 87-run victory. Dhoni's side were up and running. India breathed a sigh of relief.

***

Two days later, Australia began their campaign against Zimbabwe in Ahmedabad, playing in Group A which also included Pakistan, Sri Lanka, New Zealand, Canada and Kenya. After winning the last three World Cups, the Australians had an unbeaten streak of 29 matches in the tournament, stretching back to the group stage of the 1999 edition in England. However, with a bowling attack built around the three tearaways of Brett Lee, Mitchell Johnson and Shaun Tait, and no genuinely world-class spinner in their ranks, there were doubts about how well-suited they would be to the typically slow, low tracks of the subcontinent.

There were also concerns about the form and fitness of their captain. After breaking a finger during the 2010–11 Ashes, Ricky Ponting had missed the ODI series against England which followed and Australia's World Cup opener would be his first competitive international match for more than two months.

His team won comfortably, Johnson blowing away Zimbabwe with a spell of 4 for 19 in a 91-run victory and the reigning champions extended their unbeaten run four days later in Nagpur, sweeping aside New Zealand by seven wickets, with their pace triumvirate again to the fore.

The next day in Colombo, Sri Lanka hosted Pakistan in one of the most eagerly anticipated match-ups in Group A. They had both eased to emphatic victories in their opening fixtures – Sri Lanka beating Canada by 210 runs and Pakistan thrashing Kenya by 205 runs – and were considered among the favourites for the title in conditions where their spinners should prosper.

The two sides had met six times in previous World Cups, Pakistan winning on each occasion, and the dominance of the men in green continued as their captain Shahid Afridi took 4 for 34 with his mix of leg-spinners and fizzing googlies. It was a close encounter, though, the tightest of the tournament so far, with Afridi's dismissal of Kumar Sangakkara on 49 derailing Sri Lanka's reply when their target of 278 looked within reach.

The wicket of Mahela Jayawardene, clean bowled by Shoaib Akhtar for 2, was also a pivotal moment in Pakistan's 11-run victory. The "Rawalpindi Express" had announced that he would be retiring at the end of the tournament and, even at the age of 35, Shoaib had his sights set on beating his own world record for the fastest recorded delivery – 161.3kph, achieved against England in the 2003 World Cup in South Africa.

***

Excitement levels in India ratcheted up once more as the hosts prepared to take on England in Bangalore in their second Group B match. Andrew Strauss' side had suffered a scare in their opening fixture against the Netherlands, winning with only eight balls to spare, and weren't expected to unduly trouble their hosts, particularly considering their last ODI series in India, in December 2008, had ended in a 5–0 whitewash. What unfolded, though, was one of the most thrilling matches in World Cup history.

After Dhoni won the toss and elected to bat, Tendulkar and Sehwag were quickly into their stride.

"It was absolutely roasting, you couldn't hear yourself think because it was so loud," recalled Ajmal Shahzad, the England fast bowler. "It was like a concrete jungle, people were shaking the cages – it was mad. The pitch wasn't going to offer you anything, it was just rolled mud. I was just trying to bowl quick. It was like the quicker you bowled, the easier it got. If I was slightly off I was just getting slashed. I was like, 'Is this what I signed up for? I'm not sure about this.'"

Tim Bresnan dismissed Sehwag for a 26-ball 35 but Tendulkar, supported by half-centuries from Gautam Gambhir and Yuvraj Singh, ploughed on, bringing up his 98th international hundred, and fifth in World Cups.

England's bowlers clawed their way back late in the innings, Bresnan using the yorker to good effect to finish with 5 for 48, but India were happy with their total of 338.

Their confidence dissipated, however, as Strauss came out all guns blazing, playing what he described as the best one-day innings of his life, to set up a grandstand finish. The England captain's knock of 158 from 145 balls was his sixth ODI hundred, and would prove to be his last.

England took 15 runs off the penultimate over, leaving them needing 14 from the last with two wickets remaining and Shahzad, who was yet to face a ball, at the crease. Swann managed a two and a single from the first two deliveries of Munaf Patel's over to put Shahzad on strike, with 11 still required. "I was going in with my bowler's instinct," said Shahzad. "It was all or nothing. I wasn't going to defend it. I just took a swing."

Shahzad cleared his front leg and sent his first ball sailing back over Munaf's head for six. "It looks brilliant on the telly but the boundary was shorter than you think. Then I missed the next ball because I was trying to do the same thing!"

Shahzad scrambled a bye off the fourth ball and Swann picked up two from the fifth, leaving England requiring two from the last for a famous victory. With the ball in the slot, Swann middled a drive… but straight to the fielder. The scores finished level, only the fourth tie in World Cup history.

Given the pre-match expectations, the relieved grins on the England dressing-room balcony were understandable. But those smiles were wiped off their faces by what followed three days later at the same venue, as they suffered a shock defeat to Ireland.

"Every now and again someone wakes up and simply has the best day of their life," said Swann in his autobiography. "Kevin O'Brien was that guy against us."

No one gave Ireland a chance after they were reduced to 111 for 5 in reply to England's 327 for 8, but from that seemingly hopeless situation blossomed a match-winning knock for the ages – with the game all but up, O'Brien, the beefy 26-year-old all-rounder from Dublin, decided to chance his arm.

He brought up his half-century from 30 deliveries and, as the wheels came off for England in the field, he motored on, reaching his century in 50 balls – the fastest hundred in World Cup history. When he was dismissed for 113 in the 49th over, he'd hit 13 fours and six sixes in an innings of unadulterated mayhem.

"I remember at one stage looking up and I was 80 off 40 balls and I was like, 'Where did that come from?'" said O'Brien. "It was pretty surreal. I didn't have any clue what the record was at the time. I didn't know until after the match."

For Ireland – who had upset the odds to qualify for the Super Eight stage of the 2007 World Cup, beating Pakistan in the process – it was another prize scalp, and one which helped set in motion their promotion to Full Member status in 2018. For England, buoyed only a couple of days earlier by matching the tournament favourites, it left their quarter-final hopes hanging in the balance.

***

Back in Group A and Pakistan's bubble of optimism had been burst somewhat by a laboured victory over Canada, in which they were bowled out for 184 before winning by 46 runs, and a thrashing at the hands of New Zealand.

The Black Caps had bounced back strongly after their early defeat to Australia, their 110-run demolition of Pakistan sandwiched between victories over Zimbabwe and Canada. Their batsmen were in excellent touch, posting 302 and 358 against Pakistan and Canada respectively, with Ross Taylor's 131 not out helping the Kiwis to blast an extraordinary 100 runs off the last five overs against the former.

Sri Lanka were also showing no signs of panic after their defeat to Pakistan, trouncing Kenya and Zimbabwe and sharing the points with Australia after a downpour forced their game to be abandoned in Colombo. The experienced openers Tillakaratne Dilshan and Upul Tharanga were in formidable form, putting on 282 against Zimbabwe – a record opening stand in the World Cup – and sharing three half-century partnerships. In all, they added 800 runs in nine partnerships – the most by a pair of batsmen in a World Cup, ahead of the 699 Adam Gilchrist and Matthew Hayden put on for Australia in 2007.

Sri Lanka and New Zealand had confirmed their places in the last eight before they met each other in their final group match, but there was still much to play for with, in theory at least, an easier fixture to follow in the quarter-finals for the victors.

It was Sri Lanka's first match in the tournament played outside their home country but it mattered not as they posted 265 for 9 in Mumbai, largely thanks to a sublime 111 from their captain Sangakkara, and then easily defended it – Muralitharan returning figures of 4 for 25 to help bowl out the Kiwis for 153.

The winner of the final meaningful match in Group A, between Pakistan and Australia, would top the group. Ponting's side had extended their unbeaten World Cup streak to 34 with wins over Kenya and Canada and that abandoned match against Sri Lanka, but all was not well in the Australian camp.

"We lacked some of the intensity that had been the trademark of the great Australian teams and for the first time in my cricket life I was feeling old. Not in the body but in the message," said Ponting in his autobiography.

Pakistan scented blood and produced a brilliant all-round bowling display to restrict Australia to 176 all out in Colombo, the seamer Umar Gul taking three wickets for the third consecutive match as no batsman was able to pass 50. Ponting, caught behind for 19 off Mohammad Hafeez, had now gone 19 ODIs without a century, and the pressure was building.

Pakistan wobbled in reply, Lee's fiery spell of 4 for 28 reducing them to 142 for 6, but Umar Akmal and Abdul Razzaq calmed the nerves to see their side to a four-wicket win and top spot in the group – ahead of Sri Lanka in second place, and Australia and New Zealand in third and fourth respectively.

***

While there was little doubt who would progress from Group A as the first stage neared its conclusion, Group B was much harder to call, with six of the seven teams still harbouring hopes of a quarter-final berth as the matches ticked by.

South Africa had always boasted a premier pace attack in previous tournaments but this time it was supplemented by high-quality spin in the form of Imran Tahir. The Pakistan-born leg-spinner had made an immediate impact, taking 4 for 41 and 3 for 19 against West Indies and Netherlands respectively in two comprehensive victories which marked them out as genuine contenders for the title. Graeme Smith, the Proteas captain, said he had never had such a varied attack at his disposal.

They were considered favourites for their third match too, against an England side who had suffered that shock defeat to Ireland only four days previously.

Strauss won the toss and elected to bat in Chennai, and South Africa were immediately all over England after a masterstroke from Smith. Kevin Pietersen's difficulties against left-arm spin had been well documented but the South African captain still took everyone by surprise when he decided to open the bowling with Robin Peterson. The decision went even better than Smith could have imagined, as the spinner had Strauss caught at long on from the third delivery of the match and found Pietersen's edge three deliveries later to dismiss England's dangerman. Peterson then had Ian Bell caught and bowled in his third over as England's World Cup campaign threatened to spiral out of control.

Ravi Bopara and Jonathan Trott carried England to 171 all out but that appeared well below par against an in-form South African batting unit who had blasted 351 for 5 against the Netherlands in their previous match.

At 124 for 3, and with AB de Villiers and Faf du Plessis well set, South Africa were cruising to a third straight win until an extraordinary passage of play which saw three wickets fall with the score on 124 – two of those to Anderson who clean bowled de Villiers and JP Duminy in the space of five balls.

With the required run rate not a concern, Morne van Wyk and Dale Steyn inched towards the target, but Bresnan bowled the former and Stuart Broad finished the job, trapping Steyn lbw and having Morkel caught behind to steal a dramatic six-run victory.

Excitement at the smash-and-grab win was tempered by the news that Pietersen would play no further part in the tournament, as he returned home to undergo hernia surgery. It was a major loss to a misfiring batting line-up.

The loss proved only a minor blip to South Africa, who inflicted a first defeat of the tournament on India – despite another hundred for Tendulkar, his 99th in international cricket – before making short work of Ireland and Bangladesh to secure top spot in Group B.

For England, though, the victory was hugely significant and left them knowing that a win in their penultimate group match, a day/nighter against Bangladesh in Chittagong, would confirm their place in the last eight. The Bangladeshis came into the match with one victory and one defeat since their opening loss to India, beating Ireland by 27 runs before getting thumped by West Indies in Dhaka, where they were skittled for 58 in 18.5 overs.

England again struggled after being put into bat, Trott hitting his fourth half-century in five innings and Eoin Morgan impressing in his first outing of the tournament but no other batsman passing 18 in a modest total of 225 all out.

At 155 for 3 in the 30th over, Bangladesh were firmly in control until England's bowlers produced another inspired spell, as they had done against South Africa, to peg them back to 169 for 8. This time there was to be no great escape though, Mahmudullah and Shafiul Islam guiding Bangladesh to a two-wicket win – only their second ODI victory over England.

The result kept Bangladesh in the hunt for quarter-final qualification, while England would have to beat West Indies in their final group match and rely on other results going their way if they were to progress.

Strauss' men kept up their side of the bargain, Swann and James Tredwell sharing seven wickets against the Windies in Chennai, after yet another disappointing batting display, to claim an 18-run victory, before South Africa's 206-run demolition of Bangladesh ensured England's qualification.

As well as the Proteas, they would be joined in the last eight by India, who finished second after defeating West Indies by 80 runs in the final match in Group B, and the Windies, who lost three of their six group matches but pipped Bangladesh to fourth place by virtue of a superior net run rate.

***

After a two-day break, the tournament resumed on 23 March with the first of the quarter-finals, between Pakistan and West Indies in Dhaka. While the Pakistanis had sailed through the group stage with five wins from six, the Windies had struggled for rhythm, with their potentially explosive batting unit misfiring. The trend continued in one of the more one-sided quarter-final clashes in World Cup history.

Darren Sammy won the toss and elected to bat but the loss of the dangerous Chris Gayle in the third over, caught at mid-off by Afridi off the bowling of Gul, was a hammer blow from which West Indies never recovered. They mustered just seven fours and a six in their innings of 112 all out from 43.3 overs as Pakistan's spinners strangled the life out of them – the spin trio of Afridi, Hafeez and Saeed Ajmal returning combined figures of 27.3-5-64-8. Afridi was in the bowling form of his life, with 21 wickets at an average of 10.71. Over the course of the tournament he took two five-wicket hauls, and had two more four-wickets innings. No other bowler has taken four wickets more than twice in a single World Cup.

Pakistan made light work of their target, openers Kamran Akmal and Hafeez knocking off the runs in 20.5 overs as the Windies' underwhelming campaign came to an abrupt close.

***

A day later, Ahmedabad hosted the most hotly anticipated tie of the round, as the reigning champions and tournament favourites locked horns with a semi-final against Pakistan at stake.

"These are the moments you live for, these are the moments you dream of," said Indian all-rounder Yuvraj Singh ahead of the match. "Sometimes living in this world you don't realise that, because it becomes an everyday part of your life. But this is one of the most amazing things happening in your career, so you need to remember that."

Yuvraj came into the tournament with his place in question but he had been in scintillating form with both bat and ball in the group stage, hitting a century and three fifties and taking nine wickets with his left-arm spin, including a five-for against Ireland. However, members of India's backroom staff were beginning to become concerned about his health. "He was falling sick on and off," said team manager Ranjib Biswal in Makarand Waingankar's biography of Yuvraj. "He felt nauseous and vomited frequently. Sometimes he used to get breathless. He complained of a stiff neck."

It later emerged that Yuvraj had a cancerous tumour in his left lung. He underwent chemotherapy in 2012, making a full recovery to return to the Indian side for the

ICC World Twenty20 in October of that year. With the benefit of hindsight, his outstanding performances at the 2011 World Cup were all the more remarkable.

The sound was cacophonous in the Sardar Patel Stadium as Ponting won the toss and chose to bat. Tim Nielsen, Australia's coach, had told the Australian captain in the build-up that he felt he was batting better than he had at any point in the last two years and forecast a big score for him. His prediction proved well-founded as Ponting ended his 13-month wait for an ODI hundred, hitting 104 – his 30th century in the format – to guide his team to 260 for 6 and leave the match delicately balanced.

Half centuries from Tendulkar and Gautam Gambhir put India on track after Shane Watson's early dismissal of Sehwag but Australia took wickets at regular intervals and when Michael Clarke took a screamer at point off Lee to dismiss Dhoni for 7 and leave the score 187 for 5, the nerves were palpable among the home support. Thankfully for India, Yuvraj was the coolest man in the stadium, chipping away at the target in partnership with Suresh Raina before hitting the boundary that sealed victory with 14 balls to spare to set up a tantalising semi-final with Pakistan.

For the first time since 1992, a World Cup final would not feature Australia. Less than a week later Ponting stood down as Test and ODI captain. He continued to play on as a batsman but his century in the quarter-final would be his last in the 50-over format, as he retired 12 months later.

***

It was back to the Shere Bangla Stadium in Dhaka for the third quarter-final, the impressive South Africans returning to the venue where they had thrashed Bangladesh only a week earlier, this time to take on New Zealand.

The Black Caps' frailties against the turning ball had been exposed in their final group match against Sri Lanka and the Proteas' team selection reflected that, with Tahir – who had taken 12 wickets in four matches – supported in the spin department by Peterson, Johan Botha and Duminy.

Smith continued with his ploy of opening the bowling with Peterson and again it had an almost immediate effect, the left-arm spinner pulling off a brilliant caught and bowled to dismiss Brendon McCullum in the third over. New Zealand were creaking when Steyn removed the in-form Martin Guptill for 1 and it took a century stand between Jesse Ryder and Taylor to push the score towards respectability, the Kiwis eventually scrambling to 221 for 8.

After watching his own team struggle on a slow, turning deck, Daniel Vettori gave the first over to the off-spinner Nathan McCullum and he took a wicket with his sixth delivery when an under-edge from Hashim Amla ricocheted off the keeper's boot and looped to Vettori at slip. Given their below-par total it was just the slice of luck New Zealand needed.

Useful contributions from Smith, Kallis and de Villiers kept South Africa on course and at 108 for 2 in the 25th over, a semi-final place beckoned. But just as they had done in their group match against England, the Proteas imploded. Tim Southee started the collapse, tempting Kallis with a short delivery and Jacob Oram taking a high catch on the mid-wicket boundary, before Duminy and de Villiers fell in the space of three deliveries – the former clean bowled by McCullum and the latter run out in a mix-up which betrayed the nerves in the South African camp. Not for the first time, the Proteas were blowing their big chance on the biggest stage.

Sensing an opening, the Kiwis were rampant, Oram taking out Botha, Peterson and du Plessis in a man of the match performance of 4 for 39 as South Africa subsided to 172 all out.

"There are no words to describe how I feel," said Smith in his post-match interview. "Your guess is as good as mine – it's been happening since 1992."

New Zealand, meanwhile, could dream of a first World Cup final appearance, having fallen at the penultimate hurdle in five previous tournaments. They would play the winner of the fourth quarter-final between Sri Lanka and England.

***

Much like the first of the quarter-finals, the match proved something of a damp squib, Sri Lanka easing to a 10-wicket win after England once again failed to set a challenging target.

They were indebted to a fifth half-century of the tournament from Trott and a fortuitous 50 from Morgan, in which he was dropped on four occasions, to reach 229 for 6, but hundreds from Sri Lanka's prolific opening pair of Dilshan and Tharanga saw Sri Lanka race to their target inside 40 overs.

***

England's defeat meant New Zealand would be the sole non-Asian representative in the semi-finals. "We fly under the radar and that's always quite nice I think," said the all-rounder Jacob Oram. "Maybe they don't scout or plan quite as hard against us, because they think it'll be an easy match. We fight internally with this underdog tag. It'd be nice to be favoured. It'd be nice to be rated. But whatever people think of us doesn't really matter."

If the Kiwis were to reach their first World Cup final they would have to overcome Sri Lanka on home soil – no easy feat, and the formbook was against them. The Sri Lankans had won each of their last four World Cup encounters against New Zealand, including an 81-run victory at the semi-final stage of the 2007 tournament.

There was a carnival atmosphere in the R Premadasa Stadium in Colombo as Vettori won the toss and chose to bat, but Sri Lanka's well-balanced attack kept New

Zealand's batsmen in check, Lasith Malinga cleaning up Guptill with a brute of an inswinging yorker. But with the scoreboard reading 161 for 3 in the 40th over, and Taylor and Scott Styris well set, a total of around 250 looked within reach. It was then that wickets began to tumble, Taylor becoming the first of Ajantha Mendis' three victims before Muralitharan trapped Styris lbw with his final ball on Sri Lankan soil.

The Kiwis lost their last five wickets for 13 runs to finish on a disappointing 217, but they had shown in their quarter-final against South Africa that they were capable of defending low totals.

Sri Lanka's openers were brimming with confidence after their run spree in the tournament and Tharanga dispatched the third ball of the innings for six as he and Dilshan put on 40 for the first wicket. It took a stunning catch by Ryder at point to send Tharanga on his way but Sri Lanka continued to dominate as Dilshan went past Trott as the leading run-scorer in the competition and Sangakkara eased his way to a half-century.

By this time there was a celebratory atmosphere in the ground but the loss of three wickets for nine runs, as the key trio of Dilshan, Jayawardene and Sangakkara departed in quick succession, silenced the home crowd. Sri Lanka still required 51 to take their place in the final, with their most experienced batsmen all back in the hutch.

The scoring rate slowed as the tension rose, Southee clean bowling Chamara Silva with 35 more still needed, but Thilan Samaraweera and Angelo Mathews took their side home with 13 balls to spare, even if the winning runs needed to be hit twice. Mathews thought he had won the match when he carved the ball through the covers, only for the umpire to call dead-ball due to a firework exploding at the point of delivery. But Samaraweera sealed the victory five balls later, sending Colombo into pandemonium.

Sri Lanka would take on either India or Pakistan four days later in Mumbai, in the first all-Asian World Cup final.

***

Pakistan had a wretched World Cup record against their arch-rivals, losing all four of their previous matches, but were finding form at just the right time ahead of the semi-final clash in Mohali, just 150 miles from the Pakistani border. India, meanwhile, had yet to really hit top gear and their captain Dhoni had not made a meaningful contribution with the bat.

With a pacy pitch expected, India bolstered their seam attack by picking the left-armer Ashish Nehra in place of the off-spinner Ravichandran Aswhin. But there was still no place in Pakistan's side for Shoaib Akhtar, who had been dropped after the group-stage defeat against New Zealand.

An estimated half a billion tuned in to watch the clash, and the nerves were evident as Sehwag had a wild swish at the first delivery of the match after India elected to bat first. He continued to play his shots, hitting 38 from 25 balls, before being dismissed lbw by the left-arm quick Wahab Riaz.

Wahab was under pressure after being selected in favour of Shoaib but he responded by producing the best spell of fast bowling in the tournament, tearing through India's middle order to finish with career-best figures of 5 for 46. His dismissal of the in-form Yuvraj, who had his woodwork rearranged by an in-swinging howitzer to fall for a golden duck, reducing India to 141 for 4, was a moment of high drama. By contrast Gul, who had been impeccable up to that point in the tournament, had a day to forget, conceding 69 from eight wicketless overs.

Amongst the chaos, forever unruffled, was Tendulkar, who brought up his half-century from 67 balls and had that hundredth hundred in his sights. He received more than a helping hand from the Pakistani fielders, though, who dropped him on no less than four occasions – on 27, 45, 68 and 81. Finally, on 85, Afridi was able to hold on at short extra-cover off the bowling of Ajmal. Tendulkar's landmark would have to wait.

A handy cameo from Raina helped India finish on 260 for 9 – a total which seemed about par on a surface offering something for the bowlers. Without those fluffed chances to dismiss Tendulkar, it would have been considerably less.

After Kamran Akmal's early dismissal, Pakistan kept wickets in hand but struggled to keep up with the required rate and the loss of Umar Akmal to the first delivery of Harbhajan Singh's third spell heaped on further pressure. Umar had been one of the few Pakistani batsmen to score fluently but he was clean bowled by a ripper which pegged back his off stump, leaving Pakistan 142 for 5 and requiring around seven runs per over.

Pakistan's hopes were rapidly slipping away when Afridi hit a full toss from Harbhajan straight to Sehwag at cover and they eventually succumbed to a 29-run defeat, Misbah-ul-Haq the last man out, caught on the boundary for 56.

***

And so to Mumbai for the final, where a febrile crowd of 33,000 packed into the Wankhede Stadium, with 558 million more watching on TV across the world.

As much as the Indian players tried to shut out the outside pressure, the excitement from an expectant nation was impossible to ignore. On the eve of the match, Mike Horn, the South African-born Swiss adventurer who had been with the team for much of the tournament, gave a speech to help put things in perspective.

"While for most of us there is always another day, for Mike it was often a matter of life and death," said Tendulkar in his autobiography. "One mistake and it could all be over. The stories of how he coped with extreme pressure during his adventures – such as circumnavigating the globe at the Equator without motorised transport, or walking to the North Pole during the dark season – definitely helped us deal with our own concerns on the eve of the World Cup final."

Sri Lanka were revelling in their underdog status. For them the pressure was off, although the team were determined to give Muralitharan the send-off he deserved. The 38-year-old had battled through a succession of minor injuries in the tournament, including a hamstring problem, a side strain, a troublesome knee and a groin complaint, but Sri Lanka's coach Trevor Bayliss insisted he was fit for the final: "Such is the character of the man that he will play even with discomfort."

The noise in the stadium was deafening as Dhoni and Sangakkara walked out to the middle for the toss, so much so that match referee Jeff Crowe couldn't hear the Sri Lankan captain's call and it had to be redone. After a successful second attempt, Sangakkara won the toss and chose to bat.

Zaheer – who finished as the joint leading wicket-taker in the tournament, level with Afridi on 21 – was impeccable with the new ball, reeling off three maidens on the trot to tame Sri Lanka's explosive opening pair before making the breakthrough in his fourth, Sehwag taking a low catch at slip to dismiss Tharanga for a painstaking 2 from 20 balls.

Dilshan was also not at his most fluent and was bowled round his legs by Harbhajan for 33 to bring Jayawardene to the crease with the score 60 for 2. Jayawardene's form had been scratchy since making a century in Sri Lanka's tournament opener against Canada but he produced one of the great World Cup final knocks, batting through the innings to finish on 103 not out.

The silky right-hander found support from Sangakkara, Samaraweera, Nuwan Kulasekara and finally Thisara Perera, who hit 22 not out from nine deliveries, including a six and two fours from Zaheer's final over, to propel Sri Lanka to a more-than-respectable 274 for 6. India would need to hit a record second-innings total in a World Cup final if they were to lift the trophy.

That task looked tougher still when Malinga trapped Sehwag lbw with the second ball of the innings and then found Tendulkar's edge in his fourth over to leave India 31 for 2 and the Wankhede stunned.

Gambhir and Kohli steadied the innings with a partnership of 83 until Dilshan removed the latter for 35 with a magnificent caught and bowled. With the match hanging in the balance, Dhoni, who had yet to score a 50 in the tournament, decided to promote himself to No.5, ahead of the in-form Yuvraj.

"Something in me said I should go," said Dhoni. "I was changing into my batting shoes when Gary [Kirsten, India's coach] came in and gave me a look. 'Should I go?' 'Yes, I think you should go, man,' he said. I had played a lot with Murali for Chennai in the IPL and felt I could read him. If I got it right, I felt I would calm the others down. I knew in my heart it was justified and felt that the team trusted me."

It proved an inspired, match-defining decision, as Dhoni eased to a half-century from 52 balls, carving Muralitharan to the boundary to bring up the landmark and drop the required rate below a run a ball. A loose stroke from Gambhir saw him bowled by Perera three short of his century, but Dhoni continued to dictate the chase, with Yuvraj happy to play second fiddle.

Sangakkara had three overs from Malinga up his sleeve to try and turn the game but Dhoni hit consecutive fours off the second of those to leave India requiring just five runs from the final two overs.

Tendulkar refused to leave the dressing room until the winning runs were hit and insisted Sehwag do the same, fearing a change of position could derail the run chase. They didn't have long to wait as Dhoni sent the second ball of the penultimate over sailing over the long-on boundary with a short-arm jab that sent the country into ecstasy. India's captain finished on 91 not out from 79 balls, having scripted a six-wicket win for his side.

Fireworks lit up the Mumbai sky as Tendulkar's teammates lifted him onto their shoulders and carried him on a victory lap. As Kohli said: "Sachin Tendulkar has carried Indian cricket on his shoulders for 21 years. So it was fitting that we carried him on our shoulders after this win."

"Being carried by my teammates, waving the tricolour at my home ground, having won the World Cup – what more could I ask for?" said Tendulkar. "Life, to be honest, seemed complete. It was the greatest moment of my cricketing journey. Cricket's greatest prize was finally ours."

After the party in the stadium finally subsided, the celebrations continued long into the night at the Taj Mahal Palace hotel, with the Indian players leaving their bedroom doors open as they moved from one to the next, drinking and dancing.

Dhoni took his leave at one stage in the proceedings and surprised his teammates by returning with a shaved head, having cut off his trademark long locks. "It had been a stressful few months," he later said. "Many people were demanding that we won the World Cup at home. The bare heard was the final goodbye to the pressure we had been under. It was like we could start afresh."

Tendulkar, meanwhile, retired to bed around 5am, but some of his teammates were not yet finished. "At 7am I heard Zaheer Khan and Ashish Nehra banging on my door, wanting to share a drink. I just smiled to myself and went back to sleep."

Sachin had well and truly earned his rest.

2011

RESULTS AND STATISTICS

GROUP A TABLE

		P	W	T	L	NR	A	Pts	Net RR
1	Pakistan	6	5	0	1	0	0	10	0.758
2	Sri Lanka	6	4	0	1	1	0	9	2.582
3	Australia	6	4	0	1	1	0	9	1.123
4	New Zealand	6	4	0	2	0	0	8	1.135
5	Zimbabwe	6	2	0	4	0	0	4	0.03
6	Canada	6	1	0	5	0	0	2	-1.987
7	Kenya	6	0	0	6	0	0	0	-3.042

GROUP B TABLE

		P	W	T	L	NR	A	Pts	Net RR
1	South Africa	6	5	0	1	0	0	10	2.026
2	India	6	4	1	1	0	0	9	0.9
3	England	6	3	1	2	0	0	7	0.072
4	West Indies	6	3	0	3	0	0	6	1.066
5	Bangladesh	6	3	0	3	0	0	6	-1.361
6	Ireland	6	2	0	4	0	0	4	-0.696
7	Netherlands	6	0	0	6	0	0	0	-2.045

SRI LANKA V NEW ZEALAND

ICC WORLD CUP 2010/11 (SEMI-FINAL)

Venue: R Premadasa Stadium, Colombo
Date: 29th March 2011
Toss: New Zealand
Result: Sri Lanka won by 5 wickets
Umpires: Aleem Dar, SJ Davis
TV Umpire: M Erasmus (South Africa)
Referee: BC Broad (England)
Reserve Umpire: BR Doctrove (West Indies)
Man of the Match: KC Sangakkara

NEW ZEALAND		R	b	SRI LANKA		R	b
MJ Guptill	b Malinga	39	65	WU Tharanga	c Ryder b Southee	30	31
+BB McCullum	b Herath	13	21	TM Dilshan	c Ryder b Southee	73	93
JD Ryder	c Sangakkara b Muralitharan	19	34	*+KC Sangakkara	c Styris b McKay	54	79
LRPL Taylor	c Tharanga b Mendis	36	55	DPMD Jayawardene	lbw b Vettori	1	3
SB Styris	lbw b Muralitharan	57	77	TT Samaraweera	not out	23	38
KS Williamson	lbw b Malinga	22	16	LPC Silva	b Southee	13	25
NL McCullum	c Sangakkara b Malinga	9	9	AD Mathews	not out	14	18
JDP Oram	c Jayawardene b Dilshan	7	9	SL Malinga	did not bat		
*DL Vettori	not out	3	3	HMRKB Herath	did not bat		
TG Southee	c Sangakkara b Mendis	0	3	BAW Mendis	did not bat		
AJ McKay	b Mendis	0	2	M Muralitharan	did not bat		
Extras	(5 lb, 1 nb, 6 w)	12		Extras	(2 lb, 10 w)	12	
Total	(all out, 48.5 overs)	217		Total	(5 wickets, 47.5 overs)	220	

Fall of wickets: 1-32 (BB McCullum, 7.1 ov), 2-69 (Ryder, 18.3 ov), 3-84 (Guptill, 21.3 ov), 4-161 (Taylor, 39.1 ov), 5-192 (Williamson, 43.3 ov), 6-204 (NL McCullum, 45.1 ov), 7-213 (Styris, 46.6 ov), 8-215 (Oram, 47.4 ov), 9-217 (Southee, 48.3 ov), 10-217 (McKay, 48.5 ov)

Fall of wickets: 1-40 (Tharanga, 7.2 ov), 2-160 (Dilshan, 32.4 ov), 3-161 (Jayawardene, 33.1 ov), 4-169 (Sangakkara, 36.2 ov), 5-185 (Silva, 42.2 ov)

SRI LANKA	O	M	R	W	Wd	Nb	NEW ZEALAND	O	M	R	W	Wd	Nb
Malinga	9	0	55	3	-	1	NL McCullum	6	0	33	0	1	-
Herath	9	1	31	1	1	-	Southee	10	2	57	3	1	-
Mathews	6	0	27	0	-	-	Vettori	10	0	36	1	-	-
Mendis	9.5	0	35	3	-	-	Oram	8	1	29	0	-	-
Muralitharan	10	1	42	2	2	-	McKay	9.5	1	37	1	2	-
Dilshan	5	0	22	1	1	-	Styris	2	0	12	0	-	-
							Ryder	2	0	14	0	-	-

INDIA V PAKISTAN

ICC WORLD CUP 2010/11 (SEMI-FINAL)

Venue: Punjab Cricket Association Stadium, Mohali
Date: 30th March 2011
Toss: India
Result: India won by 29 runs
Umpires: IJ Gould, SJA Taufel
TV Umpire: BF Bowden (New Zealand)
Referee: RS Madugalle (Sri Lanka)
Reserve Umpire: RJ Tucker (Australia)
Man of the Match: SR Tendulkar

INDIA		R	b	PAKISTAN		R	b
V Sehwag	lbw b Wahab Riaz	38	25	+Kamran Akmal	c Yuvraj Singh b Khan	19	21
SR Tendulkar	c Shahid Afridi b Saeed Ajmal	85	115	Mohammad Hafeez	c Dhoni b Patel	43	59
G Gambhir	st Kamran Akmal b Mohammad Hafeez	27	32	Asad Shafiq	b Yuvraj Singh	30	39
V Kohli	c Umar Akmal b Wahab Riaz	9	21	Younis Khan	c Raina b Yuvraj Singh	13	32
Yuvraj Singh	b Wahab Riaz	0	1	Misbah-ul-Haq	c Kohli b Khan	56	76
*+MS Dhoni	lbw b Wahab Riaz	25	42	Umar Akmal	b Harbhajan Singh	29	24
SK Raina	not out	36	39	Abdul Razzaq	b Patel	3	9
Harbhajan Singh	st Kamran Akmal b Saeed Ajmal	12	15	*Shahid Afridi	c Sehwag b Harbhajan Singh	19	17
Z Khan	c Kamran Akmal b Wahab Riaz	9	10	Wahab Riaz	c Tendulkar b Nehra	8	14
A Nehra	run out (Kamran Akmal->Wahab Riaz)	1	2	Umar Gul	lbw b Nehra	2	3
MM Patel	not out	0	0	Saeed Ajmal	not out	1	5
Extras	(8 lb, 2 nb, 8 w)	18		Extras	(8 w)	8	
Total	(9 wickets, 50 overs)	260		Total	(all out, 49.5 overs)	231	

Fall of wickets: 1-48 (Sehwag, 5.5 ov), 2-116 (Gambhir, 18.5 ov), 3-141 (Kohli, 25.2 ov), 4-141 (Yuvraj Singh, 25.3 ov), 5-187 (Tendulkar, 36.6 ov), 6-205 (Dhoni, 41.4 ov), 7-236 (Harbhajan Singh, 46.4 ov), 8-256 (Khan, 49.2 ov), 9-258 (Nehra, 49.5 ov)

Fall of wickets: 1-44 (Kamran Akmal, 8.6 ov), 2-70 (Mohammad Hafeez, 15.3 ov), 3-103 (Asad Shafiq, 23.5 ov), 4-106 (Younis Khan, 25.4 ov), 5-142 (Umar Akmal, 33.1 ov), 6-150 (Abdul Razzaq, 36.2 ov), 7-184 (Shahid Afridi, 41.5 ov), 8-199 (Wahab Riaz, 44.5 ov), 9-208 (Umar Gul, 46.1 ov), 10-231 (Misbah-ul-Haq, 49.5 ov)

PAKISTAN	O	M	R	W	Wd	Nb	INDIA	O	M	R	W	Wd	Nb
Umar Gul	8	0	69	0	1	2	Khan	9.5	0	58	2	2	-
Abdul Razzaq	2	0	14	0	-	-	Nehra	10	0	33	2	1	-
Wahab Riaz	10	0	46	5	4	-	Patel	10	1	40	2	1	-
Saeed Ajmal	10	0	44	2	2	-	Harbhajan Singh	10	0	43	2	-	-
Shahid Afridi	10	0	45	0	-	-	Yuvraj Singh	10	1	57	2	-	-
Mohammad Hafeez	10	0	34	1	-	-							

INDIA V SRI LANKA

ICC WORLD CUP 2010/11 (FINAL)

Venue: Wankhede Stadium, Mumbai
Date: 2nd April 2011
Toss: Sri Lanka
Result: India won by 6 wickets
Umpires: Aleem Dar, SJA Taufel
TV Umpire: IJ Gould (England)
Referee: JJ Crowe (New Zealand)
Reserve Umpire: SJ Davis (Australia)
Man of the Match: MS Dhoni

SRI LANKA		R	b	INDIA		R	b
WU Tharanga	c Sehwag b Khan	2	20	V Sehwag	lbw b Malinga	0	2
TM Dilshan	b Harbhajan Singh	33	49	SR Tendulkar	c Sangakkara b Malinga	18	14
*+KC Sangakkara	c Dhoni b Yuvraj Singh	48	67	G Gambhir	b Perera	97	122
DPMD Jayawardene	not out	103	88	V Kohli	c and b Dilshan	35	49
TT Samaraweera	lbw b Yuvraj Singh	21	34	*+MS Dhoni	not out	91	79
CK Kapugedera	c Raina b Khan	1	5	Yuvraj Singh	not out	21	24
KMDN Kulasekara	run out (Dhoni)	32	30	SK Raina	did not bat		
NLTC Perera	not out	22	9	Harbhajan Singh	did not bat		
SL Malinga	did not bat			Z Khan	did not bat		
HKSR Kaluhalamulla	did not bat			MM Patel	did not bat		
M Muralitharan	did not bat			S Sreesanth	did not bat		
Extras	(1 b, 3 lb, 2 nb, 6 w)	12		Extras	(1 b, 6 lb, 8 w)	15	
Total	(6 wickets, 50 overs)	274		Total	(4 wickets, 48.2 overs)	277	

Fall of wickets: 1-17 (Tharanga, 6.1 ov), 2-60 (Dilshan, 16.3 ov), 3-122 (Sangakkara, 27.5 ov), 4-179 (Samaraweera, 38.1 ov), 5-182 (Kapugedera, 39.5 ov), 6-248 (Kulasekara, 47.6 ov)

Fall of wickets: 1-0 (Sehwag, 0.2 ov), 2-31 (Tendulkar, 6.1 ov), 3-114 (Kohli, 21.4 ov), 4-223 (Gambhir, 41.2 ov)

INDIA	O	M	R	W	Wd	Nb	SRI LANKA	O	M	R	W	Wd	Nb
Khan	10	3	60	2	1	-	Malinga	9	0	42	2	2	-
Sreesanth	8	0	52	0	-	2	Kulasekara	8.2	0	64	0	-	-
Patel	9	0	41	0	1	-	Perera	9	0	55	1	2	-
Harbhajan Singh	10	0	50	1	1	-	Kaluhalamulla	9	0	43	0	-	-
Yuvraj Singh	10	0	49	2	-	-	Dilshan	5	0	27	1	1	-
Tendulkar	2	0	12	0	3	-	Muralitharan	8	0	39	0	1	-
Kohli	1	0	6	0	-	-							

MOST RUNS

Player	Mat	Inns	NO	Runs	HS	Ave	BF	SR	100	50	0	4s	6s
TM Dilshan (SL)	9	9	1	500	144	62.5	551	90.74	2	2	0	61	4
SR Tendulkar (INDIA)	9	9	0	482	120	53.55	524	91.98	2	2	0	52	8
KC Sangakkara (SL)	9	8	3	465	111	93	555	83.78	1	3	0	44	5
IJL Trott (ENG)	7	7	0	422	92	60.28	522	80.84	0	5	0	28	0
WU Tharanga (SL)	9	9	2	395	133	56.42	472	83.68	2	1	0	52	2
G Gambhir (INDIA)	9	9	0	393	97	43.66	462	85.06	0	4	0	37	0
V Sehwag (INDIA)	8	8	0	380	175	47.5	310	122.58	1	1	1	49	7
Yuvraj Singh (INDIA)	9	8	4	362	113	90.5	420	86.19	1	4	1	39	3
AB de Villiers (SA)	5	5	1	353	134	88.25	326	108.28	2	1	0	31	7
AJ Strauss (ENG)	7	7	0	334	158	47.71	357	93.55	1	1	1	34	3
BJ Haddin (AUS)	7	6	0	332	88	55.33	421	78.85	0	4	0	40	5
LRPL Taylor (NZ)	8	6	1	324	131*	64.8	372	87.09	1	1	0	20	14
RN ten Doeschate (NL)	6	6	1	307	119	61.4	344	89.24	2	1	0	26	5
HM Amla (SA)	7	7	0	306	113	43.71	349	87.67	1	2	0	25	1
DPMD Jayawardene (SL)	9	7	1	304	103*	50.66	304	100	2	1	0	32	1
DS Smith (WI)	7	7	0	300	107	42.85	391	76.72	1	2	0	32	2
SR Watson (AUS)	7	6	0	290	94	48.33	314	92.35	0	3	0	32	7
V Kohli (INDIA)	9	9	1	282	100*	35.25	343	82.21	1	1	0	24	2
MJ Guptill (NZ)	8	8	2	262	86*	43.66	382	68.58	0	2	0	27	4
BB McCullum (NZ)	8	8	2	256	101	42.66	277	92.41	1	1	0	28	6
Misbah-ul-Haq (PAK)	8	6	1	248	83*	49.6	336	73.8	0	3	1	13	3
IR Bell (ENG)	7	7	0	245	81	35	307	79.8	0	2	0	16	2
CO Obuya (KENYA)	6	6	1	243	98*	48.6	347	70.02	0	2	0	21	7
MS Dhoni (INDIA)	9	8	3	241	91*	48.2	295	81.69	0	1	0	19	3
Umar Akmal (PAK)	7	6	1	240	71	48	276	86.95	0	1	0	21	5

MOST WICKETS

Player	Mat	Inns	Overs	Mdns	Runs	Wkts	BBI	Ave	Econ	SR	4	5
Shahid Afridi (PAK)	8	8	74.3	4	270	21	5/16	12.85	3.62	21.2	2	2
Z Khan (INDIA)	9	9	81.3	4	394	21	3/20	18.76	4.83	23.2	0	0
TG Southee (NZ)	8	8	72.2	9	312	18	3/13	17.33	4.31	24.1	0	0
RJ Peterson (SA)	7	7	56	5	238	15	4/12	15.86	4.25	22.4	1	0
M Muralitharan (SL)	9	8	71	1	291	15	4/25	19.4	4.09	28.4	1	0
Yuvraj Singh (INDIA)	9	9	75	2	377	15	5/31	25.13	5.02	30	0	1
Imran Tahir (SA)	5	5	39.3	2	150	14	4/38	10.71	3.79	16.9	2	0
Umar Gul (PAK)	8	8	60.3	5	272	14	3/30	19.42	4.49	25.9	0	0
KAJ Roach (WI)	6	6	46	2	195	13	6/27	15	4.23	21.2	0	1
B Lee (AUS)	7	7	54.2	6	235	13	4/28	18.07	4.32	25	2	0
SL Malinga (SL)	7	6	48.4	0	270	13	6/38	20.76	5.54	22.4	0	1
HS Baidwan (CAN)	6	6	55	3	307	13	3/35	23.61	5.58	25.3	0	0
DW Steyn (SA)	6	6	46.1	3	192	12	5/50	16	4.15	23	0	1
JDP Oram (NZ)	6	6	49.5	6	221	12	4/39	18.41	4.43	24.9	1	0
SJ Benn (WI)	6	6	47.5	3	238	12	4/18	19.83	4.97	23.9	2	0
GP Swann (ENG)	7	7	68	5	309	12	3/36	25.75	4.54	34	0	0
SW Tait (AUS)	7	7	52	3	264	11	3/35	24	5.07	28.3	0	0
MM Patel (INDIA)	8	8	65.5	1	353	11	4/48	32.09	5.36	35.9	1	0
MG Johnson (AUS)	7	7	57.3	7	231	10	4/19	23.1	4.01	34.5	2	0
JF Mooney (IRE)	6	6	45	0	259	10	4/63	25.9	5.75	27	1	0
RW Price (ZIM)	6	6	49	7	169	9	3/16	18.77	3.44	32.6	0	0
M Morkel (SA)	6	6	40.2	0	207	9	3/33	23	5.13	26.8	0	0
WD Balaji Rao (CAN)	6	6	54	0	299	9	4/57	33.22	5.53	36	1	0
TT Bresnan (ENG)	7	7	63	5	309	9	5/48	34.33	4.9	42	0	1
Harbhajan Singh (IND)	9	9	87	2	390	9	3/53	43.33	4.48	58	0	0

HIGH SCORES

Player	Runs	Balls	4s	6s	SR	Team	Opposition	Ground
V Sehwag	175	140	14	5	125	India	v Bangladesh	Dhaka
AJ Strauss	158	145	18	1	108.96	England	v India	Bengaluru
TM Dilshan	144	131	16	1	109.92	Sri Lanka	v Zimbabwe	Pallekele
AB de Villiers	134	98	13	4	136.73	South Africa	v Netherlands	Mohali
WU Tharanga	133	141	17	0	94.32	Sri Lanka	v Zimbabwe	Pallekele
LRPL Taylor	131*	124	8	7	105.64	New Zealand	v Pakistan	Pallekele
SR Tendulkar	120	115	10	5	104.34	India	v England	Bengaluru
RN ten Doeschate	119	110	9	3	108.18	Netherlands	v England	Nagpur
KJ O'Brien	113	63	13	6	179.36	Ireland	v England	Bengaluru
HM Amla	113	130	8	0	86.92	South Africa	v Netherlands	Mohali

BEST BOWLING

Player	Overs	Mdns	Runs	Wkts	Econ	Team	Opposition	Ground
KAJ Roach	8.3	0	27	6	3.17	West Indies	v Netherlands	Delhi
SL Malinga	7.4	0	38	6	4.95	Sri Lanka	v Kenya	Colombo (RPS)
Shahid Afridi	8	3	16	5	2	Pakistan	v Kenya	Hambantota
Shahid Afridi	10	0	23	5	2.3	Pakistan	v Canada	Colombo (RPS)
Yuvraj Singh	10	0	31	5	3.1	India	v Ireland	Bengaluru
Wahab Riaz	10	0	46	5	4.6	Pakistan	v India	Mohali
TT Bresnan	10	1	48	5	4.8	England	v India	Bengaluru
DW Steyn	9.4	0	50	5	5.17	South Africa	v India	Nagpur
R Rampaul	10	0	51	5	5.1	West Indies	v India	Chennai
TM Dilshan	3	1	4	4	1.33	Sri Lanka	v Zimbabwe	Pallekele

2015

SOUTHERN STARS

BY GEOFF LEMON

It was fitting, in a sporting tournament hosted between Australia and New Zealand, that the trans-Tasman rivals should end up contesting the final. The perfect result for those putting on the show. And in late March of 2015 the show had won plaudits. "The World Cup organisers might just be born of exceptional water-divining stock. They have, with the Anzac final now lined up, struck to the very core of what a global event is all about – sharing the love for the game, all drinking from the same well."

Martin Crowe, who had endured a long and lonely existence as New Zealand's only great batsman, knew that he had terminal cancer as he wrote those words and counted down the days to his country's first World Cup final.

"I will be there to share my gratitude at seeing a baton carried with such brilliance and daring. My precarious life ahead may not afford me the luxury of many more games to watch and enjoy," ran his Cricinfo essay with an honesty that slapped you sober. "I will hold back tears all day long. I will gasp for air on occasions. I will feel like a nervous parent."

Crowe was someone who achieved so much but defined himself by what he missed. The Test match triple-hundred that he never scored rather than the 299 that he did; the 1992 semi-final in an era when Pakistan couldn't possibly chase 123 from the last 90 balls, until they did.

So 23 years later, as Brendon McCullum's team finally washed away a history of six lost semi-finals at cricket's biggest tournament, it seemed to give Crowe a moment of personal catharsis alongside national one. And even though the last dance of 2015 didn't go New Zealand's way, valuing achievements over shortfalls was far easier for Crowe when it came to other people's rather than his own. He was proud on that day, and was gone within a year.

Before the final there was a lot of talk that the dimensions of the Melbourne Cricket Ground might throw off the New Zealanders, who had made their qualifying run on their home country's smaller arenas. The satirical hashtag circulating social media was #MCGSoBig, along with stories of Kiwi batsmen getting lost on their way to centre wicket practice. In the end the ground wasn't too big for the visitors, nor even the occasion, but they weren't able to bounce back from the day's biggest moment.

Few cricket matches have been lost to the fifth ball, but if ever one was, it was this. Mitchell Starc, left-arm fast, was greeted by Martin Guptill's forward defensive then a glided single. Regulation stuff. McCullum, though, came on strike. His first ball he aimed a mighty drive, missed completely, and was nearly bowled. His second he charged at the fastest bowler on the planet, aiming towards the leg side, and this time the ball missed leg stump. The fifth ball he stayed home, in two minds, playing another big drive but without a clear plan behind it. Moving his foot towards a ball that swung in, robbing him of space. Swishing an angled bat that couldn't access the line. Missing the near-yorker that took his off stump. New Zealand's talisman was broken.

In most ways, this result made perfect sense. Mitchell Starc's personal lead-up had been Grade A bonkers. He had been hoovering up wickets in the 50-over format with a simple approach: run in with a lithe and easy action, sling down a new white ball at speeds that respectively topped 150 kilometres and 93 miles an hour, add late swing from his pace and the ball's lacquer, and blow up the stumps.

Batsmen knew exactly what he was doing, but that didn't mean they could stop him doing it. A lot of his wickets came to balls hitting the stumps on the full, as high as halfway up, but even his full toss that in theory was hittable tended to swerve like a car-chase driver while approaching at a similar speed. Batsmen were caught in the headlights. In the domestic 50-over competition just before that World Cup, Starc racked up 26 wickets in six matches. Of those, 17 were bowled.

Carrying on that form, he ended his World Cup with 22 wickets at a frankly outrageous 10.18 runs each. He knocked over a batsman every 17.4 deliveries. 53 times in World Cups have bowlers taken 15 or more wickets, but nobody has come close to matching those figures. People compared him to Wasim Akram, given the left-arm pace and swing and World Cup influence. But by that stage of his career Starc had a five-wicket haul on five occasions in his first 35 matches. Wasim did it six times in 356.

However otherworldly Starc's performance, he had a more mortal presence along for the ride. New Zealand's Trent Boult was another left-arm swinger who opened the bowling. He too finished on 22 wickets in the tournament, even if his average blew out to 16.86.

Boult operated at closer to 135 kilometres an hour than 155. He was medium height and slight of frame; where the towering Starc never looked like anything but an athlete, Boult often wandered out of his hotel in a striped t-shirt and black jeans and could blend in at any bar with a group of graphic designers. He had to be a thinker as well as a sportsman, but he moved the ball more prodigiously than Starc and aimed it more consistently.

Along with his colleague Tim Southee, Boult did for plenty of teams in the World Cup. Hooping the ball into the pads of right-handers, or through them to clatter stumps. Enough movement to draw false shots to a catching cordon that was always well attended. During the pool stages New Zealand rissoled England for 123, Scotland for 146, Afghanistan for 186. Then there was Auckland against Australia. But we'll come to that.

The other key component for New Zealand was McCullum. The captain, a former wicket-keeper who had given up the gloves. His long career hadn't exactly dominated One Day Internationals, mostly bits-and-pieces scores with the occasional spike. He had started down the order, then opened the batting for some years before dropping back down to five or six.

But as the World Cup loomed, he put himself up to open again. Far from the first New Zealand pinch-hitter: Crowe's 1992 outfit had a reputation for boldness that included sending Mark Greatbatch up to swing freely at the top, as well as opening the bowling with the Dipak Patel's spin. Since then, though, McCullum felt that teams from his country had been hesitant in global tournaments, trying to play safe while merely hampering their own abilities.

He wanted his team to be fearless, and he was willing to set the example. So up he came, first to batter 65 from 49 balls against Sri Lanka. The first two balls McCullum's faced went for four, then he took 23 off a Lasith Malinga over, the containment specialist who is one of the greatest yorker exponents the game has seen. Inspired, New Zealand romped to 331.

Then, against England, where most teams might have chosen safety first chasing that small target, McCullum launched one of the most dramatic assaults in cricket history. Carving his second ball for six over point, it went from there. He ransacked England, taking 49 from runs from 12 balls against Steven Finn, and passing the 123 target in less than 13 overs. McCullum was out just before the end, with 77 from 25 balls.

The entire match was over before the scheduled halfway break. And for New Zealand, a familiar face had become a new champion. The mark of their campaign became the fast McCullum start: breakneck, never pausing, going after the opponent's best bowler. It didn't always come off, but when it did it was dramatic.

And more than being the signature of his team's campaign, his shots became the signature of the tournament. McCullum opening his front leg to a wide low stance to power inside-out sixes over cover. McCullum charging fast bowlers, standing on one foot with the other flamingoed up behind him in a Hello Sailor move, flat-batting length balls into the crowd with the sunlight flashing off his blade. McCullum with both feet off the ground to put everything into pull shots that were dumped over the leg side.

At the same time, he took that approach in the field as well. New Zealand knocked over sides because when one of his main bowlers was taking wickets, McCullum would roll the dice and keep them going in pursuit of more. He often had up to four slips in a cordon, in a game where defensiveness is the mantra. And he threw himself around to save boundaries like he was trying to stop a child going over a precipice.

The culmination of his approach came in the semi-final, a thriller over South Africa that is remembered chiefly for the image of victory and defeat in which Grant Elliott reaches out a hand to lift the fallen and despairing bowler Dale Steyn. Needing 298 in 43 overs after rain, Elliott got New Zealand home with a ball to spare, but McCullum was where it began. Facing Steyn, one of the fastest and fiercest the game had known. Carving a six from his first over. A four from his second. Then an assault on his third, 25 runs as boundaries rained. McCullum made 59 from 26 balls, and an imposing run rate was suddenly well in hand.

But before that, the group game between Australia and New Zealand was another with everything. El Superclásico. The preview that got people amped for the final. It was like a comic-book crossover between the tournament's main heroes, who each got a scene to display their special powers. First Boult dismantled Australia, turning 80 for 1 into 124 for 9. His captain let him roll as he finished his allotted overs by the 26th of the innings, grabbing five wickets on the way. Australia were all out for 151.

Then McCullum teed off on Mitchell Johnson, trying to recreate the England match. Johnson, with an Ashes whitewash fresh in his memory, was still the team's most feared bowler. He proved why when he pulverised McCullum's forearm with a bouncer, raising an obscene swelling. McCullum pulverised Johnson's bowling in reply, ending up with 50 from 24.

It was just as well for New Zealand that McCullum got that many. As soon as he fell, Starc took over the show. He finished a spell by getting Ross Taylor and Elliott in successive balls. Then as New Zealand neared the target, having lost a couple more wickets, back came Starc to bounce out Luke Ronchi, then smash through Adam Milne and Southee. There were gasps from the crowd with each rattle of the stumps: surely, ran the predominant reaction, they couldn't stuff this up? It was 146 for 9, five runs from safety, with Boult at the crease.

Boult had bowled Starc earlier, but before the Australian could return the favour, Kane Williamson hit one long to get New Zealand home. Australia had fallen short, but in the process the mantle of attack leader had indisputably passed to Starc. Which brings us back to the final, as Starc took the new ball. It's easy now to say that McCullum should have played sensibly and seen him off. Waited before taking on Josh Hazlewood from the other end.

But the fact that Starc was white-hot and shooting off sparks was exactly why McCullum had to go for him. That was all the more reason. McCullum's entire campaign had been built around doing what shouldn't have been done, and what shouldn't have been possible. It was about inspiring his team to never back down, to

Top left: Lance Klusener continued to shine on the World Cup stage.

Top right: Sachin Tendulkar, with a record 673, scored over 200 runs more than any other player during the tournament.

Bottom: South African captain Shaun Pollock realises what they have done as his side crash out after a Duckworth Lewis misreading.

Top: Kenya became the only Associates nation ever to reach the semi-final, where they were beaten by a Ganguly-inspired India.

Bottom: Ricky Ponting's brutal unbeaten 140 in the final ensured a second successive World Cup triumph.

Top: Ireland captain Trent Johnston celebrates with Eoin Morgan as his side pulls off a major upset against Pakistan.

Middle: Bermuda's Dwayne Leverock takes the catch that shook the world.

Bottom: New Zealand's Scott Styris had an all-round World Cup to remember, with 499 runs and nine wickets.

Top: Sri Lanka's Lasith Malinga bowls Makhaya Ntini for his fourth wicket in four balls but South Afirca, who needed four to win with five wickets in hand, just squeak home.

Bottom left: Adam Gilchrist and the controversial squash ball in his glove, which helped him score a blistering 149 in the final off just 104 deliveries.

Bottom right: The main architects of Aussie dominance, skipper Ponting, leading wicket-taker Glenn McGrath (a World Cup record 26), and the final's man of the match, Adam Gilchrist.

Top: Andrew Strauss scored a brilliant 158 in Bangalore as England and India tied their group game with 338 runs apiece.

Bottom: Kevin O'Brien hit an astonishing World Cup record 50-ball century and ended with 113 as Ireland chased down England's 327.

Top: Muttiah Muralitharan, whose last ODI was the World Cup final against India in Mumbai, receives a special award.

Middle: MS Dhoni hits the match-winning six, having promoted himself up the order, to finish unbeaten on 91 and take away the man of the match award.

Bottom: Sachin Tendulkar, in his last World Cup, is chaired around the field by his teammates, including his protégé Virat Kohli.

Top: Afghanistan's Shapoor Zadran hits the winning boundary in a nail-biting contest with Scotland that his side won by one wicket.

Bottom: Kumar Sangakkara celebrates a century against Australia, the third of his four successive hundreds in the tournament.

Top: Martin Guptill, having just hit a World Cup record 237*, poses with Chris Gayle, who had hit his own double century earlier in the tournament. They are the only two men to have scored World Cup double hundreds.

Middle: Mitchell Starc, player of the tournament, gets rid of the prolific and inspirational Brendon McCullum in the first over of the final.
Bottom: Michael Clarke lifts the trophy as Australia win the World Cup for the fifth time.

leap regardless. He rode forth to slay a dragon, and while you only hear songs about the winners, most people who try it end up on the wrong side of the contest.

His approach had worked until that moment, but failed in the final. Not just because he fell, but because in making himself a talisman, he made his dismissal devastating. With 93,000 people packed into the MCG, McCullum's wicket was a detonation of sound mirroring the detonation of the stumps. There was the feeling that the whole stadium might rise up for a moment, quivering with energy, before slamming back onto its foundations. Equally palpable, if not audible, was the deflation of the New Zealand part of the crowd, and of all those watching further afield. A sinkhole had opened up in their emotional landscape, dragging down half the surrounding countryside.

While New Zealand had been the team of bonhomie and derring-do, Australia had been the triumph of process. They were relentless. They made huge scores batting first and chased modest ones with ease. They shared around the runs and bowled fiercely as a unit. The only time a team made more than 233 against them was when they allowed Sri Lanka 312 in chasing a hopeless 376. The Australians were never pushed, aside from a few overs in their Pakistan quarter-final, and that memorable day in Auckland – and even that unwinnable match they nearly snatched out of the fire.

Process trumped emotion. Consistency stalled momentum. In the final, New Zealand never recovered and limped to 183. The outgoing captain Michael Clarke and the incoming Steven Smith handled the chase with ease. Clarke was dismissed just before the finish, allowing him a solo farewell in his last home international match. It was a strange farewell to a leader who didn't necessarily command public affection or by that stage even a spot in Australia's best team. George Bailey had looked after the side for years with Clarke injured or rested for one-day tours, but had been pushed out for the prize tournament.

"McCullum has won his nation's heart already. He has been simply irresistible. Clarke has one more game to win […] a better understanding from his countrymen," wrote Crowe. "In many ways, McCullum can't lose, yet he won't see it that way. And Clarke must win, and even then it may not be enough, which is madness." Australia's complicated relationship with Clarke continues well after his retirement.

***

But as compelling as their story was, the 2015 World Cup was about more than the finalists. It was about the match-ups at the smaller grounds, the local festival feel at Manuka Oval in Canberra or the grass banks of Hagley Oval in Christchurch or the cricket ground in the university at Dunedin. It was groups of neutral students and diehard expats watching the likes of Afghanistan tussle with Sri Lanka, or a then-unknown Zimbabwean named Solomon Mire against South Africa clouting Morné Morkel miles and miles into the night sky. It was about the way Indian supporters turned every Australian ground into a sea of blue, with a pink lava sunset behind them while taking on Pakistan in Adelaide, or the way the MCG became a vortex of sound and activity, dancing and playing instruments and cheering each single or a dot ball.

It was about more than just big scores, even though the numbers grab your attention. With two new balls in each innings and a limit of four outfielders during the death overs, it often got ugly for bowling sides. Three innings finished above 400, and 28 of them topped 300. Through the last 15 overs, teams batting first averaged nearly nine runs per over.

After waiting decades for the first ODI double-century, two came in one tournament, and neither Martin Guptill's nor Chris Gayle's is treated as especially memorable in cricket's pantheon. David Warner made 178 against Afghanistan and had to make reparations after hitting a kid in the second tier of the WACA with a six.

In all there were seven individual scores of 150 or more; there had been 12 in the previous ten World Cups, and never more than two in one tournament. 11 batsmen scored more than 300 runs at a strike rate over 100, whereas only three had done so in 2011, with an identical tournament format.

This was also the highest-scoring (32.9 runs per wicket) and fastest-scoring (5.65 runs per over) World Cup and the first in which more than half the runs off the bat were scored in boundaries (51.4 per cent; 12.5 per cent in sixes, 38.9 per cent in fours). Batsmen's collective strike rate was 88.9 per 100 balls against a previous highest in a World Cup of 78.3, in 2011.

Glenn Maxwell destroyed Sri Lanka at the SCG, making 102 from 53 balls in a devastating conclusion to an innings. Kumar Sangakkara couldn't chase it down that night but he did continue his world-record set of consecutive ODI centuries: 105 not out against Bangladesh, 117 not out against England, 104 against Australia, and 124 against Scotland. Zimbabwe's Brendan Taylor went on an extraordinary run against all opponents that went 40, 47, 37, 50, 121 and 138, but still couldn't take his side to the finals.

On 19 occasions out of 49, the team batting first made over 300 runs and won by a mile, with a smallest margin of 62. Ireland and Afghanistan were yet to receive Test status, and made up the Associate ranks along with Scotland and the United Arab Emirates. But only six of those 19 big losses involved Associates, while the rest were between top-ranked sides. Contrary to the claim that Associates make tournaments less competitive, most matches between big teams were one-sided. Only one was decided by fewer than 20 runs, and two either in the last over or with a couple of wickets to spare.

Of those big targets, only a few were overhauled or close to it. Sri Lanka humiliated England, mowing down 309 for the cost of a wicket as Sangakkara hit cruise control. Scotland thought they had a great chance of a breakthrough win, only for Bangladesh to chase their 318 four wickets down. Ireland, meanwhile, provided some of the thrills of the tournament, first stunning West Indies by passing 304 with overs to spare, then conjuring a way to hold off Zimbabwe when the African team was steaming towards a target of 331, only to be bowled out five runs and three balls short.

The most devastating batting performance came from South Africa's AB de Villiers. In a warm-up series against West Indies a month before the World Cup, de Villiers had broken the world speed record with a century off 31 balls. During a turbulent time in West Indies cricket, the inexperienced fast-bowling all-rounder Jason Holder had been named ODI captain aged 23. In this match, before the ball was even bowled, de Villiers would walk outside off stump, sink to one knee, then receive a full toss or a half volley on his pads which he would lap-pull over backward square leg for six. Even more extraordinary than the shot was its context; it was like watching a cobra hypnotise a mongoose, as a bewildered Holder trotted in, ignored the three unattended stumps, and bowled exactly where de Villiers had already decided that he would.

So in the World Cup a month later, the psychological dominance was fresh and forceful. De Villiers came to the crease in the 30th over. Holder had bowled well, his first five overs returning a wicket, two maidens, and costing nine runs. His next three overs went for 31. His final two overs, as he closed the innings, went for 64. He finished the day with 1 for 104, as de Villiers this time took the record for the fastest 150 in one-dayers. South Africa topped 400 against West Indies for the second time in a matter of weeks.

But for all the runs, the excitement of the 2015 World Cup came largely from the lower-scoring games and lower-drawing teams. Bangladesh in the pool stage brought England's tournament to an early close and grabbed a quarter-final spot. England had already been dismantled by New Zealand, overrun by Sri Lanka, and thumped by Australia, but even after a ton to Mahmudullah conceded 275 to Bangladesh, England couldn't believe it when they were bowled out 15 short. The seamer Rubel Hossain became the hero, knocking over the stumps of the last two batsmen with overs to spare to seal the win.

The UAE nearly pulled off a surprise, first piling on what by their standards was a massive 285, then holding Zimbabwe at bay until the 48th over. But the UAE's following game against Ireland was one of the matches of the tournament, as the unfancied team dressed in drab grey took the Irish into the last over and eight wickets down in passing 278.

The target was built on Shaiman Anwar's work as he became the first UAE player to make a World Cup century. Ireland's Kevin O'Brien, best known for his own astonishing World Cup hundred against England in 2007, was by this stage trying to reinvent himself as an all-rounder. He had all the attitude of a fast bowler with none of the speed, and his tussle with Shaiman was brilliant theatre as the batsman kept bunny-hopping around the crease, grinning at the bowler while creating angles to glide balls to third man or fine leg. When Shaiman at one stage took guard three feet outside off stump, O'Brien's face matched the red of his hair.

But O'Brien found some composure to make the chase possible, coming in at a shaky 171 for 5, then bashing a half-century from 25 balls to keep his team in touch. More wickets fell, with Amjad Javed bowling an exceptional defensive spell late in the piece as the balls remaining dwindled, and it was only by good fortune that Ireland's tailenders were able to scramble over the line.

For the UAE team, with their long-time batting champion Khurram Khan in his final series, it was timely that Shaiman stood up. His aggression was best summed up by the story of him once hitting seven sixes in an over in domestic cricket – one was from a no-ball. For the UAE, he kept on coming in at No.6 with his team in trouble, then counter-attacking with skill and bravado to find a way out. He made 67 against Zimbabwe, 106 against Ireland, 35 against India during a mighty collapse, 62 against Pakistan, and 39 against South Africa. Overmatched, he showed the capacity of the underdog.

Pakistan were the masters of the low-scoring contest, using a plethora of bowling options. The giant Mohammad Irfan, the left-arm whip of Rahat Ali, and the sharp leg-spin of Shahid Afridi all went at less than five runs per over. Whatever their batsmen made was enough. Pakistan's 235 against Zimbabwe preceded squeezing out the African team for 215. The potent South Africans were bowled out short of Pakistan's 222. Finally they stifled Ireland for 237.

This almost worked again for Pakistan in the quarter-finals, in what would be Australia's only dicey moment of the World Cup. On a decent Adelaide Oval pitch, Pakistan's all out 213 was extremely sub-par as Australia's bowlers gave nothing away. But when Clarke got a snorting bouncer from Wahab Riaz and fended it to short leg to make the score 59 for 3, concern started to bubble. Especially when Wahab found his range and worked over Shane Watson.

This contest has gone down in history. Often a figure of some fun despite having one of Australia's best one-day records, Watson stood up to the examination. But he had an especially stern invigilator. Wahab cranked up his pace on the placid surface. He zinged bouncers past the helmet, past the gloves, making Watson hop and skitter. One ball was fended over the cordon. Then came the moment. A hook, a top edge... and Rahat at fine leg dropped the straightforward catch.

Australia could have been four down, but no. Wahab kept at Watson as long as he could, but was always going to tire. The Australian all-rounder worked his way into an innings, eventually taking on Wahab to pull him flat and square for six. It was the story of Wahab's career: striving hard, looking every inch the threat, but somehow not getting to the desired result. Smith was out for a half-century, but Maxwell at the other end came in to play shots like the look-away cut over backward point. Australia made the target with him 44 not out, and Watson still there on 64.

It could so easily have been Ireland who made the quarters. The permutations of Pool B meant they were extremely unlucky to miss out. They thrashed the West Indies and Zimbabwe as well as beating the UAE, but even three wins couldn't get them a spot given other results. Had Pakistan done the right thing and beaten West Indies, the Irish would have been through.

Scotland, too, had reason to feel hard done by. Not just when Bangladesh turned on that huge chase after Kyle Coetzer had smashed 150. But after their other close one, in the single best match of the tournament. Afghanistan. Scotland. Neither of whom had ever won a World Cup match.

It was cut and thrust all day. Afghanistan's seamers kept making inroads. The solid Dawlat Zadran slid one through Coetzer, one of his three wickets. But Afghanistan's stars were undoubtedly his bowling colleagues: Hamid Hassan won fans for the way he charged in every ball and emoted with every near miss. He wore Afghan-flag facepaint and a broad headband, and was so excited when he dismissed Sangakkara while playing Sri Lanka that he did the world's least elegant cartwheel. By his side was always Shapoor Zadran: tall, built like an oak, with lustrous black hair that streamed out behind him as he ran in to bowl far more slowly than his build or his run-up suggested.

At one stage the bowlers had Scotland 144 for 8. Then a partnership between seamer Alisdair Evans and off-spinner Majid Haq took the Scots up to 206. Shapoor came back to finish with four wickets, bowling them out for 210 from the last ball.

But that soon started to look more than enough. Evans grabbed two wickets, then a run-a-ball 50 from opener Javed Ahmadi ended when he tried to clear mid-on. It started a slide of 5 for 12, as seamer Richie Berrington ran amok.

Now the score was 97 for 7, and surely Afghanistan had botched it. Except their one remaining batsman, Samiullah Shenwari, was dug well in on 24 from 65 balls. And he was not going to let anything shake his focus. He knew he had plenty of overs. He just had to get through them and allow runs to come. He blocked out maidens, took occasional singles, found even more occasional boundaries, and kept walking down to remind Dawlat to stay patient. "I can hit it," he kept saying, a reminder that his colleague didn't need to.

It worked until they had added 35, when Dawlat tried to whack Berrington down the ground and holed out. Shenwari was furious, hitting his bat on the ground and shouting after his teammate, demanding to know what he had been thinking. It didn't change anything, but it certainly let Hamid Hassan know what his job was as he came in at No.10. Survive.

So he did, with 79 needed from 90 balls. He took 13 balls to get off the mark, and played one scoring shot in his first 24 deliveries. But he was still there while Shenwari continued at the other end. From 56 needed off 44 balls, Majid Haq's final overs proved the turning point. The Scottish spinner was a joy, bowling old-fashioned off-break lobs that came in at half the pace of most spinners, floated up high and dropping on batsmen. For those who disparaged it, his bowling was remarkably effective, going at 4.8 runs an over through the tournament. But on this day he got hit: first a six in the 43rd over, then three more of them in the 45th, all swung away over the leg side.

The equation narrowed to 19 needed from 19 balls. Shenwari was a mess of emotion, periodically dropping to his haunches and trying to control his breathing as his rearguard went on. He was on 96, and looking history in the eye. But finally an error, as he went to the well once too often. His attempt at a fifth big hit was held on the boundary.

No departing batsman has ever radiated such distress. He stayed slumped for the longest moment, then almost walked back to the middle as the umpires checked how many fielders had been in the circle. When he finally had to leave the arena he collapsed to the ground as he crossed the boundary, staying there to watch from the grass, knees drawn up to his chest. He didn't remove his pads or helmet or gloves. He held his bat between his knees and literally chewed the handle as he watched the last-wicket pair.

Hamid. Shapoor. Who had done so much for this side, but it had never included much ability with the bat. Three overs for 19 runs should have been beyond them. So should one over for 10. But Berrington slipped in a wide while trying to end the 49th, and Shapoor pulled the extra ball for four. Once Hamid found a single from a yorker, Shapoor played the most famous leg glance in his nation's history. Then provided the image of the World Cup: sprinting, arms spread aeroplane-wide, hair a wild flag beside him, before crashing to his knees and falling face-first beaming into the turf. On the sidelines, Shenwari put down his gnawed bat and remembered how to use his teeth to smile instead.

Only 14 years earlier, Afghanistan didn't even have a cricket team. They had cobbled one together out of refugee camps and second-hand gear, and had built a momentum that no cricket team has ever matched. Now they celebrated a breakthrough victory on the biggest stage, by the thinnest margin, using nothing but cussedness and self-belief. It was the feelgood moment of them all.

But Australia were feeling pretty good too. After the final, the team had spent all night in celebrations, as evidenced by blurry photos of squinting players still in gold team kit as the sun rose behind them on some Melbourne rooftop terrace. Several did phone-ins to breakfast radio stations while audibly the worse for wear, but happy. An absurd fifth title had predictably been sealed on home soil. Indeed, neither Australia nor New Zealand lost on home turf, their sole defeats coming once they crossed the Tasman.

Once Australians reach a final, wrote Sharda Ugra, "some A-game gene springs to life in their DNA." But in a world where that was expected, the lasting memories of the tournament will be broader: McCullum's bravado, Starc's menace, Sangakkara's precision, Shapoor's joy, Maxwell's freestyle, Wahab's battle, Watson's survival, Shaiman's audacity, and the weeks when it all mattered.

2015

RESULTS AND STATISTICS

POOL A TABLE

		P	W	T	L	NR	A	Pts	Net RR
1	New Zealand	6	6	0	0	0	0	12	2.564
2	Australia	6	4	0	1	0	1	9	2.257
3	Sri Lanka	6	4	0	2	0	0	8	0.371
4	Bangladesh	6	3	0	2	0	1	7	0.136
5	England	6	2	0	4	0	0	4	-0.753
6	Afghanistan	6	1	0	5	0	0	2	-1.853
7	Scotland	6	0	0	6	0	0	0	-2.218

POOL B TABLE

		P	W	T	L	NR	A	Pts	Net RR
1	India	6	6	0	0	0	0	12	1.827
2	South Africa	6	4	0	2	0	0	8	1.707
3	Pakistan	6	4	0	2	0	0	8	-0.085
4	West Indies	6	3	0	3	0	0	6	-0.053
5	Ireland	6	3	0	3	0	0	6	-0.933
6	Zimbabwe	6	1	0	5	0	0	2	-0.527
7	United Arab Emirates	6	0	0	6	0	0	0	-2.032

NEW ZEALAND V SOUTH AFRICA

ICC WORLD CUP 2014/15 (SEMI-FINAL)

Venue: Eden Park, Auckland
Date: 24th March 2015
Toss: South Africa
Result: New Zealand won by 4 wickets
Umpires: IJ Gould, RJ Tucker
TV Umpire: NJ Llong (England)
Referee: DC Boon (Australia)
Reserve Umpire: BNJ Oxenford (Australia)
Man of the Match: GD Elliott

SOUTH AFRICA		R	b	NEW ZEALAND		R	b
HM Amla	b Boult	10	14	MJ Guptill	run out (Amla->de Kock)	34	38
+Q de Kock	c Southee b Boult	14	17	*BB McCullum	c Steyn b Morkel	59	26
F du Plessis	c Ronchi b Anderson	82	107	KS Williamson	b Morkel	6	11
RR Rossouw	c Guptill b Anderson	39	53	LRPL Taylor	c de Kock b Duminy	30	39
*AB de Villiers	not out	65	45	GD Elliott	not out	84	73
DA Miller	c Ronchi b Anderson	49	18	CJ Anderson	c du Plessis b Morkel	58	57
JP Duminy	not out	8	4	+L Ronchi	c Rossouw b Steyn	8	7
VD Philander	did not bat			DL Vettori	not out	7	6
DW Steyn	did not bat			MJ Henry	did not bat		
M Morkel	did not bat			TG Southee	did not bat		
Imran Tahir	did not bat			TA Boult	did not bat		
Extras	(1 b, 13 w)	14		Extras	(6 b, 2 lb, 5 w)	13	
Total	(5 wickets, 43 overs)	281		Total	(6 wickets, 42.5 overs)	299	

Fall of wickets: 1-21 (Amla, 3.4 ov), 2-31 (de Kock, 7.5 ov), 3-114 (Rossouw, 26.1 ov), 4-217 (du Plessis, 38.2 ov), 5-272 (Miller, 42.2 ov)

Fall of wickets: 1-71 (McCullum, 6.1 ov), 2-81 (Williamson, 8.5 ov), 3-128 (Guptill, 17.1 ov), 4-149 (Taylor, 21.4 ov), 5-252 (Anderson, 37.6 ov), 6-269 (Ronchi, 40.1 ov)

NEW ZEALAND	O	M	R	W	Wd	Nb	SOUTH AFRICA	O	M	R	W	Wd	Nb
Southee	9	1	55	0	1	-	Steyn	8.5	0	76	1	1	-
Boult	9	0	53	2	-	-	Philander	8	0	52	0	-	-
Henry	8	2	40	0	1	-	Morkel	9	0	59	3	1	-
Vettori	9	0	46	0	2	-	Imran Tahir	9	1	40	0	1	-
Williamson	1	0	5	0	-	-	Duminy	5	0	43	1	2	-
Elliott	1	0	9	0	-	-	de Villiers	3	0	21	0	-	-
Anderson	6	0	72	3	5	-							

AUSTRALIA V INDIA

ICC WORLD CUP 2014/15 (SEMI-FINAL)

Venue: Sydney Cricket Ground, Sydney
Date: 26th March 2015
Toss: Australia
Result: Australia won by 95 runs
Umpires: HDPK Dharmasena, RA Kettleborough
TV Umpire: M Erasmus (South Africa)
Referee: RS Madugalle (Sri Lanka)
Reserve Umpire: RK Illingworth (England)
Man of the Match: SPD Smith

AUSTRALIA		R	b	INDIA		R	b
AJ Finch	c Dhawan b Yadav	81	116	RG Sharma	b Johnson	34	48
DA Warner	c Kohli b Yadav	12	7	S Dhawan	c Maxwell b Hazlewood	45	41
SPD Smith	c RG Sharma b Yadav	105	93	V Kohli	c Haddin b Johnson	1	13
GJ Maxwell	c Rahane b Ashwin	23	14	AM Rahane	c Haddin b Starc	44	68
SR Watson	c Rahane b M Sharma	28	30	SK Raina	c Haddin b Faulkner	7	11
*MJ Clarke	c RG Sharma b M Sharma	10	12	*+MS Dhoni	run out (Maxwell)	65	65
JP Faulkner	b Yadav	21	12	RA Jadeja	run out (Smith)	16	17
+BJ Haddin	not out	7	7	R Ashwin	b Faulkner	5	13
MG Johnson	not out	27	9	Mohammed Shami	not out	1	1
MA Starc	did not bat			M Sharma	b Faulkner	0	1
JR Hazlewood	did not bat			UT Yadav	b Starc	0	5
Extras	(1 b, 7 lb, 6 w)	14		Extras	(8 lb, 2 nb, 5 w)	15	
Total	(7 wickets, 50 overs)	328		Total	(all out, 46.5 overs)	233	

Fall of wickets: 1-15 (Warner, 3.1 ov), 2-197 (Smith, 34.1 ov), 3-232 (Maxwell, 37.3 ov), 4-233 (Finch, 38.2 ov), 5-248 (Clarke, 42.1 ov), 6-284 (Faulkner, 46.3 ov), 7-298 (Watson, 47.5 ov)

Fall of wickets: 1-76 (Dhawan, 12.5 ov), 2-78 (Kohli, 15.3 ov), 3-91 (RG Sharma, 17.6 ov), 4-108 (Raina, 22.6 ov), 5-178 (Rahane, 36.2 ov), 6-208 (Jadeja, 41.5 ov), 7-231 (Dhoni, 44.3 ov), 8-232 (Ashwin, 45.4 ov), 9-232 (M Sharma, 45.5 ov), 10-233 (Yadav, 46.5 ov)

INDIA	O	M	R	W	Wd	Nb	AUSTRALIA	O	M	R	W	Wd	Nb
Mohammed Shami	10	0	68	0	2	-	Starc	8.5	0	28	2	2	1
Yadav	9	0	72	4	4	-	Hazlewood	10	1	41	1	-	-
M Sharma	10	0	75	2	-	-	Johnson	10	0	50	2	2	-
Kohli	1	0	7	0	-	-	Faulkner	9	1	59	3	1	1
Jadeja	10	0	56	0	-	-	Maxwell	5	0	18	0	-	-
Ashwin	10	0	42	1	-	-	Watson	4	0	29	0	-	-

AUSTRALIA V NEW ZEALAND

ICC WORLD CUP 2014/15 (FINAL)

Venue: Melbourne Cricket Ground, Melbourne
Date: 29th March 2015
Toss: New Zealand
Result: Australia won by 7 wickets
Umpires: HDPK Dharmasena, RA Kettleborough
TV Umpire: M Erasmus (South Africa)
Referee: RS Madugalle (Sri Lanka)
Reserve Umpire: IJ Gould (England)
Man of the Match: JP Faulkner

NEW ZEALAND		R	b	AUSTRALIA		R	b
MJ Guptill	b Maxwell	15	34	DA Warner	c Elliott b Henry	45	46
*BB McCullum	b Starc	0	3	AJ Finch	c and b Boult	0	5
KS Williamson	c and b Johnson	12	33	SPD Smith	not out	56	71
LRPL Taylor	c Haddin b Faulkner	40	72	*MJ Clarke	b Henry	74	72
GD Elliott	c Haddin b Faulkner	83	82	SR Watson	not out	2	5
CJ Anderson	b Faulkner	0	2	GJ Maxwell	did not bat		
+L Ronchi	c Clarke b Starc	0	4	JP Faulkner	did not bat		
DL Vettori	b Johnson	9	21	+BJ Haddin	did not bat		
TG Southee	run out (Maxwell)	11	11	MG Johnson	did not bat		
MJ Henry	c Starc b Johnson	0	7	MA Starc	did not bat		
TA Boult	not out	0	1	JR Hazlewood	did not bat		
Extras	(7 lb, 6 w)	13		Extras	(3 lb, 6 w)	9	
Total	(all out, 45 overs)	183		Total	(3 wickets, 33.1 overs)	186	

Fall of wickets: 1-1 (McCullum, 0.5 ov), 2-33 (Guptill, 11.2 ov), 3-39 (Williamson, 12.2 ov), 4-150 (Taylor, 35.1 ov), 5-150 (Anderson, 35.3 ov), 6-151 (Ronchi, 36.2 ov), 7-167 (Vettori, 40.6 ov), 8-171 (Elliott, 41.5 ov), 9-182 (Henry, 44.5 ov), 10-183 (Southee, 45 ov)

Fall of wickets: 1-2 (Finch, 1.4 ov), 2-63 (Warner, 12.2 ov), 3-175 (Clarke, 31.1 ov)

AUSTRALIA	O	M	R	W	Wd	Nb	NEW ZEALAND	O	M	R	W	Wd	Nb
Starc	8	0	20	2	1	-	Southee	8	0	65	0	3	-
Hazlewood	8	2	30	0	-	-	Boult	10	0	40	1	-	-
Johnson	9	0	30	3	2	-	Vettori	5	0	25	0	-	-
Maxwell	7	0	37	1	1	-	Henry	9.1	0	46	2	2	-
Faulkner	9	1	36	3	-	-	Anderson	1	0	7	0	1	-
Watson	4	0	23	0	2	-							

MOST RUNS

Player	Mat	Inns	NO	Runs	HS	Ave	BF	SR	100	50	0	4s	6s
MJ Guptill (NZ)	9	9	1	547	237*	68.37	523	104.58	2	1	0	59	16
KC Sangakkara (SL)	7	7	2	541	124	108.2	511	105.87	4	0	0	57	7
AB de Villiers (SA)	8	7	2	482	162*	96.4	334	144.31	1	3	0	43	21
BRM Taylor (ZIM)	6	6	0	433	138	72.16	405	106.91	2	1	0	43	12
S Dhawan (INDIA)	8	8	0	412	137	51.5	449	91.75	2	1	0	48	9
SPD Smith (AUS)	8	7	1	402	105	67	439	91.57	1	4	0	37	4
TM Dilshan (SL)	7	7	1	395	161*	65.83	409	96.57	2	1	2	46	3
F du Plessis (SA)	7	7	1	380	109	63.33	449	84.63	1	3	0	28	4
Mahmudullah (BDESH)	6	6	1	365	128*	73	446	81.83	2	1	0	30	6
Misbah-ul-Haq (PAK)	7	7	0	350	76	50	466	75.1	0	4	0	25	7
DA Warner (AUS)	8	8	1	345	178	49.28	287	120.2	1	0	0	38	9
CH Gayle (WI)	6	6	0	340	215	56.66	290	117.24	1	1	0	17	26
SC Williams (ZIM)	6	6	1	339	96	67.8	311	109	0	4	0	29	6
HM Amla (SA)	8	8	0	333	159	41.62	350	95.14	1	1	0	35	5
RG Sharma (INDIA)	8	8	1	330	137	47.14	360	91.66	1	2	1	33	9
BB McCullum (NZ)	9	9	0	328	77	36.44	174	188.5	0	4	1	44	17
GJ Maxwell (AUS)	8	6	1	324	102	64.8	178	182.02	1	2	0	35	14
DA Miller (SA)	8	7	2	324	138*	64.8	233	139.05	1	0	1	21	14
Shaiman Anwar (UAE)	6	6	0	311	106	51.83	340	91.47	1	2	0	34	4
GD Elliott (NZ)	9	8	1	310	84*	44.28	294	105.44	0	2	1	29	7
V Kohli (INDIA)	8	8	2	305	107	50.83	374	81.55	1	0	0	29	1
HDRL Thirimanne (SL)	7	7	1	302	139*	50.33	356	84.83	1	2	1	29	2
Mushfiqur Rahim (BDESH)	6	6	0	298	89	49.66	282	105.67	0	3	0	26	5
SK Raina (INDIA)	8	6	1	284	110*	56.8	258	110.07	1	2	0	25	8
AJ Finch (AUS)	8	8	0	280	135	35	304	92.1	1	1	1	26	6

MOST WICKETS

Player	Mat	Inns	Overs	Mdns	Runs	Wkts	BBI	Ave	Econ	SR	4	5
MA Starc (AUS)	8	8	63.5	3	224	22	6/28	10.18	3.5	17.4	1	1
TA Boult (NZ)	9	9	85	14	371	22	5/27	16.86	4.36	23.1	1	1
UT Yadav (INDIA)	8	8	64.2	5	321	18	4/31	17.83	4.98	21.4	2	0
Mohammed Shami (IND)	7	7	61	7	294	17	4/35	17.29	4.81	21.5	1	0
M Morkel (SA)	8	8	68.1	4	299	17	3/34	17.58	4.38	24	0	0
JE Taylor (WI)	7	7	57.3	2	328	17	3/15	19.29	5.7	20.2	0	0
Wahab Riaz (PAK)	7	7	66.1	4	368	16	4/45	23	5.56	24.8	1	0
DL Vettori (NZ)	9	9	75.5	5	307	15	4/18	20.46	4.04	30.3	1	0
JH Davey (SCOT)	6	6	50	2	311	15	4/68	20.73	6.22	20	1	0
Imran Tahir (SA)	8	8	76.2	5	323	15	5/45	21.53	4.23	30.5	1	1
MG Johnson (AUS)	8	8	63.3	2	326	15	4/22	21.73	5.13	25.4	1	0
TG Southee (NZ)	9	9	81	7	472	15	7/33	31.46	5.82	32.4	0	1
CJ Anderson (NZ)	9	9	36.1	1	234	14	3/18	16.71	6.47	15.5	0	0
MM Sharma (INDIA)	8	8	63	4	314	13	3/48	24.15	4.98	29	0	0
R Ashwin (INDIA)	8	8	77	6	330	13	4/25	25.38	4.28	35.5	1	0
SL Malinga (SL)	7	7	63.4	1	354	12	3/35	29.5	5.56	31.8	0	0
Sohail Khan (PAK)	7	7	61.5	3	364	12	5/55	30.33	5.88	30.9	0	1
AD Russell (WI)	7	7	54	5	343	11	3/33	31.18	6.35	29.4	0	0
DW Steyn (SA)	8	8	68.5	7	346	11	3/30	31.45	5.02	37.5	0	0
JP Faulkner (AUS)	6	6	41.5	2	197	10	3/36	19.7	4.7	25.1	0	0
Shapoor Zadran (AFG)	6	6	51	5	265	10	4/38	26.5	5.19	30.6	1	0
TL Chatara (ZIM)	6	6	59.4	5	342	10	3/35	34.2	5.73	35.8	0	0
KJ Abbott (SA)	4	4	31	1	130	9	4/21	14.44	4.19	20.6	1	0
Taskin Ahmed (BDESH)	6	6	51	1	325	9	3/43	36.11	6.37	34	0	0
JO Holder (WI)	7	7	58	6	351	9	4/27	39	6.05	38.6	1	0

HIGH SCORES

Player	Runs	Balls	4s	6s	SR	Team	Opposition	Ground
MJ Guptill	237*	163	24	11	145.39	New Zealand	v West Indies	Wellington
CH Gayle	215	147	10	16	146.25	West Indies	v Zimbabwe	Canberra
DA Warner	178	133	19	5	133.83	Australia	v Afghanistan	Perth
AB de Villiers	162*	66	17	8	245.45	South Africa	v West Indies	Sydney
TM Dilshan	161*	146	22	0	110.27	Sri Lanka	v Bangladesh	Melbourne
HM Amla	159	128	16	4	124.21	South Africa	v Ireland	Canberra
KJ Coetzer	156	134	17	4	116.41	Scotland	v Bangladesh	Nelson
HDRL Thirimanne	139*	143	13	2	97.2	Sri Lanka	v England	Wellington
DA Miller	138*	92	7	9	150	South Africa	v Zimbabwe	Hamilton
BRM Taylor	138	110	15	5	125.45	Zimbabwe	v India	Auckland

BEST BOWLING

Player	Overs	Mdns	Runs	Wkts	Econ	Team	Opposition	Ground
TG Southee	9	0	33	7	3.66	New Zealand	v England	Wellington
MA Starc	9	0	28	6	3.11	Australia	v New Zealand	Auckland
TA Boult	10	3	27	5	2.7	New Zealand	v Australia	Auckland
MR Marsh	9	0	33	5	3.66	Australia	v England	Melbourne
Imran Tahir	10	2	45	5	4.5	South Africa	v West Indies	Sydney
Sohail Khan	10	0	55	5	5.5	Pakistan	v India	Adelaide
ST Finn	10	0	71	5	7.1	England	v Australia	Melbourne
MA Starc	4.4	1	14	4	3	Australia	v Scotland	Hobart
DL Vettori	10	4	18	4	1.8	New Zealand	v Afghanistan	Napier
KJ Abbott	8	0	21	4	2.62	South Africa	v Ireland	Canberra

WORLD CUP RECORDS

BATTING

MOST RUNS

COUNTRY	PLAYER	SPAN	INNINGS	RUNS	HS
IND	SR Tendulkar	1992-2011	44	2278	152
AUS	RT Ponting	1996-2011	42	1743	140*
SL	KC Sangakkara	2003-2015	35	1532	124
WI	BC Lara	1992-2007	33	1225	116
SA	AB de Villiers	2007-2015	22	1207	162*
SL	ST Jayasuriya	1992-2007	37	1165	120
SA	JH Kallis	1996-2011	32	1148	128*
SL	TM Dilshan	2007-2015	25	1112	161*
SL	DPMD Jayawardene	1999-2015	34	1100	115*
AUS	AC Gilchrist	1999-2007	31	1085	149

BEST AVERAGE (MIN. 20 INNS)

COUNTRY	PLAYER	SPAN	INNINGS	AVERAGE
SA	AB de Villiers	2007-2015	22	63.52
AUS	MJ Clarke	2007-2015	21	63.42
WI	IVA Richards	1975-1987	21	63.31
IND	R Dravid	1999-2007	21	61.42
IND	SR Tendulkar	1992-2011	44	56.95
SL	KC Sangakkara	2003-2015	35	56.54
SA	HH Gibbs	1999-2007	23	56.15
IND	SC Ganguly	1999-2007	21	55.88
NZ	MD Crowe	1983-1992	21	55
PAK	Saeed Anwar	1996-2003	21	53.82

BEST STRIKE RATE (MIN. 20 INNS)

COUNTRY	PLAYER	SPAN	INNINGS	S/R
NZ	BB McCullum	2003-2015	27	120.84
SA	AB de Villiers	2007-2015	22	117.29
IND	N Kapil Dev	1979-1992	24	115.14
PAK	Shahid Afridi	1999-2015	24	112.45
IND	V Sehwag	2003-2011	22	106.17
PAK	Wasim Akram	1987-2003	30	101.18
AUS	AC Gilchrist	1999-2007	31	98.01
AUS	MJ Clarke	2007-2015	21	94.16
SL	TM Dilshan	2007-2015	25	92.97
AUS	ML Hayden	2003-2007	21	92.93

HIGHEST INNINGS

COUNTRY	PLAYER	RUNS	BALLS	VS	DATE	GROUND
NZ	MJ Guptill	237*	163	WI	21/03/15	Wellington
WI	CH Gayle	215	147	ZIM	24/02/15	Canberra
SA	G Kirsten	188*	159	UAE	16/02/96	Rawalpindi
IND	SC Ganguly	183	158	SL	26/05/99	Taunton
WI	IVA Richards	181	125	SL	13/10/87	Karachi
AUS	DA Warner	178	133	AFG	04/03/15	Perth
IND	N Kapil Dev	175*	138	ZIM	18/06/83	Tunbridge Wells
IND	V Sehwag	175	140	BAN	19/02/11	Dhaka
ZIM	CB Wishart	172*	151	NAM	10/02/03	Harare
NZ	GM Turner	171*	201	E AF	07/06/75	Birmingham

MOST SIXES

COUNTRY	PLAYER	SPAN	INNINGS	SIXES
SA	AB de Villiers	2007-2015	22	37
WI	CH Gayle	2003-2015	26	37
AUS	RT Ponting	1996-2011	42	31
NZ	BB McCullum	2003-2015	27	29
SA	HH Gibbs	1999-2007	23	28
SL	ST Jayasuriya	1992-2007	37	27
IND	SR Tendulkar	1992-2011	44	27
IND	SC Ganguly	1999-2007	21	25
AUS	ML Hayden	2003-2007	21	23
WI	IVA Richards	2003-2007	21	22

BEST INNINGS STRIKE RATE (25+)

COUNTRY	PLAYER	RUNS	BALLS	4s	6s	S/R	VS	DATE	GROUND
NZ	JEC Franklin	31*	8	2	3	387.5	CAN	13/03/11	Mumbai
WI	AD Russell	42*	13	3	4	323.07	PAK	21/02/15	Christchurch
NZ	BB McCullum	77	25	8	7	308	ENG	20/02/15	Wellington
AUS	MG Johnson	27*	9	4	1	300	IND	26/03/15	Sydney
NZ	JDP Oram	25	9	1	3	277.77	PAK	08/03/11	Pallekele
AUS	BJ Haddin	25	9	4	1	277.77	SL	08/03/15	Sydney
SA	DA Miller	49	18	6	3	272.22	NZ	24/03/15	Auckland
PAK	Shoaib Akhtar	43	16	5	3	268.75	ENG	22/02/03	Cape Town
AUS	GB Hogg	40*	15	3	3	266.66	SCO	14/03/07	Basseterre
SA	JP Duminy	40	15	2	4	266.66	NED	03/03/11	Mohali

MOST HUNDREDS

COUNTRY	PLAYER	SPAN	VS	100s
IND	SR Tendulkar	1992-2011	Kenya (1996), Sri Lanka (1996), Kenya (1999), Namibia (2003), England (2011), South Africa (2011)	6
SL	KC Sangakkara	2003-2015	New Zealand (2011), Bangladesh (2015), England (2015), Australia (2015), Scotland (2015)	5
AUS	RT Ponting	1996-2011	West Indies (1996), Sri Lanka (2003), India (2003), Scotland (2007), India (2011)	
IND	SC Ganguly	1999-2007	Sri Lanka (1999), Namibia (2003), Kenya (2003), Kenya (2003)	4
SA	AB de Villiers	2007-2015	West Indies (2007), South Africa (2011), Netherlands (2011), West Indies (2015)	
AUS	ME Waugh	1992-1999	Kenya (1996), India (1996), New Zealand (1996), Zimbabwe (1999)	
SL	TM Dilshan	2007-2015	Zimbabwe (2011), England (2011), Bangladesh (2015), Scotland (2015)	
SL	DPMD Jayawardene	1999-2015	New Zealand (2007), Canada (2011), India (2011), Afghanistan (2015)	

MOST 50S

COUNTRY	PLAYER	SPAN	S/R	50s
IND	SR Tendulkar	1992-2011	88.98	21
SL	KC Sangakkara	2003-2015	86.55	12
AUS	RT Ponting	1996-2011	79.95	11
SA	AB de Villiers	2007-2015	117.29	10
SA	HH Gibbs	1999-2007	87.38	
SA	JH Kallis	1996-2011	74.4	
NZ	MD Crowe	1983-1992	83.57	9
ENG	GA Gooch	1979-1992	63.25	
PAK	Javed Miandad	1975-1996	68.02	
AUS	AC Gilchrist	1999-2007	98.01	
WI	BC Lara	1992-2007	86.26	
SL	DPMD Jayawardene	1999-2015	85.93	
SL	ST Jayasuriya	1992-2007	90.66	

MOST DUCKS

COUNTRY	PLAYER	SPAN	INNINGS	DUCKS
NZ	NJ Astle	1996-2003	22	5
PAK	Ijaz Ahmed	1987-1999	26	
IRE	WK McCallan	2007	8	4
WI	KLT Arthurton	1992-1999	13	
ENG/IRE	EJG Morgan	-2007	17	
SA	AB de Villiers	2007-2015	22	
IND	K Srikkanth	1983-1992	23	
PAK	Inzamam-ul-Haq	1992-2007	33	

MOST RUNS IN A SINGLE ICC WORLD CUP

COUNTRY	PLAYER	YEAR	HOST COUNTRY	RUNS
IND	SR Tendulkar	2003	Kenya/South Africa/Zimbabwe	673
AUS	ML Hayden	2007	West Indies	659
SL	DPMD Jayawardene	2007	West Indies	548
NZ	MJ Guptill	2015	Australia/New Zealand	547
SL	KC Sangakkara	2015	Australia/New Zealand	541
AUS	RT Ponting	2007	West Indies	539
IND	SR Tendulkar	1996	India/Pakistan/Sri Lanka	523
SL	TM Dilshan	2011	Bangladesh/India/ Sri Lanka	500
NZ	SB Styris	2007	West Indies	499
SA	JH Kallis	2007	West Indies	485

FASTEST HUNDRED

COUNTRY	PLAYER	BALLS	VS	DATE	GROUND
IRE	KJ O'Brien	50	ENG	02/03/11	Bangalore
AUS	GJ Maxwell	51	SL	08/03/15	Sydney
SA	AB de Villiers	55	WI	27/02/15	Sydney
AUS	ML Hayden	66	SA	24/03/07	Basseterre
CAN	JM Davison	67	WI	23/02/03	Centurion
IND	N Kapil Dev	72	ZIM	18/06/83	Tunbridge Wells
AUS	AC Gilchrist	72	SL	28/04/07	Barbados
IND	V Sehwag	81	BER	19/03/07	Trinidad
WI	CH Lloyd	82	AUS	21/06/75	Lord's
AUS	BJ Hodge	82	NED	18/03/07	St. Kitts

PARTNERSHIPS

HIGHEST PARTNERSHIPS BY WICKET

Wkt	Runs	Partners	Team	VS	Ground	Date
1st	282	WU Tharanga, TM Dilshan	SL	ZIM	Pallekele	10 Mar 2011
2nd	372	CH Gayle, MN Samuels	WI	ZIM	Canberra	24 Feb 2015
3rd	237*	R Dravid, SR Tendulkar	IND	KEN	Bristol	23 May 1999
4th	204	MJ Clarke, BJ Hodge	AUS	NED	Basseterre	18 Mar 2007
5th	256*	DA Miller, JP Duminy	SA	ZIM	Hamilton	15 Feb 2015
6th	162	KJ O'Brien, AR Cusack	IRE	ENG	Bengaluru	2 Mar 2011
7th=	107	Shaiman Anwar, Amjad Javed	UAE	IRE	Brisbane	25 Feb 2015
7th=	107	Amjad Javed, Nasir Aziz	UAE	WI	Napier	15 Mar 2015
8th	117	DL Houghton, IP Butchart	ZIM	NZ	Hyderabad (Deccan)	10 Oct 1987
9th	126*	N Kapil Dev, SMH Kirmani	IND	ZIM	Tunbridge Wells	18 Jun 1983
10th	71	AME Roberts, J Garner	WI	IND	Manchester	9 Jun 1983

HIGHEST PARTNERSHIPS BY RUNS

Partners	Runs	Wkt	Team	VS	Ground	Date
CH Gayle, MN Samuels	372	2nd	WI	ZIM	Canberra	24 Feb 2015
SC Ganguly, R Dravid	318	2nd	IND	SL	Taunton	26 May 1999
WU Tharanga, TM Dilshan	282	1st	SL	ZIM	Pallekele	10 Mar 2011
DA Warner, SPD Smith	260	2nd	AUS	AFG	Perth	4 Mar 2015
DA Miller, JP Duminy	256*	5th	SA	ZIM	Hamilton	15 Feb 2015
HM Amla, F du Plessis	247	2nd	SA	IRE	Canberra	3 Mar 2015
SR Tendulkar, SC Ganguly	244	2nd	IND	NAM	Pietermaritzburg	23 Feb 2003
R Dravid, SR Tendulkar	237*	3rd	IND	KEN	Bristol	23 May 1999
RT Ponting, DR Martyn	234*	3rd	AUS	IND	Johannesburg	23 Mar 2003
WU Tharanga, TM Dilshan	231*	1st	SL	ENG	Colombo (RPS)	26 Mar 2011

BOWLING

MOST WICKETS

COUNTRY	PLAYER	SPAN	INNINGS	OVERS	WICKETS	AVG
AUS	GD McGrath	1996-2007	39	325.5	71	18.19
SL	M Muralitharan	1996-2011	39	343.3	68	19.63
PAK	Wasim Akram	1987-2003	36	324.3	55	23.83
SL	WPUJC Vaas	1996-2007	31	261.4	49	21.22
IND	Z Khan	2003-2011	23	198.5	44	20.22
IND	J Srinath	1992-2003	33	283.2	44	27.81
SL	SL Malinga	2007-2015	21	170.4	43	21.11
SA	AA Donald	1992-2003	25	218.5	38	24.02
NZ	JDP Oram	2003-2011	23	182.2	36	21.33
NZ	DL Vettori	2003-2015	31	281.3	36	32.44

BEST ANALYSIS

COUNTRY	PLAYER	OVERS	FIGS	ECON	VS	GROUND	DATE
AUS	GD McGrath	7	7-15	2.14	NAM	Potchefstroom	27/02/03
AUS	AJ Bichel	10	7-20	2	ENG	Port Elizabeth	02/03/03
NZ	TG Southee	9	7-33	3.66	ENG	Wellington	20/02/15
WI	WW Davis	10.3	7-51	4.85	AUS	Leeds	11/06/83
AUS	GJ Gilmour	12	6-14	1.16	ENG	Leeds	18/06/75
IND	A Nehra	10	6-23	2.3	ENG	Durban	26/02/03
NZ	SE Bond	10	6-23	2.3	AUS	Port Elizabeth	11/03/03
SL	WPUJC Vaas	9.1	6-25	2.72	BAN	Pietermaritzburg	14/02/03
WI	KAJ Roach	8.3	6-27	3.17	NED	Delhi	28/02/11
AUS	MA Starc	9	6-28	3.11	NZ	Auckland	28/02/15

LOWEST AVERAGE

COUNTRY	PLAYER	SPAN	BBI	AVE
AUS	GD McGrath	1996-2007	7-15	18.19
PAK	Imran Khan	1975-1992	4-37	19.26
SL	M Muralitharan	1996-2011	4-19	19.63
IND	Z Khan	2003-2011	4-42	20.22
SL	SL Malinga	2007-2015	6-38	21.11
SL	WPUJC Vaas	1996-2007	6-25	21.22
WI	AME Roberts	1975-1983	3-32	21.23
NZ	JDP Oram	2003-2011	4-39	21.33
IND	A Kumble	1996-2007	4-32	22.83
PAK	Wasim Akram	1987-2003	5-28	23.83

BEST STRIKE RATE (MIN. 18 MATCHES)

COUNTRY	PLAYER	SPAN	S/R	AVE
SL	SL Malinga	2007-2015	23.8	18.19
IND	Z Khan	2003-2011	27.1	19.26
AUS	GD McGrath	1996-2007	27.5	19.63
PAK	Imran Khan	1975-1992	29.9	20.22
SL	M Muralitharan	1996-2011	30.3	21.11
NZ	JDP Oram	2003-2011	30.3	21.22
SL	WPUJC Vaas	1996-2007	32	21.23
IND	A Kumble	1996-2007	33.5	21.33
SA	AA Donald	1992-2003	34.5	22.83
PAK	Wasim Akram	1987-2003	35.4	23.83

HAT TRICKS

COUNTRY	PLAYER	WICKETS	VS	DATE	GROUND
SL	SL Malinga	4	SA	28/03/07	Georgetown
IND	C Sharma	3	NZ	31/10/87	Nagpur
PAK	Saqlain Mushtaq		ZIM	11/06/99	The Oval, London
SL	WPUJC Vaas		BAN	14/02/03	Pietermaritzburg
AUS	B Lee		KEN	15/03/03	Durban
WI	KAJ Roach		NED	28/02/11	New Delhi
SL	SL Malinga		KEN	01/03/11	Colombo
ENG	ST Finn		AUS	14/02/15	Melbourne
SA	JP Duminy		SL	18/03/15	Sydney

WICKETS IN ONE WORLD CUP

COUNTRY	PLAYER	MATCHES	OVERS	WKTS	YEAR/HOST
AUS	GD McGrath	11	80.5	26	2007 (West Indies)
SL	WPUJC Vaas	10	88	23	2003 (Kenya, South Africa, Zimbabwe)
SL	M Muralitharan	10	84.4	23	2007 (West Indies)
AUS	SW Tait	11	84.3	23	2007 (West Indies)
AUS	MA Starc	8	63.5	22	2015 (Australia, New Zealand)
NZ	TA Boult	9	85	22	2015 (Australia, New Zealand)
AUS	B Lee	10	83.1	22	2003 (Kenya, South Africa, Zimbabwe)
PAK	Shahid Afridi	8	74.3	21	2011 (Bangladesh, India, Sri Lanka)
AUS	GD McGrath	11	87	21	2003 (Kenya, South Africa, Zimbabwe)
AUS	GB Hogg	11	82.5	21	2007 (West Indies)

MORE THAN ONE FIVE-WICKET HAUL

COUNTRY	PLAYER	SPAN	INNS	WKTS	5s	VS.
AUS	GJ Gilmour	1975-1975	2	11	2	ENG (Leeds, 18 Jun 1975) WI (Lord's, 21 Jun 1975)
WI	VC Drakes	2003-2003	6	16	2	CAN (Centurion, 23 Feb 2003) KEN (Kimberley, 4 Mar 2003)
SL	ALF de Mel	1983-1987	9	18	2	PAK (Leeds, 16 Jun 1983) NZ (Derby, 18 Jun 1983)
PAK	Shahid Afridi	1999-2015	24	30	2	KEN (Hambantota, 23 Feb 2011) CAN (Colombo, 3 Mar 2011)
AUS	GD McGrath	1996-2007	39	71	2	WI (Manchester, 30 May 1999) NAM (Potchefstroom, 27 Feb 2003)

WICKET-KEEPING

MOST DISMISSALS

Player	Span	Mat	Inns	Dis	Ct	St
KC Sangakkara (SL)	2003-2015	37	36	54	41	13
AC Gilchrist (AUS)	1999-2007	31	31	52	45	7
MS Dhoni (INDIA)	2007-2015	20	20	32	27	5
BB McCullum (NZ)	2003-2015	34	25	32	30	2
MV Boucher (SA)	1999-2007	25	25	31	31	0
Moin Khan (PAK)	1992-1999	20	20	30	23	7
BJ Haddin (AUS)	2011-2015	15	15	29	29	0
D Ramdin (WI)	2007-2015	16	16	26	26	0
AJ Stewart (ENG)	1992-2003	25	20	23	21	2
RD Jacobs (WI)	1999-2003	11	11	22	21	1

MOST DISMISSALS IN AN INNINGS

Player	Dis	Ct/St	Team	VS	Ground	Date
AC Gilchrist	6	6/0	AUS	NAM	Potchefstroom	27 Feb 2003
Sarfaraz Ahmed	6	6/0	PAK	SA	Auckland	7 Mar 2015
SMH Kirmani	5	5/0	IND	ZIM	Leicester	11 Jun 1983
JC Adams	5	4/1	WI	KEN	Pune	29 Feb 1996
Rashid Latif	5	4/1	PAK	NZ	Lahore	6 Mar 1996
NR Mongia	5	4/1	IND	ZIM	Leicester	19 May 1999
RD Jacobs	5	5/0	WI	NZ	Southampton	24 May 1999
Umar Akmal	5	5/0	PAK	ZIM	Brisbane	1 Mar 2015

MOST DISMISSALS IN A WORLD CUP

COUNTRY	PLAYER	INNINGS	DISMISSALS	CT	ST	YEAR/HOST
AUS	AC Gilchrist	10	21	21	0	2003 (Kenya, South Africa, Zimbabwe)
SL	KC Sangakkara	10	17	15	2	2003 (Kenya, South Africa, Zimbabwe)
AUS	AC Gilchrist	11	17	12	5	2007 (West Indies)
WI	PJL Dujon	8	16	15	1	1983 (England)
AUS	BJ Haddin	8	16	16	0	2015 (Australia, New Zealand)
PAK	Moin Khan	10	16	12	4	1999 (England, Ireland, Netherlands, Scotland)
IND	R Dravid	11	16	15	1	2003 (Kenya, South Africa, Zimbabwe)
IND	MS Dhoni	8	15	15	0	2015 (Australia, New Zealand)
SA	DJ Richardson	9	15	14	1	1992 (Australia, New Zealand)
SL	KC Sangakkara	11	15	11	4	2007 (West Indies)

PLAYER OF THE TOURNAMENT AWARDS

Since 1992, one player has been awarded this honour

Year	Player	Performance details
1992	Martin Crowe	456 runs
1996	Sanath Jayasuriya	221 runs and 7 wickets
1999	Lance Klusener	281 runs and 17 wickets
2003	Sachin Tendulkar	673 runs and 2 wickets
2007	Glenn McGrath	26 wickets
2011	Yuvraj Singh	362 runs and 15 wickets
2015	Mitchell Starc	22 wickets

NATION BY NATION BREAKDOWN

An overview of the teams' performances in every World Cup

Team/Host	1975 (8)	1979 (8)	1983 (8)	1987 (8)	1992 (9)	1996 (12)	1999 (12)	2003 (14)	2007 (16)	2011 (14)	2015 (14)
Afghanistan											GP
Australia	RU	GP	GP	W	GP	RU	W	W	W	QF	W
Bangladesh							GP	GP	S8	GP	QF
Bermuda									GP		
Canada		GP						GP	GP	GP	
East Africa†	GP										
England	SF	RU	SF	RU	RU	QF	GP	GP	S8	QF	GP
India	GP	GP	W	SF	GP	SF	S6	RU	GP	W	SF
Ireland									S8	GP	GP
Kenya							GP	GP	SF	GP	GP
Namibia								GP			
Netherlands						GP		GP	GP	GP	
New Zealand	SF	SF	GP	GP	SF	QF	SF	S6	SF	SF	RU
Pakistan	GP	SF	SF	SF	W	QF	RU	GP	GP	SF	QF
Scotland							GP		GP		GP
South Africa					SF	QF	SF	GP	SF	QF	SF
Sri Lanka	GP	GP	GP	GP	GP	W	GP	SF	RU	RU	QF
United Arab Emirates						GP					GP
West Indies	W	W	RU	GP	GP	SF	GP	GP	S8	QF	QF
Zimbabwe			GP	GP	GP	GP	S6	S6	GP	GP	GP

W – Winner
RU – Runner up
SF – Semi-finals
S6 – Super Six (1999–2003)
S8 – Super Eight (2007)
QF – Quarter-finals (1996, 2011–2015)
GP – Group stage / First round

THE WRITERS

Tanya Aldred is a freelance writer, co-editor of the *Nightwatchman* and founder of The Next Test.

Andrew Fidel Fernando is a writer based in Sri Lanka. He works for ESPNCricinfo.

Jo Harman is a cricket writer and magazine editor of *Wisden Cricket Monthly*.

Jon Hotten is the author of *The Meaning of Cricket* and is the reviews editor for *Wisden Cricket Monthly*, and is on the editorial board of the *Nightwatchman*.

Geoff Lemon is a writer and broadcaster from Melbourne whose book *Steve Smith's Men* won 2019's *Wisden* Book of the Year and MCC Book of the Year.

Suresh Menon is editor of *Wisden India Almanack* and consulting editor of *The Hindu*. His books include *Bishan: Portrait of a Cricketer, Pataudi: Nawab of Cricket,* and *Champions! How the World Cup Was Won.*

Benj Moorehead is a freelance cricket writer and editor. He is on the editorial board of the *Nightwatchman*.

Scott Oliver is a freelance writer who has contributed to *ESPNcricinfo*, has a column in *Wisden Cricket Monthly*, and compiles the 'Eyewitness' features for the *Cricketer*.

Matt Thacker is managing editor of both the *Nightwatchman* and of *Wisden Cricket Monthly*.

Telford Vice started covering cricket in South Africa in 1991. He is the author of *In the Nick of Time: Peter Kirsten's life in Cricket.*

Phil Walker was formerly editor of *All Out Cricket* magazine before becoming editor-in-chief of *Wisden Cricket Monthly*.

Andy Zaltzman, stand-up comedian and *Test Match Special* scorer, supplied a huge number of statistics for this book.